THE BOOK OF POLITICAL LISTS

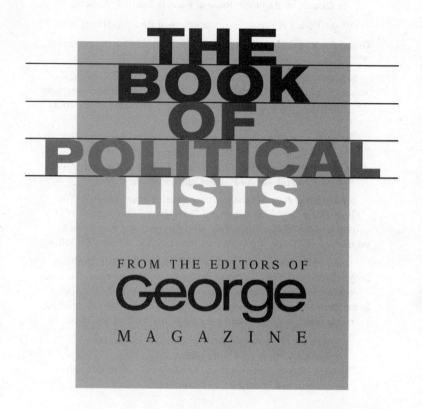

THE BOOK OF POLITICAL LISTS

FROM THE EDITORS OF

George

MAGAZINE

COMPILED BY

BLAKE ESKIN

VILLARD   NEW YORK

Library of Congress Cataloging-in-Publication Data
Eskin, Blake.
The book of political lists / from the editors of *George* magazine:
compiled by Blake Eskin.
p. cm.
Includes bibliographical references.
ISBN 0-375-75011-8 (acid-free paper)
1. Presidents—United States—Miscellanea. 2. United States—
Politics and government—Miscellanea. I. *George* (New York, N.Y.)
II. Title.
E176.1.E69 1997
973'.09'9—dc21 97-26480

Random House website address: www.randomhouse.com

Printed in the United States of America on acid-free paper

2 4 6 8 9 7 5 3

First Edition

Design by Robert Bull Design

CONTENTS

CONTENTS

INTRODUCTION
by John F. Kennedy, Jr.

Lists have long been at the heart of both the best and the worst of American politics. Thomas Jefferson made sure to include a list of the "long train of abuses and usurpations" by King George III in the Declaration of Independence as a justification for casting off British rule. In his Emancipation Proclamation, Abraham Lincoln included a list of the states rebelling against the Union and then freed the slaves in those states. In a February 1950 speech in Wheeling, West Virginia, Senator Joseph McCarthy waved what he claimed was a list of 205 known Communists employed by the State Department; that list, which never materialized, sparked a witch-hunt in Washington and around the country. And old-line liberals consider it a badge of honor to have been included on President Nixon's "enemies list."

At *George* we've always believed in the maxim that politics is too important to be left to politicians. Accordingly, this book of political lists covers federal and local governments as well as the lively intersection of politics and popular culture. Whether you're reading about Thomas Jefferson's canons for good living, Bill Maher's proposed order of presidential succession, or Harry Truman's campaigning mottos, we'll tell you everything you need to know and a few things you thought you didn't, but we'll leave the judgments up to you. Some of the lists in this book will surprise you and others may amuse, and hopefully each will offer something interesting and provocative about American politics and its fascinating cast of characters. Who knows, they may even inspire you to do something wonderful and get on a list of your own.

PRESIDENTIAL LISTS

Nobody receives more scrutiny than a president. Even after he is long dead, people are interested not just in his policies but also in how much he weighed, what he ate for breakfast, how often he went to the dentist as a child, and what his last words were. Harry Truman didn't think that he deserved so much attention. "All the president is," Truman said, "is a glorified public relations man who spends his time flattering, kissing, and kicking people to get them to do what they are supposed to do anyway."

PRESIDENTS

George Washington	Federalist-VA, 1789–1797
John Adams	Federalist-MA, 1797–1801
Thomas Jefferson	D-VA, 1801–1809
James Madison	D-VA, 1809–1817
James Monroe	D-VA, 1817–1825
John Quincy Adams	D-MA, 1825–1829
Andrew Jackson	D-TN, 1829–1837
Martin Van Buren	D-NY, 1837–1841
William Henry Harrison	Whig-OH, 1841
John Tyler	Whig-VA, 1841–1845
James Knox Polk	D-TN, 1845–1849
Zachary Taylor	Whig-KY, 1849–1850
Millard Fillmore	Whig-NY, 1850–1853
Franklin Pierce	D-NH, 1853–1857
James Buchanan	D-PA, 1857–1861
Abraham Lincoln	R-IL, 1861–1865
Andrew Johnson	R-TN, 1865–1869
Ulysses Simpson Grant	R-OH, 1869–1877
Rutherford Birchard Hayes	R-OH, 1877–1881
James Abram Garfield	R-OH, 1881
Chester Alan Arthur	R-NY, 1881–1885
Grover Cleveland	D-NY, 1885–1889
Benjamin Harrison	R-IN, 1889–1893
Grover Cleveland	D-NY, 1893–1897
William McKinley	R-OH, 1897–1901
Theodore Roosevelt	R-NY, 1901–1909
William Howard Taft	R-OH, 1909–1913
Woodrow Wilson	D-NJ, 1913–1921
Warren Gamaliel Harding	R-OH, 1921–1923
Calvin Coolidge	R-MA, 1923–1929
Herbert Hoover	R-CA, 1929–1933
Franklin Delano Roosevelt	D-NY, 1933–1945
Harry S Truman	D-MO, 1945–1953
Dwight David Eisenhower	R-KS, 1953–1961
John Fitzgerald Kennedy	D-MA, 1961–1963

Lyndon Baines Johnson	D-TX, 1963–1969
Richard Milhous Nixon	R-CA, 1969–1974
Gerald Rudolph Ford	R-MI, 1974–1977
James Earl Carter	D-GA, 1977–1981
Ronald Wilson Reagan	R-CA, 1981–1989
George Herbert Walker Bush	R-TX, 1989–1993
William Jefferson Clinton	D-AR, 1993–

FERTILE GROUND:
States That Have Given Birth to More Than One President

Most presidents were born on the eastern seaboard. In fact, Herbert Hoover, who was born in West Branch, Iowa, was the first to be born west of the Mississippi River.

Virginia 8 George Washington, Thomas Jefferson, James Madison, James Monroe, William Henry Harrison, John Tyler, Zachary Taylor, Woodrow Wilson

Ohio 7 Ulysses Grant, Rutherford Hayes, James Garfield, Benjamin Harrison, William McKinley, William Howard Taft, Warren Harding

Massachusetts 4 John Adams, John Quincy Adams, John Kennedy, George Bush

New York 4 Martin Van Buren, Millard Fillmore, Theodore Roosevelt, Franklin Roosevelt

North Carolina 2 James Polk, Andrew Johnson

Texas 2 Dwight Eisenhower, Lyndon Johnson

Vermont 2 Chester Arthur, Calvin Coolidge

Andrew Jackson was born on the border between North Carolina and South Carolina. Many sources list Waxhaw, South Carolina, as his birthplace, but both states claim him as their native son. Still others have claimed that Andrew Jackson was born at sea during his parents' journey to America from Ireland.

BORN TO LEAD:
Presidents Who Were Firstborn Males

*Psychologists and other social scientists have tried to prove
a connection between personality traits and birth order.
An unusually large number of presidents were the first born
in their families.*

George Washington
John Adams
Thomas Jefferson
James Madison
James Monroe
John Quincy Adams
James Polk
Millard Fillmore
James Buchanan ☞
Abraham Lincoln
Ulysses Grant
Chester Arthur
Theodore Roosevelt
Woodrow Wilson
Warren Harding
Calvin Coolidge
Franklin Roosevelt
Harry Truman
Lyndon Johnson
Gerald Ford
Jimmy Carter
Bill Clinton

*William Howard Taft, Richard Nixon, and John Kennedy became
the oldest boys in their families after a brother died.*

FRUIT FROM THE SAME TREE:
Presidents Known to Be Related to Other Presidents

Four pairs of presidents shared the same last name, including John Adams and his son John Quincy Adams, William Henry Harrison and his grandson Benjamin Harrison, and Theodore Roosevelt and his fifth cousin Franklin Roosevelt. Gary Boyd Roberts and other genealogists who have traced presidential lineages back a dozen and more generations have found that many other presidents share common ancestors in colonial America and England.

Franklin Roosevelt	16 other presidents		
George Bush	15		
William Howard Taft	14	**James Garfield**	5
Calvin Coolidge	14	**Warren Harding**	5
Gerald Ford	14	**John Adams**	4
Millard Fillmore	11	**William Henry Harrison**	4
Richard Nixon	10	**Theodore Roosevelt**	4
Grover Cleveland	9	**Jimmy Carter**	4
Herbert Hoover	9	**George Washington**	3
Benjamin Harrison	8	**James Madison***	2
John Quincy Adams	7	**Martin Van Buren**	2
Rutherford Hayes	7	**John Tyler**	2
Ulysses Grant	6	**Zachary Taylor***	2
Franklin Pierce	5	**Abraham Lincoln**	2

* James Madison and Zachary Taylor were second cousins.

PRESIDENTS NOT KNOWN TO BE RELATED TO OTHER PRESIDENTS

Lyndon and Andrew Johnson may have shared the same last name, but that doesn't mean they were even remotely related.

Thomas Jefferson	**Andrew Johnson**	**Dwight Eisenhower**
James Monroe	**Chester Arthur**	**John Kennedy**
Andrew Jackson	**William McKinley**	**Lyndon Johnson**
James Polk	**Woodrow Wilson**	**Ronald Reagan**
James Buchanan	**Harry Truman**	**Bill Clinton**

PRESIDENTS WITH ROYAL BLOOD

After the Revolutionary War, some Americans suggested establishing another monarchy, with George Washington as the first king of the United States. Were they aware that Washington had no fewer than three kings in his family tree? (The kings in this list are English unless otherwise noted.)

John Quincy Adams Edward III

James Buchanan Robert III of Scotland

George Bush Henry I, Henry II, Edward I; William the Lion and Robert II of Scotland

Grover Cleveland Edward I

Calvin Coolidge Henry I, Edward I, Edward III; Robert I of France

Gerald Ford Edward I; Henry I of France

Benjamin Harrison Edward I; Hugh Capet of France

William Henry Harrison Edward I

Rutherford Hayes Hugh Capet and Henry I of France

Herbert Hoover John

Thomas Jefferson Henry I, Edward III; William the Lion of Scotland

James Madison Henry II, Edward I

Franklin Pierce Henry I

Franklin Roosevelt Henry I, Edward I, Edward III; James II of Scotland; Robert I of France

Theodore Roosevelt Edward I , Edward III; James I of Scotland

William Howard Taft Robert I of France

Zachary Taylor Edward I, Edward III

George Washington Edward I, Edward III; William the Lion of Scotland

PRESIDENTS WITH ANCESTORS WHO CAME OVER ON THE *MAYFLOWER*

John Adams
John Quincy Adams
Zachary Taylor
Ulysses Grant
James Garfield

Franklin Roosevelt
Richard Nixon
Gerald Ford
George Bush

PRESIDENTS' DISTANT RELATIVES

Robert E. Lee, Confederate general   Washington's () third cousin twice removed

Winston Churchill, British prime minister   Washington's eighth cousin six times removed

Elizabeth II, queen of England   George Washington's second cousin, seven times removed

Wendell Corey, actor   John Adams

Chet Huntley, anchorman   John Adams

Nelson Eddy, actor and singer   Martin Van Buren

Glenn Ford, actor   Martin Van Buren

Dorothy and **Lillian Gish**, actresses   Zachary Taylor

Judy Garland, actress   Ulysses Grant's first cousin three times removed

Ralph Waldo Emerson, transcendentalist writer   William Howard Taft

Orson Bean, actor   Calvin Coolidge's third cousin

Jessamyn West, novelist   Richard Nixon's second cousin

GREEN IN THE WHITE HOUSE: Presidents with Irish Ancestors

George Washington   Family related to the McCarthy clan of County Cork

James Madison   On mother's side

Andrew Jackson   Parents from Carrickfergus, County Antrim

James Polk   Paternal grandparents and maternal grandmother from County Donegal

James Buchanan   Father from Ramelton, County Donegal; paternal grandfather's forebears from County Tyrone

Andrew Johnson   On mother's side

Ulysses Grant   Maternal grandfather from Golan, Ardstraw, County Tyrone; paternal grandmother from Ireland

Chester Arthur   Father from Cullybackey, County Antrim

Grover Cleveland   Maternal grandfather from County Antrim

Benjamin Harrison   On mother's side

William McKinley   Father's family from County Antrim and County Tyrone

Theodore Roosevelt   Paternal grandmother's parents from County Meath and County Donegal; maternal great-great-great-grandfather from County Donegal

Woodrow Wilson   Paternal grandfather from Dergalt, Strabane, County Tyrone

John Kennedy   Paternal and maternal grandparents from County Wexford

Richard Nixon   Paternal ancestors from New Ross, County Wexford; maternal ancestors from Carrickfergus, County Antrim

Gerald Ford   Paternal ancestors from County Monaghan

Jimmy Carter   On both parents' sides

Ronald Reagan   Paternal great-grandfather from Ballyporeen, County Tipperary; also paternal grandmother's family from Ireland

Bill Clinton   On mother's side

Clinton, whose mother's maiden name was Cassidy, gathered with hundreds of members of the Cassidy clan in a Dublin pub when he visited Ireland in 1995. The Irish government was unable to locate a direct blood relative.

SELF-MADE MEN:
Presidents Who Did Not Attend College

Nowadays a bachelor's degree is considered a requirement for skilled employment; other than Bill Gates, few Americans expect to become much of anything, let alone president, without a college diploma. Some of our greatest presidents and some of our most ineffectual ones never went to college.

George Washington	Abraham Lincoln
Andrew Jackson	Andrew Johnson
Martin Van Buren	Grover Cleveland
Zachary Taylor	Harry Truman
Millard Fillmore	

William Henry Harrison, William McKinley, and Warren Harding all attended college, but none graduated.

GENTLEMEN AND SCHOLARS:
Presidents Who Were Elected to Phi Beta Kappa

There are several ways to join the prestigious academic honor society Phi Beta Kappa, which was founded in 1776 at the College of William and Mary, in Williamsburg, Virginia. If you didn't excel in college—even if you didn't attend college—you can become an alumnus member or an honorary member, and being elected president can help.

John Quincy Adams	Grover Cleveland
Martin Van Buren	Theodore Roosevelt
Franklin Pierce	Woodrow Wilson
Rutherford Hayes	Calvin Coolidge
James Garfield	Franklin Roosevelt
Chester Arthur	George Bush

Bill Clinton

Only John Quincy Adams, Chester Arthur, Theodore Roosevelt, George Bush, and Bill Clinton were elected to Phi Beta Kappa while in college.

PRESIDENTS WHO SERVED IN THE MILITARY

Most presidents had some military experience to guide them in their role as commander in chief. The service records below are for the U.S. Army unless otherwise noted.

George Washington District adjutant, 1752–1753; lieutenant colonel, 1754; and colonel and commander in chief of Virginia militia, 1755–1758—all in British army during French and Indian Wars; commander in chief, Continental Army, 1775–1781, during Revolutionary War

James Madison Colonel, Virginia militia, Continental Army, during Revolutionary War

James Monroe ☞ Lieutenant colonel, Virginia Regiment, Continental Army, during Revolutionary War

Andrew Jackson ☞ Major general, Tennessee militia, 1802–1814; major general, 1814–1818, including service in War of 1812

William Henry Harrison Soldier, 1791–1798, 1811; brigadier general, 1812; major general, 1813–1814

John Tyler Captain during War of 1812

James Polk Colonel, 1821

Zachary Taylor First lieutenant, 1808–1842, including service in War of 1812 and Second Seminole War; commander of army in Texas and major general, 1845–1849, including service in Mexican War

Millard Fillmore Commander, Home Guard, during Civil War

Franklin Pierce
Colonel, 1846; brigadier general, 1847–1848, during Mexican War

James Buchanan   Soldier during War of 1812

Abraham Lincoln   Captain, Illinois militia, 1832, during Black Hawk War

Andrew Johnson   Brigadier general, 1862–1864, during Civil War

Ulysses Grant
Officer,1843–1854, including service in Mexican War; officer in volunteer army, 1861–1862; major general in regular army, then lieutenant general with command of all armies, 1863–1864, all during Civil War; general of the army, 1866–1867

Rutherford Hayes   Soldier, 1861–1864; brigadier general, then major general, 1864–1865, all during Civil War

James Garfield   Soldier, 1861–1862; colonel of Ohio infantry and brigadier, 1862; major general of volunteers during Civil War

Chester Arthur Brigadier general, New York militia, 1857–1862, including service in Civil War

Benjamin Harrison ☞ Soldier, 1861–1865; brigadier general, 1865, during Civil War

William McKinley Soldier, 1861–1865; major, 1865, during Civil War

Theodore Roosevelt Lieutenant colonel, Rough Riders, 1898, during Spanish-American War

Harry Truman Major, 1918–1919, during World War I

Dwight Eisenhower Officer from 1915; became commander in chief of Allied forces in western Europe in 1943 and general of the army in 1944, during World War II; chief of staff, 1945–1948

John Kennedy Lieutenant, Navy, 1941–1945, during World War II

Lyndon Johnson Lieutenant commander, Navy, 1941–1942, during World War II

Richard Nixon Lieutenant (junior grade), Navy, 1942–1946, during World War II

Gerald Ford Lieutenant commander, Navy, 1942–46, during World War II

Jimmy Carter Lieutenant, Navy, 1946–1953

Ronald Reagan Captain, 1942–1945, during World War II

George Bush Lieutenant, Navy, 1942–1945, during World War II

PRESIDENTS WHO SERVED AS GENERALS

Americans like war heroes. At times, military experience has been prized by the electorate more than political experience.
After the Gulf War, Americans encouraged Norman Schwarzkopf and Colin Powell to run for president, and Powell almost threw his hat into the ring.

George Washington	Revolutionary War (commander in chief, Continental Army)
Andrew Jackson	War of 1812 (major general)
William Henry Harrison	Indian wars, War of 1812 (major general)
Zachary Taylor	War of 1812, Indian wars, Mexican War (major general)
Franklin Pierce	Mexican War (brigadier general)
Andrew Johnson	Civil War (brigadier general)
Ulysses Grant	Civil War (general)
Rutherford Hayes	Civil War (major general)
James Garfield	Civil War (major general of volunteers)
Chester Arthur	Civil War (quartermaster general)
Benjamin Harrison	Civil War (brigadier general)
Dwight Eisenhower	World War II, NATO (supreme commander)

PRESIDENTS WHO
DID NOT SERVE IN THE MILITARY

Much has been made of Bill Clinton's objection to the Vietnam War, but Clinton is the hardly the first commander-in-chief who never served in the military.

John Adams	Woodrow Wilson
Thomas Jefferson	Warren Harding
John Quincy Adams	Calvin Coolidge
Martin Van Buren	Herbert Hoover
Grover Cleveland	Franklin Roosevelt
William Howard Taft	Bill Clinton

> *Cleveland was drafted to fight in the Civil War, but he paid a substitute $300 to serve in his stead.*

PRESIDENTS WHO WERE
GOVERNORS

Thomas Jefferson	No party–VA, 1779–1781
James Monroe	D-VA, 1799–1802, 1811
Martin Van Buren	D-NY, 1829
William Henry Harrison	Indiana Territory, 1800–1812
John Tyler	D-VA, 1825–1827
James Polk	D-TN, 1839–1841
Andrew Johnson	D-TN, 1853–1857*
Rutherford Hayes	R-OH, 1868–1872, 1876–1877
Grover Cleveland	D-NY, 1883–1885
William McKinley	R-OH, 1892–1896
Theodore Roosevelt	R-NY, 1899–1901
William Howard Taft	Philippines, 1901–1904
Woodrow Wilson	D-NJ, 1911–1913
Calvin Coolidge	R-MA, 1919–1921
Franklin Roosevelt	D-NY, 1929–1933
Jimmy Carter	D-GA, 1971–1975
Ronald Reagan	R-CA, 1967–1975
Bill Clinton	D-AR, 1979–1981, 1983–1993

* Johnson was military governor of Tennessee from 1862 to 1865.

PRESIDENTS WHO WERE CONGRESSMEN

James Madison	No party/R–VA, 1789–1797
John Quincy Adams	Federalist-MA, 1831–1848
Andrew Jackson	No party/R–TN, 1796–1797
William Henry Harrison	No party–Northwest Territory, 1799–1800; OH, 1816–1819
John Tyler	R-VA, 1817–1821
James Polk	D-TN, 1825–1839
Millard Fillmore	Whig-NY, 1833–1835, 1837–1843
Franklin Pierce	D-NH, 1833–1837
James Buchanan	No party/D–PA, 1821–1831
Abraham Lincoln	Whig-IL, 1847–1849
Andrew Johnson	D-TN, 1843–1853
Rutherford Hayes	R-OH, 1865–1867
James Garfield	R-OH, 1863–1880
William McKinley	R-OH, 1877–1884, 1885–1891
John Kennedy	D-MA, 1947–1953
Lyndon Johnson	D-TX, 1937–1949
Richard Nixon	R-CA, 1947–1950
Gerald Ford	R-MI, 1949–1973
George Bush	R-TX, 1967–1971

John Quincy Adams was the only president to serve in the lower house after his term in the White House; he represented his Massachusetts district for 17 years.

PRESIDENTS WHO WERE SENATORS

James Monroe	No party–VA, 1790–1794
John Quincy Adams	Federalist-MA, 1803–1808
Andrew Jackson	R-TN, 1797–1798, 1823–1825
Martin Van Buren	No party–NY, 1821–1828

William Henry Harrison	No party–OH, 1825–1828
John Tyler	R-VA, 1827–1836
Franklin Pierce	D-NH, 1837–1842
James Buchanan	D-PA, 1834–1845
Andrew Johnson	D-TN, 1857–1862; R-TN, 1875
Benjamin Harrison	R-IN, 1881–1887
Warren Harding	R-OH, 1915–1921
Harry Truman	D-MO, 1935–1945
John Kennedy	D-MA, 1953–1960
Lyndon Johnson	D-TX, 1949–1961
Richard Nixon	R-CA, 1950–1953

Andrew Johnson was received warmly upon his return to the Senate in 1875, even though the same body had fallen only one vote short of convicting him in an 1868 impeachment trial.

PRESIDENTS WHO
WERE CABINET MEMBERS

"Are all Cabinets congeries of little autocrats with a super-autocrat presiding over them?" —Beatrice Webb

Thomas Jefferson   George Washington's secretary of State, 1790–1793

James Madison   Thomas Jefferson's secretary of State, 1801–1809

James Monroe   James Madison's secretary of State, 1811–1817; secretary of War, 1814–1815

John Quincy Adams   James Monroe's secretary of State, 1817–1825

Martin Van Buren   Andrew Jackson's secretary of State, 1829–1831

James Buchanan   James Polk's secretary of State, 1845–1849

Ulysses Grant   Andrew Johnson's interim secretary of War, 1867–1868

William Howard Taft   Theodore Roosevelt's secretary of War, 1804–1808

Herbert Hoover   Warren Harding's and Calvin Coolidge's secretary of Commerce, 1921–1928

"IN THE PHILIPPINES". On board the Manchuria.

William Howard Taft with Alice Roosevelt

If Bob Dole had been elected in 1996, he would have been the first president whose wife had served in the Cabinet of a previous administration.

PRESIDENTS WHO WERE LAWYERS

John Adams
Thomas Jefferson
James Madison
James Monroe
John Quincy Adams
Andrew Jackson
Martin Van Buren
John Tyler
James Polk
Millard Fillmore
Franklin Pierce
James Buchanan
Abraham Lincoln

Rutherford Hayes
James Garfield
Chester Arthur
Grover Cleveland
Benjamin Harrison
William McKinley
William Howard Taft
Woodrow Wilson
Calvin Coolidge
Franklin Roosevelt
Richard Nixon
Gerald Ford
Bill Clinton

Clinton is the first president to be married to a lawyer.

PRESIDENTS WHO WERE NOT LAWYERS

It doesn't take a lawyer to sign bills into law. A mining engineer, a peanut farmer, and a haberdasher have done the job, too.

George Washington
William Henry Harrison
Zachary Taylor
Andrew Johnson
Ulysses Grant
Theodore Roosevelt
Warren Harding
Herbert Hoover

Harry Truman
Dwight Eisenhower
John Kennedy
Lyndon Johnson
Jimmy Carter
Ronald Reagan
George Bush

Truman was an administrative judge in Missouri even though he never passed the bar.

PRESIDENTS
WHO WERE MASONS

The Free and Accepted Masons, a fraternal order organized in England in the early eighteenth century, advocates philanthropy and religious tolerance. Masons have been active in U.S. politics since the Revolution, and their perceived influence in early-nineteenth-century America inspired the Anti-Masonic Party.

George Washington   Lodge No. 4, Fredricksburg, VA

James Monroe   Williamsburg Lodge No. 6, Williamsburg, VA

Andrew Jackson   Harmony Lodge No. 1, Nashville, TN

James Polk   Columbia Lodge No. 31, Columbia, TN

James Buchanan   Lodge No. 43, Lancaster, PA

Andrew Johnson   Greeneville Lodge No. 119, Greeneville, TN

James Garfield   Magnolia Lodge No. 70, Marion, OH

William McKinley   Hiram Lodge No. 21, Winchester, VA

Theodore Roosevelt   Lodge No. 806, Oyster Bay, NY

William Howard Taft   Kilwinning Lodge No. 345, Cincinnati, OH

Warren Harding   Marion Lodge No. 70, Marion, OH

Franklin Roosevelt   Holland Lodge No. 8, New York, NY

Harry Truman   Belton Lodge No. 450, Belton, MO

Lyndon Johnson   Johnson City Lodge No. 561, Johnson City, TX

Gerald Ford   Malta Lodge No. 465, Grand Rapids, MI

PRESIDENTIAL AGES ON TAKING OFFICE

The Constitution says that a president has to be at least 35 years old; only nature provides the upper limit. The presidents are ranked here by their age upon taking the oath of office.

Ronald Reagan	69
William Henry Harrison	68
James Buchanan	65
Zachary Taylor	64
George Bush	64
Dwight Eisenhower	62
John Adams	61
Andrew Jackson	61
Gerald Ford	61
Harry Truman	60
James Monroe	58
George Washington	57
Thomas Jefferson	57
James Madison	57
John Quincy Adams	57
Andrew Johnson	56
Woodrow Wilson	56
Richard Nixon	56
Benjamin Harrison	55
Warren Harding	55
Lyndon Johnson	55
Martin Van Buren	54
Rutherford Hayes	54
William McKinley	54
Herbert Hoover	54
Abraham Lincoln	52
Jimmy Carter	52
John Tyler	51
William Howard Taft	51
Calvin Coolidge	51
Franklin Roosevelt	51
Millard Fillmore	50
Chester Arthur	50
James Polk	49
James Garfield	49
Franklin Pierce	48
Grover Cleveland	47
Ulysses Grant	46
Bill Clinton	46
John Kennedy	43
Theodore Roosevelt	42

★ ★ ★

INCLEMENT INAUGURATIONS

There wasn't a professional event planner among the drafters of the Constitution, who chose March 4 (or March 5 if March 4 was a Sunday) as inauguration day, rain or shine. This choice had dire consequences: William Henry Harrison gave a lengthy outdoor address during a bad storm, fell ill afterward, and died a month later, leading to a fracas over whether Vice President John Tyler had become president or merely acting president. After Franklin Roosevelt's first term, inauguration day was moved to January 20 (or January 21 if January 20 is a Sunday) even though by then politicians knew how lovely Washington, D.C., can be when the cherry trees are blossoming.

Snowy Inaugurations

James Monroe   1817 and 1821

Andrew Jackson   1833

William Henry Harrison   1841

Franklin Pierce   1853

William Howard Taft   1909

Rainy Inaugurations

James Polk   1845

Abraham Lincoln   1865

Ulysses Grant   1869 and 1873

Benjamin Harrison   1889

William McKinley   1901

Herbert Hoover   1929

Franklin Roosevelt   1933 and 1937

Dwight Eisenhower   1957

★ ★ ★

INAUGURAL VERBIAGE
Longest Inaugural Addresses

William Henry Harrison	1841	8,445 words
William Howard Taft	1909	5,433
James Polk	1849	4,776
James Monroe	1821	4,467
Benjamin Harrison	1889	4,388

Shortest Inaugural Addresses

George Washington	1797	135 words
Franklin Roosevelt	1945	559
Abraham Lincoln	1865	698
Theodore Roosevelt	1901	985
Zachary Taylor	1849	996

INAUGURAL EGO
Inaugural Addresses That Used "I" Most Often

William Henry Harrison	1841	45 times
Abraham Lincoln	1861	44
Martin Van Buren	1837	39
William Howard Taft	1909	32
James Monroe	1821	26
George Bush	1989	26

Inaugural Addresses That Used "I" Least Often

Theodore Roosevelt	1901	0 times
Abraham Lincoln	1865	1
Franklin Roosevelt	1941	1
Dwight Eisenhower	1957	1
Bill Clinton	1997	2

SECRET SERVICE CODE NAMES

The Secret Service was established in 1865 by Abraham Lincoln. A division of the Department of the Treasury that investigates counterfeiting, the Secret Service began to protect presidents and their families in 1901, after William McKinley was assassinated. Harry Truman was the first chief executive to be assigned a code name.

Harry Truman	General	**Gerald Ford**	Passkey
Dwight Eisenhower		**Betty Ford**	Pinafore
	Providence	**Jimmy Carter**	Deacon
John Kennedy	Lancer	**Rosalynn Carter**	Dancer
Jacqueline Kennedy	Lace	**Amy Carter**	Dynamo
Caroline Kennedy	Lyric	**Ronald Reagan**	Rawhide
John F. Kennedy Jr.	Lark	**Nancy Reagan**	Rainbow
Lyndon Johnson	Volunteer	**George Bush**	Timberwolf
Lady Bird Johnson	Victoria	**Barbara Bush**	Tranquillity
Lynda Bird Johnson	Velvet	**Bill Clinton**	Eagle
Luci Baines Johnson	Venus	**Hillary Clinton**	Evergreen
Richard Nixon	Searchlight	**Chelsea Clinton**	Energy
Pat Nixon	Starlight		

If any presidential pet has been assigned a code name by the Secret Service, the name is still a secret.

NAYSAYERS: Presidents Who Vetoed the Most Bills

The following totals include pocket vetoes, in which bills sent to the president in the last ten days of a congressional session are left unsigned.

Franklin Roosevelt	635	**Ronald Reagan**	78
Grover Cleveland	584*	**Gerald Ford**	66
Harry Truman	250	**Calvin Coolidge**	50
Dwight Eisenhower	181	**Benjamin Harrison**	44
Ulysses Grant	93	**Woodrow Wilson**	44
Theodore Roosevelt	82		

* 414 in first term; 170 in second term.

PRESIDENTS WHO VETOED THE FEWEST BILLS

Totals include pocket vetoes.

John Adams	0	James Garfield	0
Thomas Jefferson	0	James Monroe	1
John Quincy Adams	0	Martin Van Buren	1
William Henry Harrison	0	George Washington	2
Zachary Taylor	0	James Polk	3
Millard Fillmore	0		

PRESIDENTS WHO HAD THE MOST VETOES OVERRIDDEN

Andrew Johnson ☛	15
Harry Truman	12
Gerald Ford	12
Franklin Roosevelt	9
Ronald Reagan	9
Grover Cleveland	7*
Richard Nixon	7
Woodrow Wilson	6
Franklin Pierce	5
Ulysses Grant	4
Calvin Coolidge	4
Herbert Hoover	3

* 2 in first term; 5 in second term.

> *Andrew Johnson's veto of the Tenure of Office Act, which required Senate approval of the dismissal of government officials whom Congress had previously confirmed, was overridden. When Johnson violated the Tenure of Office Act by dismissing his secretary of War, Congress began impeachment proceedings.*

PRESIDENTS CONCERNING WHOM RESOLUTIONS OF IMPEACHMENT HAVE BEEN INTRODUCED IN CONGRESS

John Tyler

Andrew Johnson

Grover Cleveland

Herbert Hoover

Harry Truman

Richard Nixon

Bill Clinton

Andrew Johnson's impeachment panel

PRESIDENTS WHO ASKED CONGRESS TO DECLARE WAR

The president may be the commander in chief of the armed forces, but only Congress has the power to declare war.

James Madison   War of 1812 (1812) House, 79–49; Senate, 19–13

James Polk   Mexican War (1846) House, 173–14; Senate, 40–2

William McKinley   Spanish-American War (1898) House, 310–6; Senate, 42–35

William McKinley and his War Cabinet

Woodrow Wilson   World War I (1917) House, 375–5; Senate, 82–6

Franklin Roosevelt   World War II (1941) House, 388–1; Senate, 82–0—against Japan
House, 393–0; Senate, 88–0—against Germany
House, 399–0; Senate, 90–0—against Italy

NO MORE YEARS:
Presidents Defeated in Bids for Another Term

John Adams ☞ 1800
John Quincy Adams 1828
Martin Van Buren 1840, 1848
Millard Fillmore 1852, 1856
Grover Cleveland 1888
Benjamin Harrison 1892
Theodore Roosevelt 1912
William Howard Taft 1912
Herbert Hoover 1932
Gerald Ford 1976
Jimmy Carter 1980
George Bush 1992

Grover Cleveland lost his bid for reelection in 1888 to Benjamin Harrison, but voters returned him to office four years later.

TYRANNY OF THE MINORITY:
Presidents Who Won with Less Than 50% of the Popular Vote

Presidents are not directly elected by the people. Instead, each state casts electoral votes for a candidate, which correspond in number to the state's representation in Congress, and a plurality in any state gives a candidate all of the state's electoral votes. Not only is it possible to become president without the support of a majority of Americans, but it has happened many times.

John Quincy Adams	1824	30.9%
James Polk	1844	49.6
Zachary Taylor	1848	47.3
James Buchanan	1856	45.3
Abraham Lincoln	1860	39.8
Rutherford Hayes	1876	48.0
James Garfield	1880	48.3
Grover Cleveland ☞	1884	48.5
Benjamin Harrison	1888	47.8
Grover Cleveland	1892	46.0
Woodrow Wilson	1912	41.8
Woodrow Wilson	1916	49.2
Harry Truman	1948	49.5
John Kennedy	1960	49.7
Richard Nixon	1968	43.4
Bill Clinton	1992	43.0
Bill Clinton	1996	49.2

Three men—John Quincy Adams, Rutherford Hayes, and Benjamin Harrison—became president even though their main opponent won a greater percentage of the popular vote. In fact, Samuel Tilden, who ran against Hayes in 1876, won 51% of the vote, but the disputed election was settled by a bipartisan commission that voted along party lines.

PRESIDENTIAL ELECTIONS:
Percentages of the Electoral Vote

George Washington	1789	100%	Theodore Roosevelt	1904	70.6
George Washington	1792	100	Bill Clinton	1996	70.4
James Monroe	1820	99.6	James Madison	1808	69.7
Ronald Reagan	1984	97.6	Bill Clinton	1992	68.8
Richard Nixon	1972	96.6	Andrew Jackson	1828	68.2
Franklin Roosevelt	1936	94.4	William Howard Taft	1908	66.5
Thomas Jefferson	1804	92.1	William McKinley	1900	65.3
Abraham Lincoln	1864	91.0	Grover Cleveland	1892	62.4
Ronald Reagan	1980	90.9	James Polk	1844	61.8
Lyndon Johnson	1964	90.3	William McKinley	1896	60.6
Franklin Roosevelt	1932	88.9	Abraham Lincoln	1860	59.4
Dwight Eisenhower	1956	86.1	James Madison	1812	59.0
Franklin Pierce	1852	85.8	James Buchanan	1856	58.8
Franklin Roosevelt	1940	84.6	Benjamin Harrison	1888	58.1
James Monroe	1816	84.3	James Garfield	1880	58.0
Herbert Hoover	1928	83.6	Martin Van Buren	1836	57.8
Dwight Eisenhower	1952	83.2	Harry Truman	1948	57.1
Woodrow Wilson	1912	81.9	John Kennedy	1960	56.4
Franklin Roosevelt	1944	81.4	Zachary Taylor	1848	56.2
Ulysses Grant	1872	81.2	Richard Nixon	1968	55.9
William Henry Harrison			Jimmy Carter	1976	55.2
1840		79.6	Grover Cleveland	1884	54.6
George Bush	1988	79.2	Thomas Jefferson	1800	52.9
Andrew Jackson	1932	76.6	Woodrow Wilson	1916	52.2
Warren Harding	1920	76.1	John Adams	1796	51.4
Ulysses Grant	1868	72.8	Rutherford Hayes	1876	50.1
Calvin Coolidge	1924	71.9	John Quincy Adams	1824	32.2

Nixon carried every state but Massachusetts in 1972. After Watergate and Nixon's resignation, that state's McGovern supporters put bumper stickers on their cars saying DON'T BLAME ME, I'M FROM MASSACHUSETTS.

PRESIDENTIAL ELECTIONS:
Presidents Who Did Not Carry a Majority of the States

It's possible to carry only the 11 most populous of the 50 states and lose the other 39 and still become president. This has never happened. (See "States That Could Guarantee the Presidency in the Year 2000," page 204.)

John Quincy Adams 🖝
    1824 7 out of 24 states
Zachary Taylor 🖝 1848
    15 out of 30 states
James Garfield 1880
    19 out of 38 states
John Kennedy 1960
    22 out of 50 states
Jimmy Carter 1976
    23 out of 50 states

In 1824, none of the candidates won a majority of the electoral vote. The House of Representatives was called on to decide the election, and John Quincy Adams won with the support of the backers of the candidate Henry Clay and the New York congressional delegation, the head of which had what he believed was a divinely inspired epiphany telling him to vote for Adams.

PRESIDENTS WHO CAME TO POWER WITHOUT THEIR PARTIES' CONTROLLING BOTH HOUSES OF CONGRESS

In parliamentary democracies such as England, Israel, and Japan, the head of government is also the head of the largest party in the legislature. In the United States, presidents are elected separately from Congress, and often the American people are of two minds, putting one party in the White House and the other in charge of Congress—and letting the two branches of government fight it out.

President	Year	House(s) in Which the President's Party Was in the Minority
Zachary Taylor	1850	House and Senate
Millard Fillmore	1850	House and Senate
Rutherford Hayes	1878	House

Grover Cleveland	1886	House
Richard Nixon	1970	House and Senate
Gerald Ford	1974	House and Senate
Ronald Reagan	1980	House
George Bush	1988	House and Senate

PRESIDENTS WHOSE PARTIES LOST CONTROL OF ONE OR BOTH HOUSES OF CONGRESS DURING THEIR TERMS IN OFFICE

The use of the Contract with America in the 1994 elections was an unusual display of unity and organization by a party to win a majority in Congress, but the voting patterns behind it were no aberration. Voters have often chosen to remove the president's party from power when they were dissatisfied with the president's performance.

President	Year	House(s) in Which the President's Party Became the Minority
George Washington	1792	House
John Tyler ☞	1842	House
James Polk	1846	House
Franklin Pierce	1854	House
James Buchanan	1858	House
Ulysses Grant	1874	House
Rutherford Hayes	1878	Senate
Chester Arthur	1882	House
Benjamin Harrison	1890	House
Grover Cleveland	1894	House and Senate
William Howard Taft	1910	House
Woodrow Wilson	1918	House and Senate
Harry Truman	1946	House and Senate
Dwight Eisenhower	1954	House
Ronald Reagan	1986	Senate
Bill Clinton	1994	House and Senate

PRESIDENTS WITH FACIAL HAIR

*Shaving was in fashion when the United States was founded,
and shaving is once again the norm; bearded presidential
advisers, like Robert Reich and C. Everett Koop, are
the exception rather than the rule. But in the second half of the
19th century and in the early 20th century, beards meant power
just as Ohio meant power. In those days our country
was led by a parade of fuzzy-faced men.*

Abraham Lincoln	1861–1865	Beard
Ulysses Grant	1869–1877	Beard
Rutherford Hayes	1877–1881	Beard
James Garfield	1881	Beard
Chester Arthur	1881–1885	Mustache and sideburns
Grover Cleveland	1885–1889; 1893–1897	Mustache
Benjamin Harrison	1889–1893	Beard
Theodore Roosevelt	1901–1909	Mustache
William Howard Taft	1909–1913	Mustache

*Of the nine presidents with facial hair, only one, Cleveland, was
a Democrat; all the others were Republicans.*

PRESIDENTS WHO WERE ILL OR INJURED

Before 1967, when the 25th Amendment was ratified, there was no clear constitutional procedure for the temporary transfer of power when a president became ill or incapacitated.

Grover Cleveland   During his second term Cleveland underwent surgery to remove cancerous tissue from his jaw. Cleveland wanted to keep his condition secret because the economy was also ailing. He arranged to use the yacht of his friend Commodore Elias Benedict, the *Oneida,* as a makeshift floating hospital. He was back on the job in a month; the operation was not publicly known until 1917, when one of the surgeons published a complete account in the *Saturday Evening Post.*

Theodore Roosevelt   TR was blinded in the left eye in 1904 while sparring with a White House aide. Roosevelt kept his blindness a secret for the rest of his life.

Woodrow Wilson   Wilson fell ill in September 1919 while on a tour of the country and suffered a severe stroke a few days later. While recuperating, Wilson refused to hand off his duties to Vice President Thomas Marshall. His wife Edith (☞) was the gatekeeper to the president during his recovery, and she was thought to have had considerable control over the course of public affairs.

Warren Harding   Harding fell ill in 1923, en route from Alaska to California on the Voyage of Understanding, a national tour devoted to plugging his presidential policies. He was thought to be a victim of food poisoning. Six weeks later, while the president's wife, Florence, read a favorable magazine profile to her husband, the president had a stroke and died. Florence Harding forbade an autopsy, and several years later an author accused her of poisoning her husband, but most historians do not believe this to be true.

Calvin Coolidge ☛ Coolidge fell into a deep depression after his son Calvin Jr. died in 1924 of blood poisoning as a result of a blister he got from running around without socks on the White House tennis court. Coolidge became withdrawn, delegated authority to others, and gave no more annual addresses to Congress.

Franklin Roosevelt Before he became president, FDR was partly paralyzed as a result of polio and often used a wheelchair, though as a rule photographers were not permitted to photograph him in the chair. Despite his desire to project a robust image, during his 12-year-plus reign, Roosevelt suffered from sinusitis, impacted wisdom teeth, bronchitis, several bouts of flu, systolic and diastolic hypertension, anemia, gallbladder problems, bronchial pneumonia, pulmonary disease, and congestive heart failure. He died in office of a cerebral hemorrhage, thought to have been brought on by his heart problems and high blood pressure.

Dwight Eisenhower Ike had a heart attack in September 1955. The president claimed this was his first, but Dr. Thomas Mattingly, a cardiologist at Walter Reed Army Medical Center, believed it may have been his third and that the two earlier ones (one in 1953, when Ike was president) were reported as mysterious illnesses. In June 1956, while running for a second term, Eisenhower underwent surgery for ileitis, or inflammation of the intestine. In November 1957, after greeting the arriving president of Morocco, Ike had a slight stroke. While campaigning for Nixon in 1960, he experienced ventricular fibrillation; his wife, Mamie, wanted him to stop campaigning, but he didn't.

John Kennedy   JFK aggravated his wartime back injury in May 1961 while planting trees in Canada and was forced to walk on crutches for a time afterward. Kennedy used several therapeutic methods, including swimming in a heated White House pool and applying mustard plasters, and he wore a brace that some say prevented his ducking the fatal shot in November 1963. He also had suffered from Addison's disease, failure of the adrenal cortex, since 1947. This condition gave his skin a permanent "tan" and was treated with daily cortisone shots.

Ronald Reagan   In July 1985, Reagan underwent an operation to have a cancerous polyp removed from his colon. In accordance with the 25th Amendment, Vice President George Bush became acting president for eight hours while Reagan was under anesthesia. A few days later the president had a cancerous bump removed from his nose. He had several nose carcinomas and colon polyps removed during the remainder of his second term and underwent prostate surgery in 1987.

George Bush   In May 1991, Bush felt dizzy while jogging and was found to have an irregular heartbeat brought about by Graves' disease, a thyroid condition that also afflicted the president's wife, Barbara. In January 1992, while on a trip to Japan, Bush suffered from an intestinal flu. Ignoring his doctor's advice, he attended a state dinner, at which he vomited on Japanese prime minister Kiishi Miyazawa and fainted.

Bill Clinton   Clinton tore a tendon in his knee after falling down the stairs late at night at the Florida home of golfer Greg Norman. Recuperation lasted a couple of months, during which time he used both a wheelchair and crutches.

Many Americans were concerned that Bush would need a heart operation in 1991 and Dan Quayle would become acting president for a few hours.

PRESIDENTS WITH THE MOST U.S. PUBLIC SCHOOLS NAMED AFTER THEM

John Kennedy	103	Dwight Eisenhower	31
Thomas Jefferson	75	Theodore Roosevelt	26
George Washington	61	Andrew Jackson	23
Woodrow Wilson	57	Herbert Hoover	22
Abraham Lincoln	37	James Madison	22

> *The children on* The Brady Bunch *attended Millard Fillmore Junior High Shcool.*

NICKNAMES OF ANDREW JACKSON

Old Hickory
The Hero of New Orleans
The Farmer of Tennessee
King Mob
King Andrew the First
Duel Fighter
Land Hero of 1812
Mischievous Andy
Pointed Arrow
Sage of the Hermitage
Sharp Knife

SOME FOREIGN PLACES NAMED FOR PRESIDENTS

George Washington	Cape Washington, Antarctica Washington Land, Greenland
James Monroe	Monrovia, Liberia
James Buchanan	Buchanan, Liberia
Abraham Lincoln	Lincoln Island, South China Sea (in Chinese, Howu)
Rutherford Hayes	Presidente Hayes (department), Paraguay
Grover Cleveland	Clevelând, Brazil
Theodore Roosevelt	Rio Roosevelt, Brazil
Woodrow Wilson	Avenue du Président Wilson, Paris
Franklin Roosevelt	Avenue Franklin D. Roosevelt, Paris
Dwight Eisenhower	Mount Eisenhower, Alberta, Canada
John Kennedy	Avenue du Président Kennedy, Paris

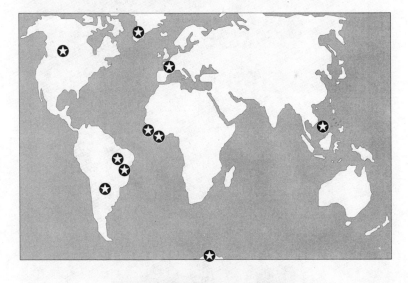

PRESIDENTS AND OBESITY

Presidents have long sponsored fitness awards for students, but they have not always practiced what they preached. Here the presidents are ranked according to body-mass index (BMI), a formula used by doctors to determine obesity. To compute BMI, a president's (or any person's) weight in kilograms is divided by the square of his height in meters. A BMI of 25 or more means the president may have been, or may be, overweight; a BMI of more than 30 means he was, or is, obese.

Obese

William Howard Taft	42.3	Zachary Taylor	30.2
Grover Cleveland	34.6	Theodore Roosevelt	30.2
William McKinley	31.1		

Overweight

Chester Arthur	28.7	Gerald Ford	26.2
Bill Clinton	28.3	Lyndon Johnson	26.0
Herbert Hoover	27.7	Rutherford Hayes	26.0
John Quincy Adams	27.2	James Monroe	25.6
James Buchanan	26.9	George Washington	25.5
James Polk	26.4	Dwight Eisenhower	25.3
Harry Truman	26.3		

Not Overweight

Andrew Johnson	24.9	John Kennedy	22.6
James Garfield	24.9	Jimmy Carter	22.4
George Bush	24.8	Thomas Jefferson	22.0
Ronald Reagan	24.2	Abraham Lincoln	21.7
Millard Fillmore	24.2	William Henry Harrison	21.2
Richard Nixon	23.9	Calvin Coolidge	21.2
Franklin Roosevelt	23.6	Franklin Pierce	20.6
Woodrow Wilson	23.5	Andrew Jackson	19.0
Warren Harding	23.5	James Madison	17.0
Ulysses Grant	23.3		

John Tyler was slim, and John Adams, Martin Van Buren, and Benjamin Harrison were all quite fat—Adams was called His Rotundity by detractors—but there is no record of their presidential weight.

Woodrow Wilson and William Howard Taft

INTERPRESIDENTIAL INSULTS

Presidents have not always sounded presidential
when referring to their peers.

Thomas Jefferson on **John Adams** (1787, in a letter to James Madison) "He is vain, irritable, and a bad calculator of the force and probable effect of the motives which govern men."

William Henry Harrison on **John Quincy Adams** "It is said he is a disgusting man to do business. Coarse, dirty, and clownish in his address and stiff and abstracted in his opinions, which are drawn from books exclusively."

James Buchanan on **John Quincy Adams** (1822, in a letter to his friend Hugh Hamilton) "His disposition is as perverse and mulish as that of his father."

Jefferson on **Andrew Jackson** "I feel much alarmed at the prospect of seeing General Jackson President. He is the most unfit man I know for such a place."

John Quincy Adams on **Jackson** (1833, in a comment to Josiah Quincy) "A barbarian who cannot write a sentence of grammar and can hardly spell his own name."

John Quincy Adams on **Martin Van Buren** (1829) "His principles are all subordinate to his ambitions."

John Quincy Adams on **William Henry Harrison** "active but shallow mind, a political adventurer not without talents but self-sufficient, vain, and indiscreet"

Jackson on **William Henry Harrison** (1841) "our present imbecile chief"

John Quincy Adams on **James Polk** (1834) "He has no wit, no literature, no point of argument, no gracefulness of delivery, no elegance of language, no philosophy, no pathos, no felicitous impromptus."

Jackson on **Polk** "I never betrayed a friend or was guilty of the black sin of ingratitude. Mr. Polk cannot say as much."

Abraham Lincoln on **Polk** (1848, regarding the Mexican War) "He is a bewildered, confounded, and miserably perplexed man."

Polk on **Zachary Taylor** (1849) "General Taylor is, I have no doubt, a well-meaning old man. He is, however, uneducated, exceedingly ignorant of public affairs, and I should judge, of very ordinary capacity."

Harry Truman on **Millard Fillmore** "At a time we needed a strong man, what we got was a man that swayed with the slightest breeze."

Theodore Roosevelt on **Franklin Pierce** (1887) "A small politician, of low capacity and mean surroundings, proud to act as the servile tool of men worse than himself but also stronger and abler."

Truman on **Pierce** "He was another one that was a complete fizzle. . . . Pierce didn't know what was going on, and even if he had, he wouldn't of known what to do about it."

Truman on **Pierce** (1952) "Pierce was the best looking President the White House ever had—but as president he ranks with Buchanan and Calvin Coolidge."

Ulysses Grant on **Buchanan** (letter to a friend) "our present granny executive"

Grant on **Andrew Johnson** (1868, to Senator John Brooks Henderson) "I would impeach him because he is such an infernal liar."

James Garfield on **Grant** (1874) "He has done more than any other president to degrade the character of Cabinet officers by choosing them in the model of the military staff, because of their pleasant personal relation to him and not because of their national reputation and the public needs."

Grant on **Garfield** (1867) "Garfield has shown that he is not possessed of the backbone of an angleworm."

Rutherford Hayes on **Garfield** (1883) "He was not executive in his talents—not original, not firm, not a moral force. He leaned on others—could not face a frowning world; his habits suffered from Washington life. His course at various times when trouble came betrayed weakness."

Woodrow Wilson on **Chester Arthur** "a non-entity with side whiskers"

TR on **Benjamin Harrison** (1890)   "Damn the president! He is a cold-blooded, narrow-minded, prejudiced, obstinate, timid old psalm-singing Indianapolis politician."

TR on **William McKinley** (1898, regarding the Spanish-American War)   "McKinley has no more backbone than a chocolate éclair."

Wilson on **TR**   "He is the most dangerous man of the age."

Warren Harding on **TR** (1912)   "eminent fakir"

TR on **William Howard Taft**   "a flub-dub with a streak of the second-rate and the common in him"

TR on **Wilson** (1919)   "He is a silly doctrinaire at times and an utterly selfish and cold-blooded politician always."

TR on **Wilson**   "byzantine logothete"

TR on **Wilson**   "infernal skunk in the White House"

Taft on **Wilson** (1916)   "I regard him as a ruthless hypocrite, and as an opportunist, who has not convictions he would not barter at once for votes."

Wilson on **Harding**   "He has a bungalow mind."

Calvin Coolidge on **Herbert Hoover** (1929)   "That man has offered me unsolicited advice for six years, all of it bad."

Hoover on **Franklin Roosevelt**   "chameleon on plaid"

Truman on **Dwight Eisenhower** (1952)   "The General doesn't know any more about politics than a pig knows about Sunday."

Eisenhower on **Lyndon Johnson** (1960)   "He doesn't have the depth of mind nor the breadth of vision to carry great responsibility. . . . Johnson is superficial and opportunistic."

Truman on **Richard Nixon**   "Richard Nixon is a no-good lying bastard. He can lie out of both sides of his mouth at the same time, and if he ever caught himself telling the truth, he'd lie just to keep his hand in."

Gerald Ford on **Jimmy Carter** (1976)   "Jimmy Carter wants to speak loudly and carry a fly swatter."

PRESIDENTS WHO LIVED THE LONGEST AFTER THEIR TERMS IN OFFICE—AND WHAT THEY DID WITH THEIR TIME

A quick glance at before-and-after pictures of any president reveals that this high-stress job ages the officeholder quickly. Several presidents, like James Polk and Lyndon Johnson, did not survive four more years after leaving office. By contrast, some of those too old to have had Bob Hope as a golfing partner survived many years in retirement.

Herbert Hoover   **32 years**   Served as chairman of relief organizations during World War II; after World War II, served as coordinator of European Food Program and chairman of Commission on Organization of the Executive Branch

John Adams   **25 years**   Retired to Quincy, Massachusetts, and read a lot of books

Millard Fillmore   **21 years**   Traveled; met Pope Pius IX; as Know-Nothing candidate for president in 1856, carried only Maryland

Martin Van Buren   **21 years**   Failed to win Democratic presidential nomination in 1841; as Free Soil candidate for president in 1848, won 10% of vote

Gerald Ford   **20 years and counting**   Wrote memoirs; played golf

Harry Truman   **20 years**   Wrote memoirs; sold family farm to shopping-center developers

Richard Nixon   **20 years**   Wrote books; traveled; worked at reestablishing reputation

James Madison   **19 years**   Edited papers on Constitutional Convention; helped found, and served as rector of, University of Virginia; helped organize American Colonization Society, which returned free African Americans to Africa

John Quincy Adams   **19 years**   Served 17 years in U.S. House of Representatives

Jimmy Carter   **18 years and counting**   Serves as freelance mediator of international disputes; established Carter Center to promote peace, human rights, and conflict resolution; writes books and poetry; works on behalf of Habitat for Humanity; teaches Sunday school

Thomas Jefferson 17 years Founded University of Virginia and designed its buildings

John Tyler 17 years Retired to Virginia plantation; served as Overseer of Roads; served in Confederate congress

William Howard Taft 17 years Taught law at Yale University; served as chief justice of the United States for nine years

A SAMPLER OF PRESIDENTS' LAST WORDS

Thomas Jefferson "I resign my spirit to God, my daughter to my country."

John Quincy Adams "This is the last of earth! I am content."

William Henry Harrison (to John Tyler) "Sir, I wish you to understand the true principles of government. I wish them carried out. I ask nothing more."

Ulysses Grant "Water."

Grover Cleveland "I have tried so hard to do the right."

Theodore Roosevelt "Put out the light."

Woodrow Wilson "I'm a broken machine, but I'm ready."

Franklin Roosevelt "I have a terrific headache."

Dwight Eisenhower "I've always loved my wife. I've always loved my children. I've always loved my grandchildren. And I have always loved my country."

> *Both John Adams and Thomas Jefferson died on July 4, 1826, 50 years to the day after the signing of the Declaration of Independence. Jefferson died at Monticello, his Virginia plantation, early in the afternoon. Adams, who outlasted him by a few hours, did not learn of his death. His last words were "Thomas—Jefferson—still surv—"*

PRESIDENTIAL AGES AT DEATH

John Adams	90	George Washington	67
Herbert Hoover	90	Benjamin Harrison	67
Harry Truman	88	Woodrow Wilson	67
James Madison	85	Andrew Johnson	66
Thomas Jefferson	83	Zachary Taylor	65
Richard Nixon	81	Franklin Pierce	64
John Quincy Adams	80	Lyndon Johnson	64
Martin Van Buren	79	Ulysses Grant	63
Andrew Jackson	78	Franklin Roosevelt	63
Dwight Eisenhower	78	Theodore Roosevelt	60
James Buchanan	77	Calvin Coolidge	60
Millard Fillmore	74	William McKinley	58
James Monroe	73	Warren Harding	57
William Howard Taft	72	Abraham Lincoln	56
John Tyler	71	Chester Arthur	56
Grover Cleveland	71	James Polk	53
Rutherford Hayes	70	James Garfield	49
William Henry Harrison	68	John Kennedy	46

PRESIDENTIAL BURIAL GROUNDS

Many presidents were buried temporarily near their place of death and reinterred weeks or years later. Below is a list of their final resting places.

George Washington	Mount Vernon, VA
John Adams	Hancock Cemetery, Quincy, MA
Thomas Jefferson	Monticello, Charlottesville, VA
James Madison	Madison Cemetery, Montpelier Station, VA
James Monroe	Hollywood Cemetery, Richmond, VA
John Quincy Adams	Hancock Cemetery, Quincy, MA
Andrew Jackson	The Hermitage, near Lebanon, TN
Martin Van Buren	Kinderhook Cemetery, Kinderhook, NY
William Henry Harrison	William Henry Harrison Memorial State Park, North Bend, OH
John Tyler	Hollywood Cemetery, Richmond, VA

James Polk	Tennessee State Capitol, Nashville, TN
Zachary Taylor	Taylor family cemetery, Louisville, KY
Millard Fillmore	Forest Lawn Cemetery, Buffalo, NY
Franklin Pierce	Old North Cemetery, Concord, NH
James Buchanan	Woodward Hill Cemetery, Lancaster, PA
Abraham Lincoln	Lincoln Monument, Springfield, IL
Andrew Johnson	Andrew Johnson Cemetery, Greeneville, TN
Ulysses Grant	Grant's Tomb, New York, NY
Rutherford Hayes	Spiegel Grove, Fremont, OH
James Garfield	James Garfield Monument, Cleveland, OH
Chester Arthur	Rural Cemetery, Albany, NY
Grover Cleveland	Princeton Cemetery, Princeton, NJ
Benjamin Harrison	Crown Hill Cemetery, Indianapolis, IN
William McKinley	Westlawn Cemetery, Canton, OH
Theodore Roosevelt	Young Memorial Cemetery, Oyster Bay, NY
William Howard Taft	Arlington National Cemetery, Arlington, VA
Woodrow Wilson	Washington National Cathedral, Washington, DC
Warren Harding	Marion Memorial Cemetery, Marion, OH
Calvin Coolidge	Plymouth Cemetery, Plymouth Notch, VT
Herbert Hoover	Hoover Memorial–Burial Site, West Branch, IA
Franklin Roosevelt	Hyde Park Rose Garden, Hyde Park, NY
Harry Truman	Harry S Truman Library, Independence, MO
Dwight Eisenhower	Eisenhower Memorial Center, Abilene, KS
John Kennedy	Arlington National Cemetery, Arlington, VA
Lyndon Johnson	LBJ Ranch, Stonewall, TX
Richard Nixon	Richard Nixon Library and Birthplace, Yorba Linda, CA

Just in case you missed it, Grant ☞ is buried in Grant's Tomb.

FIRST FAMILY LISTS

P RESIDENTS COME FROM REMARKABLE families. Their parents are elected officials, their brothers drink too much, their children join the ballet, and even their dogs write books. Juggling family life and political life can be a tremendous burden; as Theodore Roosevelt said, "I can be president—or I can attend to Alice," referring to his oldest daughter. The lists in this chapter examine the people (and the furry and feathery creatures) that have made up the first families.

PRESIDENTS WHO MARRIED OLDER WOMEN

George Washington

Millard Fillmore

Benjamin Harrison*

Warren Harding

Richard Nixon

---

* Harrison was no longer president at the time of the marriage.

> *The biggest difference in age between a president and his wife was 28 years. Forty-nine-year-old Grover Cleveland wedded 21-year-old Frances Folsom in 1886.*

FIRST LADIES:
The Oldest and the Youngest

All ages are given as of inauguration day, except Frances Cleveland's and Julia Tyler's, whose ages are given as of the dates of their weddings, when their husbands were in the White House.

The Oldest

Anna Harrison*	65	Florence Harding	60
Barbara Bush	64	Margaret Taylor	60
Abigail Fillmore	62	Bess Truman	60

---

* Wife of William Henry Harrison.

The Youngest

Frances Cleveland	21	Edith Roosevelt	40
Julia Tyler	24	Dolley Madison	40
Jacqueline Kennedy	31		

> *The only other president to marry while in the White House was Woodrow Wilson, whose first wife died during his first term.*

FIRST LADIES WHO LIVED THE LONGEST

On average, women live longer than men. In 1900, the average man lived 46.3 years and the average woman 48.3 years. Recent figures put male life expectancy at 72.3 years and female life expectancy at 79 years. The longest-living first ladies are ranked here by their age at death.

Bess Truman	97	**Lady Bird Johnson**	84 and counting
Edith Wilson	89	**Frances Cleveland**	83
Anna Harrison	88	**Helen Taft**	82
Sarah Polk	87	**Mamie Eisenhower**	82
Edith Roosevelt	87	**Dolley Madison**	81
Lucretia Garfield	85	**Pat Nixon**	81

FIRST LADIES WHO GRADUATED FROM COLLEGE

Like her husband, Herbert, Lou Hoover was an engineer and she worked closely with him.

Lucy Hayes

Lucretia Garfield

Frances Cleveland

Grace Coolidge

Lou Hoover

Jacqueline Kennedy

Lady Bird Johnson

Pat Nixon

Rosalynn Carter

Nancy Reagan

Hillary Rodham Clinton

Barbara Bush dropped out of Smith College to marry George.

FIRST LADIES WHO BELONGED TO THE DAUGHTERS OF THE AMERICAN REVOLUTION

Julia Grant	Mamie Eisenhower
Caroline Harrison	Rosalynn Carter
Edith Roosevelt	Nancy Reagan
Florence Harding	Barbara Bush
Eleanor Roosevelt	

> *Eleanor Roosevelt quit the Daughters of the American Revolution in 1939, after the organization prevented the African American opera singer Marian Anderson from singing in Constitution Hall in Washington, DC. (The concert took place at the Lincoln Memorial instead.)*

FIRST LADY FILL-INS

When the presidents' wives could not or would not serve as the White House hostess, other women filled that role.

Dolley Madison ☞ The widowed Thomas Jefferson called on his Virginia neighbor and the wife of his secretary of State to serve as his dinner-party hostess.

Emily Donelson Andrew Jackson's wife, Rachel, died when Jackson was president-elect. Emily Donelson was his niece.

Angelica Van Buren Martin Van Buren was widowed. Angelica was his daughter-in-law.

Jane Harrison William Henry

Harrison's wife, Anna, skipped the inauguration on account of illness but outlasted her husband by 24 years. Jane was Harrison's daughter-in-law.

Priscilla Tyler   John Tyler's wife, Letitia, had suffered a stroke and died while her husband was in office. Priscilla, Tyler's daughter-in-law, was relieved of her duties when the president married Julia Gardiner.

Bettie Bliss   Zachary Taylor's wife, Margaret, refused to take part in Washington society. Bettie Bliss was the Taylors' daughter.

Mary Abigail Fillmore   Millard Fillmore's wife, Abigail, did not want to serve as hostess and refused every invitation to social events. Mary Abigail was the Fillmores' daughter.

Harriet Lane   James Buchanan never married. Harriet Lane was his niece.

Martha Patterson   Andrew Johnson's wife, Eliza, feigned illness during his presidency. Martha Patterson was his daughter.

Mary Arthur McElroy   Chester Arthur was widowed. Mary McElroy was his sister.

Emily Donelson

Angelica Van Buren

Rose Cleveland   Grover Cleveland's sister, Rose, acted as hostess until the president married Frances Folsom.

Helen Woodrow Bones   After Woodrow Wilson's wife, Ellen, died, Helen Bones served as hostess and introduced the president to Edith Bolling Galt, whom he married a year later.

13 WOMEN WHO REJECTED FUTURE PRESIDENTS

If they had only known, they might have become first ladies.

1. **Betsy Fauntleroy**   Fauntleroy was courted by George Washington. She thought he wasn't rich enough.

2. **Mary Eliza "Polly" Phillipse**   Phillipse also rejected a proposal by Washington. She married a Virginian named Roger Morris, and they supported the English during the Revolution.

3. **Hannah Quincy**   Quincy grew tired of waiting for a proposal from John Adams, a struggling young lawyer and her constant suitor, so she married a doctor instead. She was widowed twice.

4. **Rebecca Burwell**   Thomas Jefferson meant to propose to Burwell while they were dancing one evening—but he was too anxious to make a coherent proposal. She later married and had two daughters, one of whom became the wife of John Marshall.

5. **Kitty Floyd**   The teenage daughter of a representative in the Continental Congress, Floyd agreed to marry James Madison. But after he announced his plan to retire from the Congress, Floyd ended the engagement and married William Clarkson, who was studying medicine. She sent Madison a Dear John letter, which she sealed with dough made of rye flour.

6. **Ellen Randolph**   Randolph was a granddaughter of Thomas Jefferson. After Martin Van Buren's wife, Hannah, died of tuberculosis, it was widely reported that Van Buren, then a

senator, courted Randolph, who was in her mid-20s. Van Buren may have proposed to her, though neither confirmed this. She married someone else in 1825.

7. **Anne Coleman**   Coleman was engaged to James Buchanan. After an argument, Coleman broke off the engagement and went to Philadelphia to stay with relatives. She died there several months later, possibly a suicide victim. Buchanan wrote down the story behind their disagreement, but the papers were burned at his request upon his death.

8. **Mary Owens**   The daughter of a wealthy Kentucky farmer, Owens was courted by Abraham Lincoln for several years. She was rubbed the wrong way by Lincoln's rough manners, and he was displeased by her gaining weight and losing her teeth.

9. **Sara Word**   Word met Andrew Johnson when he was on the lam from his indentured servitude, and he helped her sew a quilt. Her concerned parents made her break off her relationship with the 16-year-old.

10. **Fanny G. Perkins**   Perkins turned down a young Rutherford Hayes because she didn't want to live in Ohio and he refused to move to Connecticut. She ended up marrying another man and moving to Ohio.

11. **Frances Ann Cannon**   Cannon dated John Kennedy when he was at Harvard. Some family members thought they might marry, but she became engaged to the writer John Hersey.

12. **Phyllis Brown**   Brown dated Gerald Ford for four years and introduced him to modeling. She didn't want to leave New York for Grand Rapids, and they broke up. She married several times.

13. **Jane Wyman**   In her testimony at their divorce proceedings, Wyman blamed the disintegration of her marriage to Ronald Reagan on Reagan's growing political involvement with the Screen Actors Guild, which he wanted her to share. She later married the bandleader Freddie Karger (and divorced and remarried him) and starred on the TV soap opera *Falcon Crest*.

PRESIDENTS WHO HAD (OR WERE ACCUSED OF HAVING) MISTRESSES

George Washington   The British spread rumors linking George Washington to a woman named Mary Gibbons.

Thomas Jefferson   When Jefferson went to Paris, he is believed to have courted a married Englishwoman named Maria Cosway. She was his houseguest, without her husband, for four months while Jefferson was in London. Jefferson is also believed by some to have kept Sally Hemings, a black slave, as his mistress, and to have fathered several children with her.

James Garfield   ☛ Garfield had an affair in 1862 with Mrs. Lucia Gilbert Calhoun, an 18-year-old reporter for *The New York Times*. He confessed his affair to his wife, and she forgave him.

Woodrow Wilson   Wilson met Mary Hulbert Peck while in Bermuda. They became friendly and maintained a correspondence, and she later divorced her husband. After his first wife died, he kept up with Peck, but his second wife, Edith, forced him to cut ties with her. Peck ended up as a door-to-door salesperson.

Warren Harding   Carrie Phillips, who had a long affair with Harding before his presidency, was shipped off to Asia during his campaign. She also received $25,000 up front and a $2,000 monthly payment to stay quiet. Harding's affair with Nan Britton, who bore his child in 1919, continued while he was in the White House, and the Secret Service guarded the Oval Office when she visited.

Franklin Roosevelt   Before he became president, Roosevelt had an affair with Lucy Page Mercer, his wife's secretary. Eleanor Roosevelt and FDR's mother forced them to end the relationship, and Roosevelt and Mercer did not see each other for many years. FDR also had an affair with his own secretary, Marguerite "Missy" LeHand, who had the next bedroom over from his in the New York governor's mansion. He was also rumored to have had an affair with Crown Princess Marta of Norway, who lived at the White House during World War II.

Dwight Eisenhower   Kay Summersby was Eisenhower's driver in England during and after World War II. Harry Truman told the story that Ike wanted to resign from the army so he could divorce his wife and marry Summersby, but General George Marshall insisted he would ruin him if he did. Summersby wrote a book about her affair with General Eisenhower, called *Past Forgetting*.

John Kennedy   Kennedy had a reputation as a womanizer; he is believed to have had affairs with many women, including the actresses Marilyn Monroe and Angie Dickinson; Judith Exner Campbell (who was mobster Sam "Momo" Giancana's mistress); and White House secretaries Priscilla Weir and Jill Cowan, who were referred to as Fiddle and Faddle.

Lyndon Johnson   LBJ had a 30-year affair with Alice Glass, who did not believe in marriage but lived with Texas media mogul Charles E. Marsh and their two children. Her relationship with Johnson began in the late 1930s and ended in 1967, over disagreements about the Vietnam War.

Richard Nixon   Nixon was rumored to have had an affair with a Chinese cocktail waitress named Marianna Liu, whom he met in Hong Kong when he was vice president. In 1969, sponsored by associates of the president, she immigrated to Nixon's hometown of Whittier, California. Liu says that they did not have an affair and never slept together.

George Bush During the 1992 campaign, rumors that Jennifer Fitzgerald, a longtime aide to Bush, had been his mistress were denied by both of them.

Bill Clinton Gennifer Flowers claims she had a 12-year affair with Clinton and sold her story to a supermarket tabloid. The Clintons went on *60 Minutes* during the 1992 campaign to refute her charges and other widespread rumors of marital infidelity. As a result of Paula Jones's lawsuit against the president, he reportedly admitted in a deposition to having a relationship with Flowers. Reports also surfaced of an affair with former White House intern Monica Lewinsky. The president has denied having an improper relationship with Lewinsky, who visited the Oval Office 37 times.

PRESIDENTS WHO HAD LOTS OF CHILDREN, INCLUDING THOSE WHO DIED YOUNG

John Tyler	14	John Adams	5
William Henry Harrison	10	Thomas Jefferson	6
Rutherford Hayes ☞	8	Zachary Taylor	6
James Garfield	7	Andrew Johnson	5
Theodore Roosevelt	6	Grover Cleveland	5
Franklin Roosevelt	6	Ronald Reagan	5*
George Bush	6		

* Includes one whom the president adopted.

PRESIDENTS WHO HAD NO BIOLOGICAL CHILDREN

Some people would put Warren Harding on this list; but while he had no children by his wife, Florence, he did have a child by his mistress Nan Britton.

George Washington
James Buchanan
Andrew Jackson
James Polk
James Madison

Washington and Jackson both adopted children.

PRESIDENTS ACCUSED OF HAVING ILLEGITIMATE CHILDREN

George Washington   Washington provided financial support to the family of Captain Thomas Posey. Posey's son Lawrence resembled the father of our country, and it was rumored that Posey promised to raise the boy in exchange for money. Other rumors circulated that Washington had fathered Alexander Hamilton, his secretary of the Treasury. Neither of these rumors seems to have any foundation.

Thomas Jefferson ☞ Jefferson is alleged to have had a long relationship with Sally Hemings, a slave he owned. Hemings bore seven children, and some historians believe that four or five were fathered by Jefferson.

Grover Cleveland In 1874, Cleveland, a bachelor, had a son with Maria Halpin, a widow who worked for a Buffalo department store. The boy was named after Cleveland's close friend Oscar Folsom. Halpin wanted to raise young Oscar, but the boy was instead sent to an orphanage until he was adopted. Cleveland won the presidential election in 1884 despite the negative publicity about his having a son out of wedlock. Two years later Cleveland married Frances Folsom, the daughter of his friend Oscar.

Warren Harding Harding's affair with Nan Britton, thirty years his junior, began in 1917. Their daughter, Elizabeth Ann Christian, was supposedly conceived on a couch in Harding's chambers in the Senate in early 1919. Harding did not visit his daughter, and he paid child support via Secret Service couriers. Harding left no money to Elizabeth when he died, and Nan Britton wrote the bestseller *The President's Daughter* for revenge and profit. Harding is also believed to have had a daughter, Marion Louis Hodder, by Susan Pearle around 1895. He sent money to pay for this child's upbringing as well.

Lyndon Johnson In June 1987, Steven Mark Brown claimed he was the child and heir of LBJ and sued Lady Bird Johnson for $10.5 million. His mother, Madeline Brown, says that she and Johnson had an affair that lasted more than two decades.

Bill Clinton A woman named Bobbie Ann Williams claims Clinton had sex with her in 1984 and is the father of her son Danny.

CHIPS OFF THE OLD BLOCK:
Presidents' Children Who Served in the Government

John Quincy Adams   Son of John Adams
  Minister to the Netherlands, 1794–1796
  Minister to Germany, 1796–1801
  Senator (Federalist-MA), 1803–1808
  Minister to St. Petersburg, 1809–1811
  Negotiator of Treaty of Ghent, 1914
  Minister to Great Britain, 1815–1817
  Secretary of State, 1817–1825
  President, 1825–1829
  Congressman (Federalist-MA), 1831–1848

Charles Francis Adams   Son of John Quincy Adams
  Congressman (R-MA), 1859–1861
  Minister to Great Britain, 1861–1868

John Van Buren   Son of Martin Van Buren
  Congressman (D-NY), 1841–1843

John Scott Harrison   Son of William Henry Harrison
  Congressman (Whig-OH), 1853–1857

David Gardiner Tyler   Son of John Tyler
  Congressman (D-VA), 1893–1897

Robert Todd Lincoln   Son of Abraham Lincoln
  Secretary of War, 1881–1885
  Minister to Great Britain, 1889–1893

Frederick Dent Grant   Son of Ulysses Grant
  Minister to Austria-Hungary, 1889–1893

James Rudolph Garfield   Son of James Garfield
  Secretary of the Interior, 1907–1909

Russell Benjamin Harrison   Son of Benjamin Harrison
  State legislator, Indiana 1921–1923, 1924–1927

Theodore Roosevelt Jr.   Son of TR
  Assistant secretary of the Navy, 1921–1924
  Governor of Puerto Rico, 1929–1932
  Governor general of the Philippines, 1932–1933

Robert Alphonso Taft   Son of William Howard Taft
Senator (R-OH), 1939–1953

Charles Phelps Taft   Son of William Howard Taft
Mayor of Cincinnati, 1955–1957

Herbert Hoover Jr.   Son of Herbert Hoover
Undersecretary of State for Middle Eastern Affairs, 1954–1957

Franklin Delano Roosevelt Jr.   Son of FDR
Congressman (D-NY), 1949–1955
Undersecretary of Commerce, 1963–1965
Chairman of the Equal Employment Opportunity Commission, 1965–1966

James Roosevelt   Son of FDR
Congressman (D-CA), 1955–1965

Elliott Roosevelt   Son of FDR
Mayor of Miami Beach, 1965–1967

George W. Bush   Son of George Bush
Governor of Texas, 1995–

Other presidential progeny, like Maureen Reagan and Jeb Bush, have been unsuccessful candidates for public office.

FATHERLESS FATHERS OF OUR COUNTRY

The following presidents lost their fathers in infancy or childhood.

George Washington   Augustine Washington, a planter, traveled to England on business a lot, and George didn't see him very much. Augustine died when the future president was 11.

Andrew Jackson   ☞
Andrew Jackson *père* left

northern Ireland for America in 1765. Two years later he hurt himself lifting a log and died while his wife, Elizabeth, was pregnant with Andrew.

Andrew Johnson Jacob Johnson worked as, among other things, a Presbyterian church sexton. In late 1811, he rescued two men from an icy pond near Raleigh, North Carolina, and got sick. He was ringing church bells at a funeral in January 1812 when he collapsed and died. Andrew, who was then three, grew up poor and at 14 was apprenticed to a tailor as an indentured servant.

Rutherford Hayes Rutherford *père*, a storekeeper in Delaware, Ohio, died of a fever five weeks before his son was born. The future president was raised by his mother, Sophia, and her brother, Sardis Birchard.

James Garfield Abram Garfield was a farmer and a champion wrestler. He fell ill while fighting a forest fire and died soon after, when James was a year and a half old. James, who grew up poor, was raised by his mother, Eliza, and an uncle, Amos Boynton.

Herbert Hoover Jesse Clark Hoover was a blacksmith and farm-equipment salesman. He died of a heart ailment when his son was six. Herbert's mother, Hulda, died three years later, and Herbert grew up with uncles in Iowa and Oregon.

Gerald Ford In 1915, Leslie King, a wool merchant, left his wife, Dorothy, and their two-year-old son, Leslie Jr. A year later Dorothy married Gerald Rudolph Ford, who adopted Leslie King Jr. and renamed him Gerald Rudolph Ford Jr.

Bill Clinton William Jefferson Blythe, a traveling salesman, died in a car accident three months before his son was born. The future president's mother, Virginia, married Roger Clinton when her son was four. Roger Clinton never adopted Virginia's first son, but Bill eventually took his stepfather's last name.

PRESIDENTS' FATHERS
WHO HELD PUBLIC OFFICE

Spence Monroe Father of James Monroe
  Circuit judge
John Adams Father of John Quincy Adams
  President of the United States
Benjamin Harrison Father of William Henry Harrison
  Governor of Virginia
John Tyler Father of John Tyler
  Governor of Virginia
Nathaniel Fillmore Father of Millard Fillmore
  Magistrate
Benjamin Pierce Father of Franklin Pierce
  Governor of New Hampshire
Jacob Johnson Father of Andrew Johnson
  Constable
John Scott Harrison Father of Benjamin Harrison
  Congressman
Alphonso Taft Father of William Howard Taft
  Secretary of War
  Attorney general
  Minister to Austria and Russia
Joseph P. Kennedy Father of John Kennedy
  Ambassador to Great Britain
Sam Ealy Johnson Father of Lyndon Johnson
  State legislator, Texas
Prescott Bush Father of George Bush
  Senator

> *William Henry Harrison's father was also a signer of the Declaration of Independence.*

★ ★ ★

COUPLES MARRIED IN THE WHITE HOUSE

The White House is a good place for cementing all sorts of alliances.

Lucy Payne Washington, sister of James Madison, and Supreme Court Justice **Thomas Todd,** March 29, 1812

Maria Monroe, daughter of James Monroe, and **Samuel Gouverneur,** March 9, 1820

John Adams II, son of John Quincy Adams, and **Mary Catherine Adams,** February 25, 1828

Mary Eastin, niece of Andrew Jackson, and **Lucien J. Polk,** April 10, 1832

Delia Lewis, daughter of Jackson adviser William Berkeley Lewis, and **Alphonse Pageot,** November 29, 1832

Lizzie Tyler, daughter of John Tyler, and **William Waller,** January 31, 1842

Nellie Grant, daughter of Ulysses Grant, and **Algernon C.F. Sartoris,** May 21, 1874

Emily Platt, niece of Rutherford Hayes, and Colonel **Russell Hastings,** June 19, 1878

Grover Cleveland and **Frances Folsom,** June 2, 1886

Alice Roosevelt, daughter of Theodore Roosevelt, and Congressman **Nicholas Longworth,** February 17, 1906

Jessie Wilson, daughter of Woodrow Wilson, and **Francis Sayre,** November 25, 1913

Eleanor Wilson, daughter of Woodrow Wilson, and secretary of the Treasury **William Gibbs McAdoo,** May 7, 1914

Alice Wilson, niece of Woodrow Wilson, and the Reverend **Isaac Stuart McElroy Jr.,** August 7, 1918

Harry Hopkins, Franklin Roosevelt's former secretary of Commerce and **Louise Gill Macy,** July 30, 1942

Lynda Bird Johnson, daughter of Lyndon Johnson, and **Charles S. Robb,** December 9, 1967

Tricia Nixon, daughter of Richard Nixon, and **Edward F. Cox,** June 12, 1971

> *Lyndon Johnson's other daughter, Luci Baines Johnson, married Patrick Nugent in August 1966. They had a church ceremony—he is Catholic—but the reception was held at the White House.*

EMBARRASSING PRESIDENTIAL RELATIVES

Every family has its black sheep. As the following list shows, the presidents are not so good at hiding them.

George Washington   Washington's mother, **Mary Ball Washington,** falsely complained that she was destitute and neglected by George.

John Adams   John Quincy Adams followed his father to the presidency, but John Adams's second and third sons were hardly as successful. Debt-ridden and despairing, **Charles Adams** drank himself to death a month after his father's term ended, and Charles's brother **Thomas Boylston Adams** similarly died a debtor and an alcoholic.

James Madison   Madison's stepson **Payne Todd** had a gambling problem and once owed $40,000, a debt that the president had to cover. Dolley Madison was forced to give up the family house as a result of her son's pastime.

James Monroe   The first in a long line of problem presidential brothers, **Joseph Monroe** married no fewer than three times. He fell into debt and looked to his brother James to bail him out. President Monroe hired Joseph as his secretary so he could keep watch over him. The president had other family troubles: his wife, **Elizabeth Kortright Monroe,** was a snob; his daughter **Eliza,** to the consternation of others, spoke her mind; and his daughter **Maria** married **Samuel Gouverneur,** Elizabeth's nephew, who took pleasure in alcohol and gambling.

John Quincy Adams   Adams's son **George Washington Adams** suffered from paranoia, hallucinations, and other mental troubles. He met his end on a ferry traveling from Massachusetts to New York. He accused his fellow passengers of plotting against him and soon afterward either jumped or fell overboard. Six weeks later his body washed up on City Island, in the Bronx.

William Henry Harrison   One of Harrison's six sons, **John Cleves Symmes Harrison,** was appointed by the Jackson administration to serve as receiver of the Vincennes, Indiana, Land Office. He was dismissed from the post following accusations that he had embezzled about $12,000 from the government. Another of Harrison's sons, **John Scott Harrison,** died an alcoholic at 35.

Abraham Lincoln   Lincoln's wife, **Mary Todd Lincoln,** had three brothers in the Confederate army, which led some to question her loyalty to the Union. During the war, in jealous outbursts, she harangued the wives of General Edward Ord and General Ulysses Grant. As first lady, she splurged on clothing and furnishings at government expense. In 1875, after the assassination of her husband and the death of two of her sons, she was committed to an institution.

Ulysses Grant ❧ The general's brother **Orville Grant** was a beneficiary of the rampant corruption in the Grant administration. Orville was nearly indicted, along with the president's secretary, Orville E. Babcock, for receiving stolen goods in connection with the Whiskey Ring scandal.

William McKinley After her mother and two daughters died, **Ida Saxton McKinley,** the wife of the president, was afflicted by seizures. The president would cover her face with a handkerchief whenever she was stricken in public.

Theodore Roosevelt TR's brother **Elliott Roosevelt** was an alcoholic who occasionally had seizures. Elliott's wife, Anna, tried to get him declared legally insane. When TR was assistant secretary of the Navy, Elliott disappeared and shacked up in New York with another woman. He died in New York after a fall in 1894.

Lyndon Johnson LBJ took political advice from his younger brother but also kept a close eye on him. **Sam Houston Johnson** was twice divorced and lived either with his brother or with one of his sisters. He had a drinking problem, got into a couple of car accidents, and passed bad checks while his brother was president. During the 1964 campaign, he responded to the suggestion that Senator John Pastore (D-RI) be Lyndon's running mate by quoting his brother as saying, "How can an Italian from a stinky state like Rhode Island possibly help me?" In an effort to keep him out of trouble, the Secret Service kept tabs on Sam Houston's comings and goings and on those of his visitors.

Richard Nixon   In the mid-1950s, when Nixon was vice president, his brother, **Donald Nixon,** borrowed $205,000 from Howard Hughes to sustain his chain of hamburger restaurants. When he was president, Richard had the Secret Service tap Donald's phone in order to monitor his activities. Donald had connections to the financier and longtime fugitive Robert Vesco, who made an illegal contribution to one of Richard's presidential campaigns. Donald's son **Donald Nixon Jr.** worked as an aide to Vesco.

Jimmy Carter   Carter's brother, **Billy Carter,** a brewer and buffoon, took more than $200,000 from the Libyan government and had to register with the U.S. government as a foreign agent. When asked whether he was alienating the president's Jewish supporters, he replied that the Jews could "kiss my ass." In 1979, Billy distinguished himself by urinating on the tarmac at the Atlanta airport. He also took part in undistinguished international events, such as the Vancouver World Belly Flop and Cannonball Diving Contest. He spent some time in rehab. **William T.C. Spann,** the president's nephew, was sentenced to 14 years in prison for armed robbery, a crime he committed while under the influence of drugs.

Ronald Reagan   Reagan's daughter **Patti Davis** was critical of her father's politics. After he left office, Patti posed nude in *Playboy* magazine and also participated in a *Playboy* video, in which she was shown kickboxing naked. Her book *Bondage* contained passages describing kinky sex. Since Ronald Reagan's Alzheimer's condition has deteriorated, however, Patti has reconciled with the family. Her brother, **Ron Reagan Jr.,** has also received his share of unwanted attention. At his father's inauguration, Ron refused to shake outgoing president Jimmy Carter's hand because he had "the morals of a snake," and for years he was dogged by rumors (even after he married) that he was homosexual, which he persistently denied.

Bill Clinton Clinton's half brother, **Roger Clinton Jr.,** is a college dropout who has played in a rock band. When Bill was governor of Arkansas, Roger was arrested for dealing cocaine. He was sentenced to two years in prison and agreed to testify in related cases.

PRESIDENTS' RELATIVES WHO WROTE BOOKS

Alice Roosevelt Longworth (daughter of Theodore Roosevelt) *Crowded Hours*

Helen Taft (wife of William Howard Taft) *Recollections of Full Years*

Edith Wilson (wife of Woodrow Wilson) *My Memoir*

Eleanor Roosevelt (wife of Franklin Roosevelt) *This is My Story; This I Remember; India and the Awakening East; On My Own; You Learn by Living; The Autobiography of Eleanor Roosevelt; UN; Today and Tomorrow* (with William DeWitt)

Margaret Truman (daughter of Harry Truman) *Bess W. Truman; First Ladies; Harry S Truman; Murder at the FBI; Murder at the Kennedy Center; Murder at the National Cathedral; Murder at the National Gallery; Murder at the Pentagon; Murder in Georgetown; Murder in the CIA; Murder in the Smithsonian; Murder in the Supreme Court; Murder in the White House; Murder on Embassy Row; Murder on the Potomac; Souvenir, Margaret Truman's Own Story* (with Margaret Cousins); *Where the Buck Stops; White House Pets; Women of Courage*

Lady Bird Johnson (wife of Lyndon Johnson)   *A White House Diary; Wildflowers Across America* (with Carlton B. Lees)

Julie Nixon Eisenhower (daughter of Richard Nixon)   *Pat Nixon: The Untold Story; Special People*

Betty Ford (wife of Gerald Ford)   *Betty, a Glad Awakening* (with Chris Chase); *The Times of My Life* (with Chris Chase)

Rosalynn Carter (wife of Jimmy Carter)   *First Lady from Plains*

Nancy Reagan (wife of Ronald Reagan)   *My Turn: The Memoirs of Nancy Reagan* (with William Novak)

Patti Davis (daughter of Ronald Reagan)   *Angels Don't Die: My Father's Gift of Love; Bondage; Deadfall; Home Front; A House of Secrets; The Way I See It*

Barbara Bush (wife of George Bush)   *Barbara Bush: A Memoir; C. Fred's Story; Millie's Book*

Hillary Rodham Clinton (wife of Bill Clinton)   *It Takes a Village*

WHITE HOUSE DOGS

Abraham Lincoln 🐾   Fido

Warren Harding	Laddie Boy, an Airedale terrier
Herbert Hoover	King Tut, a watchdog
Franklin Roosevelt	Fala, a Scottish terrier
Harry Truman	Mike, an Irish setter
Dwight Eisenhower	Heidi, a weimaraner
John Kennedy	Charlie, a Welsh terrier
	Pushinka, presented by Nikita Khrushchev
	Shannon, presented by Eamon De Valera
Lyndon Johnson	Him and Her, beagles
Richard Nixon	King Timahoe, an Irish setter
George Bush	Millie, author of a book
Bill Clinton	Buddy, a Labrador retriever

The best known vice presidential dog was Checkers, Richard Nixon's pet when he was Dwight Eisenhower's running mate in 1952. The cocker spaniel, which had been given to the Nixons by a political supporter, was the decoy subject of a speech in which Nixon responded to charges that he had maintained a secret slush fund.

★ ★ ★

WHITE HOUSE BIRDS

Martha Washington	parrot
Thomas Jefferson	mockingbird
Dolley Madison	parrot
Ulysses Grant	parrot
William McKinley	double-yellow-headed parrot
Florence Harding	Bob, a canary
Calvin Coolidge	Enoch, a goose
	Nip and Tuck, canaries
John Kennedy	Bluebell and Maybelle, parakeets
Lyndon Johnson	lovebirds

BEYOND SOCKS:
Unusual White House Pets

Foreign dignitaries and political supporters alike have given presidents a variety of exotic pets, many of which have ended up at the Smithsonian Institution's National Zoological Park in Washington.

Louisa Adams
Wife of John Quincy Adams

silkworms

Martin Van Buren

tiger cubs

William Henry Harrison

His Whiskers, a billy goat

Tad Lincoln
Son of Abraham Lincoln

Jack, a turkey that was granted a presidential pardon after being sentenced to serve as Christmas dinner

Andrew Johnson

mice

Alice Roosevelt
Daughter of Theodore Roosevelt

Emily Spinach, a snake

Quentin Roosevelt
Son of TR

snakes

William Howard Taft

Pauline Wayne, a cow

Woodrow Wilson

Old Ike, a lawnmowing, tobacco-chewing ram

Calvin Coolidge

Rebecca and Horace, raccoons

John Kennedy

Zsa Zsa, a rabbit

THEODORE ROOSEVELT'S WHITE HOUSE MENAGERIE

TR was a lover of nature, and he encouraged this passion in his children. During his presidency the White House was overrun with animals.

Horses Bleistein, Renown, Roswell, Rusty, Jocko, Root, Grey Dawn, Wyoming, Yagenka, and Algonquin, a pony

Dogs Pete, a bull terrier; Sailor Boy, a Chesapeake Bay retriever; Skip, a mongrel; and Manchu, a spaniel

Snakes Emily Spinach and others

Cats Tom Quartz; Slippers

Badger Josiah

Guinea pigs Dewey Sr., Dewey Jr., Bob Evans, Bishop Doan, Father O'Grady, et al.

> *TR also had lions, a hyena, a wildcat, bears, parrots, a zebra, an owl, lizards, rats, roosters, and a raccoon.*

VICE PRESIDENTS AND CABINET MEMBERS
LISTS

THE EXECUTIVE BRANCH OF THE government is more than just one person. The president is surrounded by dozens of capable men and women who offer him advice on every topic under the sun. Paradoxically, the second highest office, the vice presidency, is often the least desirable. Vice presidents often stay in the background while in office and are quickly forgotten afterward, and the ambitious avoid the job when they can. When asked whether he would be willing to become Jimmy Carter's running mate, Morris Udall said, "I am against vice in all forms, including the vice presidency."

VICE PRESIDENTS

John Adams	1789–1797
Thomas Jefferson	1797–1801
Aaron Burr	1801–1805
George Clinton	1805–1812*
Elbridge Gerry	1813–1814*
Daniel D. Tompkins	1817–1825
John C. Calhoun	1825–1832†
Martin Van Buren	1833–1837
Richard Mentor Johnson	1837–1841
John Tyler	1841‡
George Mifflin Dallas	1845–1849
Millard Fillmore	1849–1850‡
William Rufus de Vane King	1853*
John Cabell Breckinridge	1857–1861
Hannibal Hamlin	1861–1865
Andrew Johnson	1865‡
Schuyler Colfax	1869–1873
Henry Wilson	1873–1875*
William Almon Wheeler	1877–1881
Chester Alan Arthur	1881‡
Thomas Andrews Hendricks	1885*
Levi Parsons Morton	1889–1893
Adlai Ewing Stevenson	1893–1897
Garret Augustus Hobart	1897–1899*
Theodore Roosevelt	1901‡
Charles Warren Fairbanks	1905–1909
James Schoolcraft Sherman	1909–1912*
Thomas Riley Marshall	1913–1921
Calvin Coolidge	1921–1923‡
Charles Gates Dawes	1925–1929
Charles Curtis	1929–1933
John Nance Garner	1933–1941
Henry Agard Wallace	1941–1945
Harry S Truman	1945‡
Alben William Barkley	1949–1953
Richard Milhous Nixon	1953–1961

Lyndon Baines Johnson	1961–1963[‡]
Hubert Horatio Humphrey	1965–1969
Spiro T. Agnew	1969–1973[†]
Gerald Rudolph Ford	1973–1974[‡]
Nelson Aldrich Rockefeller	1974–1977
Walter F. Mondale	1977–1981
George Bush	1981–1989
James Danforth Quayle	1989–1993
Albert Arnold Gore Jr.	1993–

[*] Died in office.
[†] Resigned.
[‡] Became president.

VICE PRESIDENTS
WHO BECAME PRESIDENT

John Adams
Thomas Jefferson
Martin Van Buren
John Tyler
Millard Fillmore ☞
Andrew Johnson
Chester Arthur
Theodore Roosevelt
Calvin Coolidge
Harry Truman
Lyndon Johnson
Richard Nixon
Gerald Ford
George Bush

Only two major-party losing vice presidential candidates—John Tyler and Franklin Roosevelt—later became president.

VICE-PRESIDENTS WHO DIDN'T SERVE FULL TERMS

George Clinton   In poor health during his second term; died of pneumonia

Elbridge Gerry   Died after suffering a stroke in his coach while returning home from the Senate

Daniel Tompkins   Started drinking heavily after being named in a scandal involving reimbursement of war expenses and was a no-show in the Senate for the last two years of his term (although he did not resign); eventually drank himself to death

John Calhoun   Fell out with the president over the Peggy Eaton scandal and nullification of federal laws; resigned to join the Senate

John Tyler   Became president when William Henry Harrison died

Millard Fillmore   Became president when Zachary Taylor died

Rufus King   Convalescing in Cuba at the time of the inauguration, took the oath of office in Havana; died of tuberculosis six weeks later after returning to his Alabama plantation

Andrew Johnson   Became president after Abraham Lincoln was assassinated

Henry Wilson   Died after having a stroke while presiding over the Senate

Chester Arthur   Became president after James Garfield died

Thomas Hendricks   Died of a stroke in his home state of Indiana six months after the inauguration

Garret Hobart   Entered office with a heart condition and died after a heart attack

Theodore Roosevelt   Became president after William McKinley was assassinated

James Sherman   Died of Bright's disease, a kidney condition, one week before standing for reelection

Calvin Coolidge Became president after Warren Harding died

Harry Truman Became president after Franklin Roosevelt died

Lyndon Johnson Became president after John Kennedy was assassinated

Spiro Agnew Resigned in the face of charges that he accepted kickbacks; on the day of his resignation, pleaded no contest to one charge of tax evasion and was fined

Gerald Ford Became president after Richard Nixon resigned

STATES FROM WHICH VICE PRESIDENTS HAVE BEEN CHOSEN

New York **11** Aaron Burr, George Clinton, Daniel Tompkins, Martin Van Buren, Millard Fillmore, William Wheeler, Chester Arthur, Levi Parsons, Theodore Roosevelt, James Sherman, Nelson Rockefeller

Indiana **5** Schuyler Colfax, Thomas Hendricks, Charles Fairbanks, Thomas Marshall, Dan Quayle

Massachusetts **4** John Adams, Elbridge Gerry, Henry Wilson, Calvin Coolidge

Kentucky **3** Richard Johnson, John Breckinridge, Alben Barkley

Texas **3** John Garner, Lyndon Johnson, George Bush

Illinois **2** Adlai Stevenson, Charles Dawes

Minnesota **2** Hubert Humphrey, Walter Mondale

Tennessee **2** Andrew Johnson, Al Gore

Virginia **2** Thomas Jefferson, John Tyler

Alabama **1** Rufus King

California **1** Richard Nixon

Iowa **1** Henry Wallace

Kansas 1 Charles Curtis

Maine 1 Hannibal Hamlin

Maryland 1 Spiro Agnew

Michigan 1 Gerald Ford

Missouri 1 Harry Truman

New Jersey 1 Garret Hobart

Pennsylvania 1 George Dallas

South Carolina 1 John Calhoun

> *Ohio has sent seven presidents to the White House, but never a vice president.*

★ ★ ★

LOSING MAJOR-PARTY VICE PRESIDENTIAL CANDIDATES

In the beginning, the presidential candidate who came in second in the count of electoral votes became vice president. Since 1804, presidential candidates have been paired with vice presidential candidates.

Rufus King 1804

Rufus King 1808

Charles Jared Ingersoll 1812

John Eager Howard 1816

Richard Stockton 1820

Nathan Sanford and **Nathaniel Macon** 1824

Richard Rush 1828

John Sergeant 1832

Francis Granger and **John Tyler** 1836

Richard Johnson 1840

Theodore Frelinghuysen 1844

William Orlando Butler and **Charles Francis Adams** 1848

William A. Graham 1852
William Lewis Dayton and **Andrew Jackson Donelson** 1856
Herschel V. Johnson, Joseph Lane, and **Edward Everett** 1860
George Hunt Pendleton 1864
Francis Preston Blair Jr. 1868
Benjamin Gratz Brown 1872
Thomas Hendricks 1876
William English 1880
John Alexander Logan 1884
Allen Granberry Thurman 1888
Whitelaw Reid 1892
Arthur Sewall 1896
Adlai Stevenson 1900
Henry Gassaway Davis 1904
John Worth Kern 1908
Nicholas Butler and **Hiram Warren Johnson** 1912
Charles Fairbanks 1916
Franklin Roosevelt 1920
Charles W. Bryan and **Burton Kendall Wheeler** 1924
Joseph Taylor Robinson 1928
Charles Curtis 1932
Frank Knox 1936
Charles Linza McNary 1940
John W. Bricker 1944
Earl Warren 1948
John J. Sparkman 1952
Estes Kefauver 1956
Henry Cabot Lodge 1960
William E. Miller 1964
Edmund S. Muskie and **Curtis Le May** 1968
R. Sargent Shriver Jr. 1972
Bob Dole 1976
Walter Mondale 1980
Geraldine Ferraro 1984
Lloyd Millard Bentsen Jr. 1988
Dan Quayle and **James Stockdale** 1992
Jack French Kemp and **Pat Choate** 1996

VICE PRESIDENTS WHO WERE OLDER THAN THEIR PRESIDENTS

George Clinton 4 years older than Thomas Jefferson; 12 years older than James Madison

Elbridge Gerry ☞ 7 years older than James Madison

Richard Johnson 2 years older than Martin Van Buren

George Dallas 3 years older than James Polk

Rufus King 18 years older than Franklin Pierce

Andrew Johnson 3 months older than Abraham Lincoln

William Wheeler 3 years older than Rutherford Hayes

Chester Arthur 2 years older than James Garfield

Thomas Hendricks 18 years older than Grover Cleveland

Levi Morton 9 years older than Benjamin Harrison

Adlai Stevenson 2 years older than Grover Cleveland

Charles Fairbanks 6 years older than Theodore Roosevelt

James Sherman 2 years older than William Howard Taft

Thomas Marshall 2 years older than Woodrow Wilson

Charles Curtis 15 years older than Herbert Hoover

John Garner 13 years older than Franklin Roosevelt

Alben Barkley 7 years older than Harry Truman

Lyndon Johnson 9 years older than John Kennedy

Nelson Rockefeller 5 years older than Gerald Ford

John Breckinridge was the youngest vice president. He was only 36 on inauguration day in 1857.

VICE PRESIDENTS WHO WERE CONGRESSMEN AND THEIR TERMS IN THE HOUSE

Elbridge Gerry	No party–MA, 1789–1793
Daniel Tompkins	No party–NY, 1805*
John Calhoun	R-SC, 1811–1817
Richard Johnson	D-KY, 1807–1819, 1829–1837
John Tyler	R-VA, 1817–1821
Millard Fillmore	Whig-NY, 1833–1835, 1837–1843
William King	No party–NC, 1811–1816
John Breckinridge	D-KY, 1851–1855
Andrew Johnson	D-TN, 1843–1853
Schuyler Colfax	R-IN, 1855–1869
William Wheeler	R-NY, 1861–1863, 1869–1877
Thomas Hendricks	D-IN, 1851–1855
Levi Morton	R-NY, 1879–1881
Adlai Stevenson	D-IL, 1875–1877, 1879–1881
James Sherman	R-NY, 1887–1891, 1893–1909
Charles Curtis	R-KS, 1893–1907
John Garner	D-TX, 1803–1833
Richard Nixon	R-CA, 1947–1950
Lyndon Johnson	D-TX, 1937–1949
Gerald Ford	R-MI, 1949–1973
George Bush	R-TX, 1967–1971
Dan Quayle	R-IN, 1977–1981
Al Gore	D-TN, 1977–1985

* Resigned before taking seat.

VICE PRESIDENTS WHO WERE SENATORS AFTER SERVING AS VICE PRESIDENT

John Calhoun didn't get along well with Andrew Jackson, his immediate superior, and resigned the vice presidency so he could join the Senate. The others waited until their terms as VP ended.

John Calhoun	D-SC, 1832–1843, 1845–1850
John Breckinridge*	D-KY, March–December 1861
Hannibal Hamlin†	R-ME, 1869–1881
Andrew Johnson†‡	R-TN, March–July 1875
Alben Barkley†‡	D-KY, 1955–1956
Hubert Humphrey†‡	D-MN, 1971–1978

* Expelled from the Senate.
† Also served in the Senate prior to becoming vice president.
‡ Died in office.

NUMBER OF TIE-BREAKING VOTES CAST BY VICE PRESIDENTS

In his capacity as president of the Senate, the vice president casts a vote only when there is an equal number of yea and nay votes.

John Adams	29
Thomas Jefferson	3
Aaron Burr	3
George Clinton	11
Elbridge Gerry	8
Daniel Tompkins	5
John Calhoun	28
Martin Van Buren	4
Richard Johnson	14
John Tyler	0
George Dallas	19
Millard Fillmore ☞	5
Rufus King	0
John Breckinridge	10

Hannibal Hamlin	7
Andrew Johnson	0
Schuyler Colfax	13
Henry Wilson	1
William Wheeler	5
Chester Arthur	3
Thomas Hendricks	0
Levi Morton	4
Adlai Stevenson	2
Garret Hobart	1
Theodore Roosevelt	0
Charles Fairbanks	0
James Sherman	4
Thomas Marshall	10
Calvin Coolidge	0
Charles Dawes	2
Charles Curtis	3
John Garner	3
Henry Wallace	4
Harry Truman	1
Alben Barkley	7
Richard Nixon	8
Lyndon Johnson	0
Hubert Humphrey	4
Spiro Agnew	2
Gerald Ford	0
Nelson Rockefeller	0
Walter Mondale	1
George Bush	7
Dan Quayle	0
Al Gore	3*

In the 1962 film Advise and Consent, *the vice president (Lew Ayres) is about to cast a tie-breaking vote on the confirmation of the nominee for secretary of State, Robert Leffingwell (Henry Fonda), when he learns that the president (Franchot Tone) has died. Since he has become the president, the tie is not broken and the nomination fails.*

---

* In first term.

PRESIDENTIAL SUCCESSION

When Ronald Reagan was shot in 1981, Secretary of State Alexander Haig said, "As of now, I am in control here, pending return of the vice president." He was getting ahead of himself. According to the Presidential Succession Act of 1947, this is the order of who becomes chief executive in the absence of every person listed before him or her. The order of cabinet members depends upon the year the department was established.

Vice president

Speaker of the House

President pro tempore of the Senate

Secretary of State

Secretary of the Treasury

Attorney general

Secretary of the Interior

Secretary of Agriculture

Secretary of Labor

Secretary of Health and Human Services

Secretary of Housing and Urban Development

Secretary of Transportation

Secretary of Energy

Secretary of Education

Secretary of Veterans Affairs

BILL MAHER'S PROPOSED ORDER OF PRESIDENTIAL SUCCESSION

Maher is the host of the TV talk show Politically Incorrect.

Vice president

Speaker of the House

President pro tempore of the Senate

Secretary of State

Secretary of the Treasury

Commissioner (or acting commissioner) of Major League Baseball

Secretary of Defense

Attorney general

Secretary of the Interior

Secretary of Agriculture

Secretary of Commerce

Secretary of Labor

First Lady of Country Music

Secretary of Health and Human Services

Secretary of Craft Services

Secretary of Blandishments

Secretary of Empty Threats

Secretary of Cutting Remarks

Secretary of Backhanded Compliments

Surgeon general

Surgeon general type

Dick Morris + 1

Miss Hawaiian Tropic

Miss Hawaiian Tropic, first runner-up

WOMEN IN THE CABINET

Frances Perkins   Franklin Roosevelt's secretary of Labor, 1933–1945

Oveta Culp Hobby   Dwight Eisenhower's secretary of Health, Education, and Welfare, 1953–1955

Marion B. Folsom   Eisenhower's secretary of Health, Education, and Welfare, 1955–1958

Carla Anderson Hills   Gerald Ford's secretary of Housing and Urban Development, 1975–1977

Juanita M. Kreps   Jimmy Carter's secretary of Commerce, 1977–1979

Patricia Roberts Harris   Carter's secretary of Housing and Urban Development, 1977–1979, and secretary of Health Education and Welfare/Health and Human Services, 1979–1981

Shirley Hufstedler   Carter's secretary of Education, 1979–1981

Elizabeth Hanford Dole   Ronald Reagan's secretary of Transportation, 1983–1987

Margaret M. Heckler   Reagan's secretary of Health and Human Services, 1983–1985

Ann D. McLaughlin   Reagan's secretary of Labor, 1987–1989

Elizabeth Hanford Dole   George Bush's secretary of Labor, 1989–1991

Lynn Martin   Bush's secretary of Labor, 1991–1993

Barbara H. Franklin   Bush's secretary of Commerce, 1992–1993

Janet Reno   Bill Clinton's attorney general, 1993–

Hazel R. O'Leary   Clinton's secretary of Energy, 1993–1997

Donna E. Shalala   Clinton's secretary of Health and Human Services, 1993–

Madeleine Albright   Clinton's secretary of State, 1997–

Alexis Herman   Clinton's secretary of Labor, 1997–

Frances Perkins, the first woman to serve in the Cabinet, turned the smallest and sleepiest executive department into a powerhouse after New Deal–era labor laws were passed.

AFRICAN AMERICANS IN THE CABINET

Robert C. Weaver   Lyndon Johnson's secretary of Housing and Urban Development, 1966–1969

William T. Coleman Jr.   Gerald Ford's secretary of Transportation, 1975–1977

Patricia Harris   Jimmy Carter's secretary of Housing and Urban Development, 1977–1979, and secretary of Health Education and Welfare/Health and Human Services, 1979–1981

Samuel R. Pierce Jr.   Ronald Reagan's secretary of Housing and Urban Development, 1981–1989

Louis W. Sullivan   George Bush's secretary of Health and Human Services, 1989–1993

Mike Espy   Bill Clinton's secretary of Agriculture, 1993–1994

Ronald H. Brown   Clinton's secretary of Commerce, 1993–1996

Hazel O'Leary   Clinton's secretary of Energy, 1993–1997

Jesse Brown   Clinton's secretary of Veterans Affairs, 1993–1997

Alexis Herman   Clinton's secretary of Labor, 1997–

Robert Weaver also was a member of Franklin Roosevelt's "black Cabinet," a panel of advisers on Negro affairs that also included Mary McLeod Bethune and Frank Horne.

CABINET MEMBERS WITH TIGERS TATTOOED ON THEIR TUSHES

George Shultz

FOREIGN-BORN CABINET MEMBERS

First-generation immigrants can serve in any political office other than that of president and vice president.

Alexander Hamilton Born in Nevis, British West Indies; George Washington's secretary of the Treasury, 1789–1795

James McHenry Born in Ballymena, Ireland; Washington's and John Adams's secretary of War, 1796–1800

Albert A.A. Gallatin ☞ Born in Geneva, Switzerland; Thomas Jefferson's and James Madison's secretary of the Treasury, 1801–1814

George Washington Campbell Born in Tongue, Scotland; Madison's secretary of the Treasury, 1814

Alexander J. Dallas Born in Jamaica, British West Indies; Madison's secretary of the Treasury, 1814–1816 (and acting secretary of War, 1815)

William J. Duane Born in Clonmel, Ireland; Andrew Jackson's secretary of the Treasury, 1833

Henry D. Gilpin Born in Lancaster, England; Martin Van Buren's attorney general, 1840–1841

Jacob Dolson Cox Born in Montreal, Canada; Ulysses Grant's secretary of the Interior, 1869–1870

Carl Schurz   Born in Liblar-am-Rhein, Germany; Rutherford Hayes's secretary of the Interior, 1877–1881

James Wilson   Born in Ayrshire, Scotland; William McKinley's, Theodore Roosevelt's, and William Howard Taft's secretary of Agriculture, 1897–1913

Oscar S. Straus   Born in Otterberg, Germany; Roosevelt's secretary of Commerce and Labor, 1906–1909

Franklin K. Lane   Born in Charlottetown, Prince Edward Island, Canada; Woodrow Wilson's secretary of the Interior, 1913–1920

William B. Wilson   Born in Blantyre, Scotland; Wilson's secretary of Labor, 1913–1921

James J. Davis   Born in Thedegar, Wales; Warren Harding's, Calvin Coolidge's, and Herbert Hoover's secretary of Labor, 1921–1930

Francis Biddle   Born in Paris, France; Franklin Roosevelt's attorney general, 1941–1945

Christian A. Herter   Born in Paris, France; Dwight Eisenhower's secretary of State, 1959–1961

C. Douglas Dillon   Born in Geneva, Switzerland; John Kennedy's and Lyndon Johnson's secretary of the Treasury, 1961–1965

Anthony J. Celebrezze   Born in Anzi, Italy; Kennedy's and Johnson's secretary of Health, Education, and Welfare, 1962–1965

George W. Romney   Born in Chihuahua, Mexico; Richard Nixon's secretary of Housing and Urban Development, 1969–1972

Henry A. Kissinger   Born in Fürth, Germany; Nixon's and Gerald Ford's secretary of State, 1973–1977

W. Michael Blumenthal   Born in Berlin, Germany; Jimmy Carter's secretary of the Treasury, 1977–1979

Madeleine Albright   Born in Prague, Czechoslovakia; Bill Clinton's secretary of State, 1997–

CABINET NOMINATIONS REJECTED BY THE FULL SENATE

When there is an obvious likelihood that a nominee for a Cabinet position will not be approved by the Senate, a president will usually withdraw the nomination before it comes to a vote.

Roger Brooke Taney ☞ Andrew Jackson's nominee for secretary of the Treasury. The Senate rejected the nomination, 28–18, on June 23, 1834. Taney had served as Jackson's attorney general from 1831–1833. A year later his nomination for associate justice of the Supreme Court was also rejected by the Senate. Later he became chief justice of the United States and wrote the opinion in the Dred Scott case.

Caleb Cushing ☞ John Tyler's nominee for secretary of the Treasury. The Senate voted against him three times—27–19, 27–10, 29–2—on March 3, 1843.

David Henshaw Tyler's nominee for secretary of the Navy. The Senate rejected him, 34–6, on January 15, 1844. After the nomination was rejected, Henshaw retired to private life.

James M. Porter ☞ Tyler's nominee for secretary of War. The Senate rejected the nomination, 38–3, on January 30, 1844, after Porter had served nearly ten months as acting secretary. In 1847, he became the first president of the Schuylkill and Susquehanna Railroad and in 1849 was elected to the Pennsylvania state legislature.

James S. Green   Tyler's nominee for secretary of the Treasury. The Senate rejected the nomination on June 15, 1844; the vote was not recorded.

Henry Stanbery   Andrew Johnson's nominee for attorney general. The Senate rejected the nomination, 29–11, on June 2, 1868, because of Stanbery's liberal interpretation of Reconstruction legislation. After the nomination was rejected, he resumed his law practice in Cincinnati.

Charles B. Warren   Calvin Coolidge's nominee for attorney general. The Senate rejected the nomination twice, 41–39 on March 10, 1925, and 46–39 six days later. Warren, nominated just after the Teapot Dome investigation had begun, was considered to have uncomfortably close ties to the "sugar trust."

Lewis L. Strauss   Dwight Eisenhower's nominee for secretary of Commerce. The Senate rejected the nomination, 49–46, on June 19, 1959. Strauss had served as acting secretary of Commerce since 1958 but was denied a permanent appointment because of his abrasive manner as head of the Atomic Energy Commission. He found an enemy in Senator Clinton Presba Anderson of New Mexico, who campaigned to defeat the nomination. Strauss later became an adviser to Barry Goldwater.

John Tower   George Bush's nominee for secretary of Defense. The Senate rejected the nomination, 53–47, on March 9, 1989, due to concerns about possible conflicts of interest (Tower had been a defense-company consultant) and accounts of alcoholism and womanizing. Tower died in a plane crash in 1991.

SHADY CABINET MEMBERS—AND OTHER PRESIDENTIAL ADVISERS

Edmund Randolph
George Washington's sec-
retary of State, 1794–1795.
Randolph was forced to resign when his fellow Cabinet members learned that
he had solicited bribes
from the French to stop
the Whiskey Rebellion.
(Randolph had been attor-
ney general from 1790 to
1794.)

John B. Floyd James
Buchanan's secretary of War, 1857–1861. Floyd was involved
in questionable land deals, and he was in the habit of sign-
ing contracts without reading them first. Vice President
John Breckinridge tried to fire Floyd during a war bonds
scandal, but the War secretary refused to be fired.

William W. Belknap Ulysses Grant's secretary of War,
1869–1876. Belknap arranged for a friend to receive an Indian trading-post concession; the friend kicked back half his
income. The deal was arranged by his wife, who could not
satisfy her expensive tastes on a Cabinet salary. Belknap was
impeached by the House but resigned before the Senate
voted and, as a result, was not convicted.

Harry M. Daugherty Warren Harding's and Calvin Coolidge's
attorney general, 1921–1923. Daugherty was Harding's men-
tor, campaign manager, and chief adviser. He maintained
the Green House, where Harding's Ohio cronies would retire
to drink (which was constitutionally prohibited at the time)
and receive bribes in return for pardons, appointments,
judgeships, and other favors. His henchman, Jess Smith,
killed himself in his apartment after being discovered selling
illegal liquor permits. Coolidge asked Daugherty to resign

during an investigation of his conduct. He was never indicted.

Albert B. Fall   Harding's secretary of the Interior, 1921–1923. Fall was at the center of the Teapot Dome scandal. As head of Interior, he controlled the three government oil reserves, one of which was located under Teapot Dome, Wyoming. Fall leased drilling rights to friends, who kicked back hundreds of thousands of dollars to him. He resigned during a Senate investigation and in 1929 was finally convicted of accepting a bribe and spent a year in prison. Fall was the first former Cabinet member to be convicted of a felony.

Sherman Adams   Dwight Eisenhower's chief of staff, 1953–1958. Adams resigned after it became clear that he had accepted gifts—including free hotel accommodations, a Persian rug, and a vicuña coat—from textile executive Bernard Goldfine, who was being investigated for Federal Trade Commission violations.

Earl Butz   Richard Nixon's and Gerald Ford's secretary of Agriculture, 1971–1976. Butz told the singer Pat Boone his theory of why the Republican Party did not appeal to black voters: "because coloreds only want three things . . . first, a tight pussy, second, loose shoes, and third, a warm place to shit." He resigned shortly after *Rolling Stone* printed this remark. In 1981, he pleaded guilty to tax evasion and later served as an adviser on natural resources to Ronald Reagan.

Bert Lance   Jimmy Carter's head of the Office of Management and Budget, 1977. Lance, a Georgia banker, had lent nearly $5 million to the Carter peanut farms at very favorable rates. A few months after he was named to head OMB, Lance was accused of unsound banking practices and resigned. In 1979, he was indicted for bank fraud but was not convicted.

Raymond J. Donovan   Ronald Reagan's secretary of Labor, 1981–1985. Donovan was confirmed despite numerous allegations that he and his construction company had links to organized crime and racketeering. In 1984, he became the first sitting Cabinet official to be indicted on criminal charges, which were related to his company's alleged mob ties. He resigned and was eventually acquitted.

James G. Watt   Reagan's secretary of the Interior, 1981–1983. Watt made a series of offensive remarks, the last of which, a description of an Interior Department panel as consisting of "a black, a woman, two Jews, and a cripple," led to his resignation.

Edwin Meese III   Reagan's attorney general, 1985–1988. Meese was alleged to have taken money from people whom he helped to find federal jobs, but a preconfirmation investigation found no basis for criminal charges. An ethical cloud remained over the Justice Department throughout his tenure.

Mike Espy   Bill Clinton's secretary of Agriculture, 1993–1994. Espy resigned amid accusations of accepting gifts from Arkansas's Tyson Foods and others with an interest in Agriculture Department business and of charging personal travel expenses to the government. He was indicted in August 1997 and pleaded not guilty.

PRESIDENTIAL POLLS

From time to time, historians are asked to pass judgment on the relative merits of our political leaders. Politicians know that they will be judged by history, and some of them govern with an eye to how their decisions and behavior will be regarded in the future. Rating presidents may seem like comparing apples and oranges, because the country has grown and changed in so many ways since the days of George Washington. Those at the top would be proud, and those at the bottom would at least be grateful at not having to submit to another election.

RIDINGS-McIVER
PRESIDENTIAL POLL, 1997

For this poll, 719 historians and former politicians were invited to rank the presidents on five factors: leadership qualities, accomplishments and crisis management, political skill, appointments, and character and integrity.

1. Abraham Lincoln
2. Franklin Roosevelt
3. George Washington
4. Thomas Jefferson
5. Theodore Roosevelt
6. Woodrow Wilson
7. Harry Truman
8. Andrew Jackson
9. Dwight Eisenhower
10. James Madison
11. James Polk
12. Lyndon Johnson
13. James Monroe
14. John Adams
15. John Kennedy
16. Grover Cleveland
17. William McKinley
18. John Quincy Adams
19. Jimmy Carter
20. William Howard Taft

21. Martin Van Buren
22. George Bush
23. Bill Clinton
24. Herbert Hoover
25. Rutherford Hayes
26. Ronald Reagan
27. Gerald Ford
28. Chester Arthur
29. Zachary Taylor
30. James Garfield
31. Benjamin Harrison
32. Richard Nixon
33. Calvin Coolidge
34. John Tyler
35. William Henry Harrison
36. Millard Fillmore
37. Franklin Pierce
38. Ulysses Grant
39. Andrew Johnson
40. James Buchanan
41. Warren Harding

RIDINGS-McIVER
PRESIDENTIAL POLL:
Character and Integrity, 1997

1. Abraham Lincoln 👆
2. George Washington
3. John Adams
4. John Quincy Adams
5. Jimmy Carter
6. James Madison
7. Thomas Jefferson
8. Woodrow Wilson
9. Harry Truman
10. Dwight Eisenhower
11. Herbert Hoover
12. Theodore Roosevelt
13. James Monroe
14. William Howard Taft
15. Franklin Roosevelt
16. Grover Cleveland
17. Gerald Ford
18. Andrew Jackson
19. William McKinley
20. James Polk

21. Calvin Coolidge
22. Rutherford Hayes
23. Zachary Taylor
24. George Bush
25. Martin Van Buren
26. James Garfield
27. John Tyler
28. Benjamin Harrison
29. William Henry Harrison
30. Andrew Johnson
31. Millard Fillmore
32. Ulysses Grant
33. Chester Arthur
34. John Kennedy
35. Franklin Pierce
36. James Buchanan
37. Lyndon Johnson
38. Bill Clinton
39. Ronald Reagan
40. Warren Harding
41. Richard Nixon 👇

PRESIDENTIAL POLL, 1982

The Chicago Tribune *asked 49 distinguished historians to rank the presidents. It published the results on January 10, 1982.*
(This list includes presidents through Jimmy Carter.)

20. William Howard Taft
21. Herbert Hoover
22. Rutherford Hayes
23. Gerald Ford
24. Chester Arthur
25. Benjamin Harrison
26. Jimmy Carter
27. Calvin Coolidge
28. Zachary Taylor
29. John Tyler
30. Ulysses Grant

1. Abraham Lincoln
2. Franklin Roosevelt
3. George Washington
4. Theodore Roosevelt
5. Thomas Jefferson
6. Andrew Jackson
7. Woodrow Wilson
8. Harry Truman
9. Dwight Eisenhower
10. William McKinley
11. James Polk
12. Lyndon Johnson
13. Grover Cleveland
14. John Adams*
15. John Kennedy*
16. James Monroe
17. James Madison
18. Martin Van Buren
19. John Quincy Adams

31. Millard Fillmore
32. Andrew Johnson
33. James Garfield
34. Richard Nixon
35. Franklin Pierce
36. James Buchanan
37. Warren Harding
38. William Henry Harrison

---

* Tied.

PRESIDENTIAL POLL, 1962

Arthur Schlesinger Jr. conducted a poll of 75 historians. The results were published in the New York Times Magazine *on July 29, 1962. (This list includes the presidents through Dwight Eisenhower, but excludes William Henry Harrison and James Garfield, since each died within months of his inauguration.)*

Great

1. Abraham Lincoln
2. George Washington
3. Franklin Roosevelt
4. Woodrow Wilson
5. Thomas Jefferson

Near Great

6. Andrew Jackson
7. Theodore Roosevelt
8. James Polk
9. Harry Truman
10. John Adams
11. Grover Cleveland

Average

12. James Madison
13. John Quincy Adams
14. Rutherford Hayes
15. William McKinley
16. William Howard Taft
17. Martin Van Buren
18. James Monroe
19. Herbert Hoover
20. Benjamin Harrison
21. Chester Arthur
22. Dwight Eisenhower
23. Andrew Johnson

Below Average

24. Zachary Taylor
25. John Tyler
26. Millard Fillmore
27. Calvin Coolidge
28. Franklin Pierce
29. James Buchanan

Failure

30. Ulysses Grant
31. Warren Harding

PRESIDENTIAL POLL, 1948

Earlier, Arthur Schlesinger Jr. had conducted a poll of 55 historians. The results were published in Life *magazine on November 1, 1948. (This list includes the presidents through Franklin Roosevelt, excluding William Henry Harrison and James Garfield.)*

Great

1. Abraham Lincoln
2. George Washington
3. Franklin Roosevelt
4. Woodrow Wilson
5. Thomas Jefferson
6. Andrew Jackson

Near Great

7. Theodore Roosevelt
8. Grover Cleveland
9. John Adams
10. James Polk

Average

11. John Quincy Adams
12. James Monroe
13. Rutherford Hayes
14. James Madison
15. Martin Van Buren
16. William Howard Taft
17. Chester Arthur
18. William McKinley
19. Andrew Johnson
20. Herbert Hoover
21. Benjamin Harrison

Below Average

22. John Tyler
23. Calvin Coolidge
24. Millard Fillmore
25. Zachary Taylor
26. James Buchanan
27. Franklin Pierce

Failure

28. Ulysses Grant
29. Warren Harding

HOW THEY WOULD'VE DONE:
The Also-Rans

Countless professional scholars have tried to identify the best and the worst of the presidents, but amateur historian Leslie Southwick, a judge on the Mississippi State Court of Appeals, has been bold enough to rank the men who were defeated in general elections. He first published his speculative rankings in 1984 in his book Presidential Also-Rans and Running Mates; *a revised edition was published in 1997. Third-party candidates with 10% of the vote are included, as are losing vice presidential candidates whose running mates died within four years of the election (and therefore would have succeeded to the presidency). The list also includes losing candidates who later won. The names of the winning candidate(s) they faced appear in parentheses.*

Superior

1. **Charles Evans Hughes** (Woodrow Wilson)
2. **Stephen A. Douglas** (Abraham Lincoln)
3. **Henry Clay** (John Quincy Adams, Andrew Jackson, James Polk)

Above Average

4. **DeWitt Clinton** (James Madison)
5. **Wendell Willkie** (Franklin Roosevelt)
6. **William Lowndes** (John Quincy Adams)
7. **Adlai Stevenson** (Dwight Eisenhower)
8. **Alton B. Parker** (Theodore Roosevelt)
9. **James M. Cox** (Warren Harding)
10. **Daniel Webster** (Martin Van Buren)
11. **Alfred E. Smith** (Herbert Hoover)
12. **Thomas E. Dewey** (FDR, Harry Truman)

Satisfactory

13. **Winfield Scott Hancock** (James Garfield)
14. **William H. Crawford** (John Quincy Adams)
15. **Hubert Humphrey** (Richard Nixon)
16. **Hugh Lawson White** (Van Buren)

Satisfactory (continued)

17. **John Wesley Davis**   (Calvin Coolidge)
18. **Charles Pinckney**   (Thomas Jefferson, Madison)
19. **Herschel Johnson**   (Lincoln)
20. **Alfred Mossman Landon**   (FDR)
21. **John Calhoun**   (John Quincy Adams)
22. **Horatio Seymour**   (Ulysses Grant)
23. **Walter Mondale**   (Ronald Reagan)
24. **Benjamin Fitzpatrick**   (Lincoln)
25. **James Gillespie Blaine**   (Grover Cleveland)
26. **Samuel J. Tilden**   (Rutherford Hayes)
27. **Bob Dole**   (Bill Clinton)
28. **Rufus King**   (James Monroe)
29. **Lewis Cass**   (Zachary Taylor)
30. **Winfield Scott**   (Franklin Pierce)
31. **B. Gratz Brown**   (Grant)
32. **Michael S. Dukakis**   (George Bush)

Unsatisfactory

33. **Barry M. Goldwater**   (Lyndon Johnson)
34. **John Bell**   (Lincoln)
35. **H. Ross Perot**   (Clinton)
36. **Charles McNary**   (FDR)
37. **Robert Marion La Follette**   (Coolidge)
38. **John McLean**   (Van Buren)
39. **George S. McGovern**   (Nixon)
40. **George Brinton McClellan**   (Lincoln)
41. **John Breckinridge**   (Lincoln)
42. **Burton Wheeler**   (Coolidge)
43. **John Charles Frémont**   (James Buchanan)

Probable Failure

44. **George Corley Wallace**   (Nixon)
45. **William Jennings Bryan**   (William McKinley, William Howard Taft)
46. **Horace Greeley**   (Grant)

HOW THEY WOULD'VE DONE:
The Also-Rans' Running Mates

Leslie Southwick has also assessed the leadership abilities of the losing vice presidential candidates. He has divided the candidates into three categories.

Superior

Thomas Pinckney
Albert Gallatin
Earl Warren

Henry Cabot Lodge
Lloyd Bentsen

Satisfactory

Richard Rush
John Sergeant
Francis Granger
Theodore Frelinghuysen
Charles Francis Adams
William Graham
William Dayton
Benjamin Fitzpatrick
Herschel Johnson
G. H. Pendleton
B. Gratz Brown
Henry Davis

John Kern
Hiram Johnson
Nicholas Butler
Frank Orren Lowden
Joseph Robinson
Frank Knox
John Sparkman
Estes Kefauver
Edmund Muskie
Thomas F. Eagleton
Jack Kemp

Unsatisfactory or Uncertain

John Langdon
Jared Ingersoll
John E. Howard
Nathan Sanford
Nathaniel Macon
Philip Pendleton Barbour
Silas Wright
William Butler
Andrew Jackson Donelson
Edward Everett
Joseph Lane
Francis Blair
William English

John Logan
A. G. Thurman
Whitelaw Reid
Arthur Sewall
Charles Bryan
Burton Wheeler
Charles McNary
John Bricker
William Miller
Curtis LeMay
Sargent Shriver
Geraldine Ferraro

A RANKING OF THE FIRST LADIES

Abraham Lincoln is ranked at the top in the presidential polls, but his wife, Mary Todd Lincoln, belongs at the bottom, according to this 1982 poll of historians. Recent first ladies tended to receive extreme marks; their reputations will probably mellow as they recede from popular memory. (This list ranks the first ladies, and the first lady fill-ins, through Nancy Reagan.)

1. **Eleanor Roosevelt** Wife of Franklin Roosevelt

Eleanor Roosevelt with singer Marian Anderson

2. **Abigail Adams** Wife of John Adams
3. **Lady Bird Johnson** Wife of Lyndon Johnson
4. **Dolley Madison** Wife of James Madison
5. **Rosalynn Carter** Wife of Jimmy Carter
6. **Betty Ford** Wife of Gerald Ford
7. **Edith Wilson** Second wife of Woodrow Wilson
8. **Jacqueline Kennedy** Wife of John Kennedy
9. **Martha Washington** Wife of George Washington
10. **Edith Roosevelt** Wife of Theodore Roosevelt
11. **Lou Hoover** Wife of Herbert Hoover

12. **Lucy Hayes**   Wife of Rutherford Hayes
13. **Frances Cleveland**   Wife of Grover Cleveland
14. **Louisa Adams**   Wife of John Quincy Adams
15. **Bess Truman**   Wife of Harry Truman
16. **Ellen Wilson**   First wife of Woodrow Wilson
17. **Grace Coolidge**   Wife of Calvin Coolidge
18. **Martha Jefferson Randolph**   Daughter of Thomas Jefferson
19. **Helen Taft**   Wife of William Howard Taft
20. **Julia Grant**   Wife of Ulysses Grant
21. **Eliza Johnson**   Wife of Andrew Johnson
22. **Sarah Polk**   Wife of James Polk
23. **Anna Harrison**   Wife of William Henry Harrison
24. **Elizabeth Monroe**   Wife of James Monroe
25. **Mary Arthur McElroy**   Sister of Chester Arthur
26. **Emily Donelson**   Niece of Andrew Jackson
27. **Julia Tyler**   Second wife of John Tyler
28. **Abigail Fillmore**   Wife of Millard Fillmore
29. **Harriet Lane**   Niece of James Buchanan
30. **Lucretia Garfield**   Wife of James Garfield
31. **Mamie Eisenhower**   Wife of Dwight Eisenhower
32. **Martha Patterson**   Daughter of Andrew Johnson
33. **Margaret Taylor**   Wife of Zachary Taylor
34. **Caroline Harrison**   Wife of Benjamin Harrison
35. **Letitia Tyler**   First wife of John Tyler
36. **Angelica Van Buren**   Daughter-in-law of Martin Van Buren
37. **Pat Nixon**
    Wife of Richard Nixon
38. **Jane Pierce**
    Wife of Franklin Pierce
39. **Nancy Reagan**
    Wife of Ronald Reagan
40. **Ida McKinley**
    Wife of William McKinley
41. **Florence Harding**
    Wife of Warren Harding
42. **Mary Lincoln** ☞
    Wife of Abraham Lincoln

CONGRESSIONAL LISTS

"IT COULD PROBABLY BE SHOWN BY facts and figures," said Mark Twain, "that there is no distinctly native American criminal class except Congress." There is a shred of truth in Twain's cynical observation, since plenty of members (or former members) of Congress have been convicted of a crime, but the Congress has also been home to the most honest and distinguished patriots this country has known. And most men and women who have served in Congress are little known outside their own districts.

SPEAKERS OF THE HOUSE

Frederick Augustus Conrad Muhlenberg	No party–PA, 1789–1791
Jonathan Trumbull	Federalist-CT, 1791–1793
Frederick Muhlenberg	No party–PA, 1793–1795
Jonathan Dayton	Federalist-NJ, 1795–1799
Theodore Sedgwick	Federalist-MA, 1799–1801
Nathaniel Macon	D-NC, 1801–1807
Joseph Bradley Varnum	No party–MA, 1807–1811
Henry Clay	R-KY, 1811–1814
Langdon Cleves	R-SC, 1814–1815
Henry Clay	R-KY, 1815–1820
John W. Taylor	R-NY, 1820–1821
Philip Barbour	R-VA, 1821–1823
Henry Clay	R-KY, 1823–1825
John Taylor	R-NY, 1825–1827
Andrew Stevenson	D-VA, 1827–1834
John Bell	Whig-TN, 1834–1835
James Polk	D-TN, 1835–1839
Robert Mercer Taliaferro Hunter	Whig-VA, 1839–1841
John White	Whig-NY, 1841–1843
John Winston Jones	D-VA, 1843–1845
John Davis	D-IN, 1845–1847
Robert Charles Winthrop	Whig-MA, 1847–1849
Howell Cobb	D-GA, 1849–1851
Linn Boyd	D-KY, 1851–1855
Nathaniel Prentiss Banks	Know Nothing–MA, 1856–1857
James Lawrence Orr	D-SC, 1857–1859
William Pennington	R-NJ, 1860–1861
Galusha Aaron Grow	R-PA, 1861–1863
Schuyler Colfax	R-IN, 1863–1869
Theodore Medad Pomeroy	R-NY, 1869*
James Blaine	R-ME, 1869–1875
Michael Crawford Kerr	D-IN, 1875–1876[†]
Samuel Jackson Randall	D-PA, 1876–1881

Joseph Warren Keifer	R-OH, 1881–1883
John Griffin Carlisle	D-KY, 1883–1889
Thomas Brackett Reed	R-ME, 1889–1891
Charles Frederick Crisp	D-GA, 1891–1895
Thomas Reed	R-ME, 1895–1899
David Bremner Henderson	R-IA, 1899–1903
Joseph Gurney Cannon	R-IL, 1903–1911

James Beauchamp "Champ" Clark	D-MO, 1911–1919
Frederick Huntington Gillett	R-MA, 1919–1925
Nicholas Longworth	R-OH, 1925–1931
John Garner	D-TX, 1931–1933
Henry Thomas Rainey	D-IL, 1933–1934[†]

Joseph Wellington Byrns	D-TN, 1935–1936[†]
William Brockman Bankhead	D-AL, 1936–1940[†]
Samuel Taliaferro Rayburn	D-TX, 1940–1947
Joseph William Martin Jr.	R-MA, 1947–1949
Sam Rayburn	D-TX, 1949–1953
Joseph Martin	R-MA, 1953–1955
Sam Rayburn	D-TX, 1955–1961[†]
John W. McCormack	D-MA, 1962–1971
Carl Albert	D-OK, 1971–1977
Thomas P. "Tip" O'Neill Jr.	D-MA, 1977–1987
James Wright Jr.	D-TX, 1987–1989
Thomas Foley	D-WA, 1989–1995
Newt Gingrich	R-GA, 1995–

* Served for one day.
[†] Died in office.

Henry Clay became Speaker of the House for the first time when he was only 34 years old.

SPEAKERS OF THE HOUSE WHO WERE CABINET MEMBERS

Henry Clay   John Quincy Adams's secretary of State, 1825–1829

John Bell   William Henry Harrison's and John Tyler's secretary of War, 1841

Howell Cobb   James Buchanan's secretary of the Treasury, 1857–1860

James Blaine   James Garfield's and Benjamin Harrison's secretary of State, 1881, 1889–1892

John Carlisle   Grover Cleveland's secretary of the Treasury, 1893–1897

Robert Hunter served as secretary of State for the Confederate States of America, 1861–1862.

SPEAKERS OF THE HOUSE
WITH ETHICS PROBLEMS

Newt Gingrich's recent problems are far from unique. Speakers of the House found themselves in trouble long before Watergate focused our attention on government ethics.

Henry Clay   Clay was accused of making a secret bargain in the election of 1824, trading support for John Quincy Adams for a Cabinet position (secretary of State). Congressman George Kremer of Pennsylvania made the accusation in writing but wouldn't make it in person.

John Taylor   During his presidential campaign against Andrew Jackson, Taylor was accused of keeping a girlfriend in a Baltimore hotel and sleeping there with her.

John White   In his final term in the House, White gave a speech that he presented as his own but was actually an old one of Aaron Burr's. When the truth surfaced, the Speaker killed himself.

James Blaine   Blaine was cleared in the Crédit Mobilier scandal but was tarred with many accusations of graft in his 1884 presidential campaign against Grover Cleveland.

David Henderson Henderson resigned as Speaker after he was found to be having a sexual relationship with a senator's daughter.

John McCormack McCormack retired at the end of a session after a staff member, Martin Sweig, was charged with misusing the Speaker's office to peddle influence. In 1970, Sweig was convicted of perjury.

Tip O'Neill O'Neill was implicated in 1978 in the Tongsun Park bribery scandal. Although the Korean rice broker paid for two of O'Neill's birthday parties, the Speaker was cleared of wrongdoing.

Jim Wright Wright resigned midsession after an ethics investigation took issue with the startlingly high royalty paid on the Speaker's book *Reflections of a Public Man* (which was sold in bulk to lobbyists) and with the salary and perks paid to Wright's wife, Betty, by a Texas developer.

Newt Gingrich Gingrich received a reprimand and a $300,000 fine for promoting partisan ideology in his college course, which was financed by tax-exempt funds, and for passing along untrue information to the investigation by the House Ethics Committee. Gingrich has also been accused of using GOPAC, a political action committee he masterminded, as his own slush fund, but the ethics committee did not recommend reprimanding Gingrich for his involvement with GOPAC.

SENATE MAJORITY LEADERS

Shelby Moore Cullom	R-IL, 1911–1913
John Kern	D-IN, 1913–1917
Thomas Staples Martin	D-VA, 1917–1919
Henry Cabot Lodge	R-MA, 1919–1924
Charles Curtis	R-KS, 1924–1929
James E. Watson	R-IN, 1929–1933
Joseph Robinson	D-AR, 1933–1937

Alben Barkley	D-KY, 1937–1947
Wallace H. White Jr.	R-ME, 1947–1949
Scott Wike Lucas	D-IL, 1949–1951
Ernest W. McFarland	D-AZ, 1951–1953
Robert Taft	R-OH, 1953
William Knowland	R-CA, 1953–1955
Lyndon Johnson	D-TX, 1955–1961
Michael Mansfield	D-VT, 1961–1977
Robert C. Byrd	D-WV, 1977–1981
Howard Henry Baker Jr.	R-TN, 1981–1985
Robert Dole	R-KS, 1985–1987
Robert Byrd	D-WV, 1987–1989
George J. Mitchell	D-ME, 1989–1995
Bob Dole	R-KS, 1995–1996
Trent Lott	R-MS, 1996–

SENATE MINORITY LEADERS

Thomas Martin	D-VA, 1911–1913
Jacob H. Gallinger	R-NH, 1913–1918
Henry Cabot Lodge	R-MA, 1918–1919
Thomas Martin	D-VA, 1919
Oscar Underwood	D-AL, 1920–1923
Joseph Robinson	D-AR, 1923–1933
Charles McNary	R-OR, 1933–1945
Wallace White Jr.	R-ME, 1945–1947
Alben Barkley	D-KY, 1947–1949
Kenneth S. Wherry	R-NE, 1949–1951
Henry Styles Bridges	R-NH, 1951–1953
Lyndon Johnson	D-TX, 1953–1955
William Knowland	R-CA, 1955–1959
Everett McKinley Dirksen	R-IL, 1959–1969
Hugh Scott	R-PA, 1969–1977
Howard Baker Jr.	R-TN, 1977–1981
Robert Byrd	D-WV, 1981–1987
Bob Dole	R-KS, 1987–1995
Thomas A. Daschle	D-SD, 1995–

SENATE DEMOCRATIC WHIPS

J. Hamilton Lewis	IL, 1913–1919
Peter Goelet Gerry	RI, 1919–1929
Morris Sheppard	TX, 1929–1933
J. Hamilton Lewis	IL, 1933–1939
Sherman Minton	IN, 1939–1941
Joseph Lister Hill	AL, 1941–1947
Scott Lucas	IL, 1947–1949
Francis J. Myers	PA, 1949–1951
Lyndon Johnson	TX, 1951–1953
Earle C. Clements	KY, 1953–1957
Mike Mansfield	MT, 1957–1961
Hubert Humphrey	MN, 1961–1965
Russell Billiu Long	LA, 1965–1969
Edward M. Kennedy	MA, 1969–1971
Robert Byrd	WV, 1971–1977
Alan Cranston	CA, 1977–1991
Wendell H. Ford	KY, 1991–

SENATE REPUBLICAN WHIPS

James Wadsworth	NY, 1915
Charles Curtis	KS, 1915–1924
Wesley Livsey Jones	WA, 1924–1929
Simeon Davison Fess	OH, 1929–1933
Felix Hébert	RI, 1933–1935
Kenneth Wherry	NE, 1943–1949
Leverett Saltonstall	MA, 1949–1957
Everett Dirksen	IL, 1957–1959
Thomas H. Kuchel	CA, 1959–1969
Hugh Scott	PA, 1969
Robert P. Griffin	MI, 1969–1977
Ted Stevens	AK, 1977–1985
Alan K. Simpson	WY, 1985–1993
Trent Lott	MS, 1993–1996
Don Nickles	OK, 1996–

There was no Republican Senate whip from 1935 to 1943.

SENATORS WHO
SERVED THE LONGEST

Strom Thurmond	D-SC, December 1954–April 1956	
	D, R-SC, November 1956–	42 years
Carl Hayden	D-AZ, March 1927–January 1969	41
John C. Stennis	D-MS, November 1947–January 1989	41
Robert Byrd	D-WV, January 1959–	39
Richard B. Russell	D-GA, January 1933–January 1971	38
Russell Long	D-LA, December 1948–January 1987	38
Francis Warren	R-WY, November 1890–March 1893	
	March 1895–November 1929	37
James O. Eastland	D-MS, June 1941–September 1941	
	January 1943–December 1978	36
Warren Magnuson	D-WA, December 1944–January 1981	36
Claiborne Pell	D-RI, January 1961–January 1997	36
Kenneth D. McKellar	D-TN, March 1917–January 1953	35
Milton Young	R-ND, March 1945–January 1981	35
Ellison D. Smith	D-SC, March 1909–November 1944	35
Allen J. Ellender	D-LA, January 1937–July 1972	35
William Boyd Allison	R-IA, March 1873–August 1908	35

> *The shortest term of service was Rebecca Ann Felton's. Felton, the first woman senator, was appointed to fill a vacancy. She was sworn in on November 21, 1922, and stepped down a day later in favor of the man who had been elected to fill the seat.*

THE OLDEST SENATORS
TO BE REELECTED

Senators who were over 80 at their last election, ranked by age.

Strom Thurmond	R-SC	93	**John Tyler Morgan**	D-AL	82
Theodore Green	D-RI	87	**Edmund Winston Pettus**	D-AL	82
Justin Smith Morrill	R-VT	86	**William P. Whyte**	D-MD	82
Carl Hayden	D-AZ	85	**John Stennis**	D-MS	81
Carter Glass	D-VA	84	**David Baird**	R-NJ	81

> *Strom Thurmond has not ruled out running for another term. If he does, he might become the first 100-year-old senator.*

THE FIVE MOST
OUTSTANDING SENATORS

A Senate committee that was formed in 1955 looked back over the history of the upper house to choose the five men they admired most. These senators' portraits were hung in the Senate Reception Room after the committee made its report.

1. **John Calhoun** R-SC, 1832–1843, 1845–1850
2. **Henry Clay** R-KY, 1806–1807, 1810–1811, 1831–1842, 1849–1852
3. **Robert La Follette Sr.** R-WI, 1906–1925
4. **Robert Taft** R-OH, 1939–1953
5. **Daniel Webster** Federalist, Whig–MA, 1827–1841, 1845–1850

LIMBLESS LEGISLATORS' LEAGUE

Disability has not been a barrier to holding public office. No fewer than 14 senators have managed quite well without an arm or a leg (or, in some cases, both).

James Henderson Berry (D-AR, 1885–1907)   Lost one leg in the Civil War

Max Cleland (D-GA, 1997–)   Lost both legs and right arm in the Vietnam War

John Warwick "Lame Lion" Daniel (D-VA, 1887–1910)   Injured in the Civil War and used crutches

Bob Dole (R-KS, 1969–1996)   Lost use of right arm in Italy during World War II

Paul H. Douglas (D-IL, 1949–1967)   Lost use of left arm in Pacific during World War II

Wade Hampton (D-SC, 1879–1891)   Had leg amputated after injuries suffered in an accident during a mule ride

Daniel K. Inouye (D-HI, 1963–)   Lost right arm during World War II

Richard Johnson (R-KY, 1819–1829)   Lost use of hand in War of 1812

Bob Kerrey (D-NE, 1989–)   Lost part of right leg in Vietnam War

Gouverneur Morris (Federalist-NY, 1800–1803)   Had one leg amputated and replaced with a wooden leg as a result of injuries suffered in a carriage accident

Charles E. Potter (R-MI, 1952–1959)   Lost both legs in the Battle of the Bulge

John Stennis (R-MN, 1947–1989)   Had one leg amputated late in life

Charles Taft (R-GA, 1809–1819)   Had one leg amputated and replaced with a wooden leg as a result of injuries suffered in a fall from a horse

James Kimble Vardaman (D-MS, 1913–1919)   Had one arm mangled in a corn sheller during childhood

Max Cleland, who lives alone, could not find a Washington apartment that was suitable for a triple amputee. He eventually settled in Alexandria, Virginia.

★ ★ ★

THE LONGEST 20TH-CENTURY SENATE FILIBUSTERS

This list is limited to 20th-century speeches. In the 19th-century Senate, many speeches lasted several days, but Senate records do not reveal the exact length of such marathon orations.

Senator, Party, and State	Date	Length	Subject
Strom Thurmond R-SC	August 28–29, 1957	24 hr., 18 min.	Civil Rights Act
Wayne Lyman Morse Ind.-R	April 24–25, 1953	22 hr., 26 min.	Tidelands oil bill
Robert La Follette Sr. R-WI	May 29–30, 1908	18 hr., 23 min.	Aldrich-Vreeland Currency Act
William Proxmire D-WI	September 28–29, 1981	16 hr., 12 min.	Public debt ceiling bill
Huey Long D-LA	June 12–13, 1935	15 hr., 30 min.	National Industrial Recovery Act
Alfonse M. D'Amato R-NY	October 5–6, 1992	15 hr., 14 min.	Tax bill
Robert Byrd D-WV	June 9–10, 1964	14 hr., 13 min.	Civil Rights Act of 1964

Filibusterers do not have to keep to the topic at hand. Some senators have read from a phone book. Huey Long gave recipes for New Orleans–style fried oysters and pot likker during his 1935 anti-NIRA speech.

★ ★ ★

WILLIAM PROXMIRE'S FAVORITE FLEECINGS

William Proxmire (D-WI) was elected to the Senate in 1957 to replace Joseph McCarthy. From the 1970s until his retirement in 1988, Proxmire gave out Golden Fleece Awards for what he believed were the most egregious examples of federal pork-barrel spending. Here are some of his all-time favorites.

$97,000 to the National Institute of Mental Health to study Peruvian brothels

$84,000 to the National Science Foundation to study why people fall in love

$500,000 to the National Science Foundation to study why rats, monkeys, and humans clench their teeth

$2,500 to the National Endowment for the Humanities to study why people lie and cheat on tennis courts

$46,000 to the Department of Agriculture to study how long it takes to cook breakfast

$219,592 to the Department of Education to develop a curriculum to teach students to distinguish between fact and fiction on television

$823,000 to the Department of Education to develop a curriculum to teach the skill of viewing television critically

$102,000 to the National Institute of Alcohol Abuse to study the effect of tequila and gin on sunfish

$120,000 to the National Highway Traffic Safety Administration to study the possibility of designing back-wheel-steering motorcycles

$140,000 to the National Aeronautics and Space Administration to write a 6,000-word article on the Viking Mars project*

$140,000 to the Department of the Interior to build a wave-making machine for a Salt Lake City swimming pool

---

* The article's author received a $20,000 payment and $4,000 in expenses.

20TH-CENTURY
HOUSE MAJORITY LEADERS

Sereno E. Payne	R-NY, 1901–1911
Oscar Wilder Underwood	D-AL, 1911–1915
Claude Kitchin	D-NC, 1915–1919
Franklin Wheeler Mondell	R-WY, 1919–1923
Nicholas Longworth	R-OH, 1923–1925
John Q. Tilson	R-CT, 1925–1931
Henry Rainey	D-IL, 1931–1933
Joseph Byrns	D-TN, 1933–1935
William Bankhead	D-AL, 1935–1937

Sam Rayburn	D-TX, 1937–1940
John McCormack	D-MA, 1940–1947
Charles A. Halleck	R-IN, 1947–1949

John McCormack	D-MA, 1949–1953
Charles Halleck	R-IN, 1953–1955
John McCormack	D-MA, 1955–1961
Carl Albert	D-OK, 1951–1971
Thomas Hale Boggs Sr.	D-LA, 1971–1973
"Tip" O'Neill Jr.	D-MA, 1973–1977
Jim Wright	D-TX, 1977–1987
Tom Foley	D-WA, 1987–1989
Richard A. Gephardt	D-MO, 1989–1995
Richard Armey	R-TX, 1995–

20TH-CENTURY HOUSE MINORITY LEADERS

James D. Richardson	D-TN, 1901–1903
John Sharp Williams	D-MS, 1903–1908
Champ Clark	D-MO, 1908–1911
James Robert Mann	R-IL, 1911–1919
Champ Clark	D-MO, 1919–1921
Claude Kitchin	D-NC, 1921–1923
Finis J. Garrett	D-TN, 1923–1929
John Garner	D-TX, 1929–1931

Bertrand H. Snell	R-NY, 1931–1939
Joseph Martin	R-MA, 1939–1947
Sam Rayburn	D-TX, 1947–1949
Joseph Martin	R-MA, 1949–1953
Sam Rayburn	D-TX, 1953–1955
Joseph Martin	R-MA, 1955–1959
Charles Halleck	R-IN, 1959–1965
Gerald Ford	R-MI, 1965–1974
John Rhodes	R-AZ, 1974–1981
Robert H. Michel	R-IL, 1981–1995
Richard Gephardt	D-MO, 1995–

HOUSE DEMOCRATIC WHIPS

Oscar Underwood	AL, 1901
James Tilghman Lloyd	MO, 1901–1908*
Thomas Montgomery Bell	GA, 1913–1915*
William A. Oldfield	AR, 1921–1928
John McDuffie	AL, 1928–1933
Arthur H. Greenwood	IN, 1933–1935
Patrick J. Boland	PA, 1935–1942
Robert C. Word Ramspeck	GA, 1942–1945
John Sparkman	AL, 1946–1947
John McCormack	MA, 1947–1949
James Percy Priest	TN, 1949–1953
John McCormack	MA, 1953–1955
Carl Albert	OK, 1955–1962
Hale Boggs Sr.	LA, 1962–1971
Tip O'Neill	MA, 1971–1973
John J. McFall	CA, 1973–1977
John Brademas	IN, 1977–1981
Tom Foley	WA, 1981–1987
Anthony Lee "Tony" Coelho	CA, 1987–1989
William H. Gray III	PA, 1989–1991
David E. Bonior	MI, 1991–

* There was no Democratic House whip from 1908 to 1913 or from 1915 to 1921.

HOUSE REPUBLICAN WHIPS

James A. Tawney	MN, 1897–1905
James Watson	IN, 1905–1909
John W. Dwight	NY, 1909–1913
Charles H. Burke	SD, 1913–1915
Charles Mann Hamilton	NY, 1915–1919
Harold Knutson	MN, 1919–1923
Albert H. Vestal	IN, 1923–1931
Carl G. Bachmann	WV, 1931–1933
Harry Lane Englebright	CA, 1933–1943
Leslie Cornelius Arends	IL, 1943–1975
Robert Michel	IL, 1975–1981
Trent Lott	MS, 1981–1989
Richard Cheney	WY, 1989
Newt Gingrich	GA, 1989–1995
Tom DeLay	TX, 1995–

CONGRESSMEN WHO SERVED THE LONGEST

Congressman, Party, and State	Years in Office	Years/Months/Days
Jamie L. Whitten D-MS	November 4, 1941–January 3, 1995	53/2/0
Carl Vinson D-GA	November 3, 1914–January 3, 1965	50/2/0
Emanuel Celler D-NY	March 4, 1923–January 3, 1973	49/10/0
Sam Rayburn D-TX	March 4, 1913–November 16, 1961	48/8/0
John W. Wright Patman D-TX	March 4, 1929–March 7, 1976	47/0/15
Sidney R. Yates D-IL	January 3, 1949–January 3, 1963	
	January 3, 1965–	46/10/0
Joseph G. Cannon R-IL	January 4, 1873–January 3, 1891	
	March 4, 1893–March 3, 1913	
	March 4, 1915–March 3, 1923	46/0/0
Adolph J. Sabath D-IL	March 4, 1907–November 6, 1952	45/8/0
Charles E. Bennett D-FL	January 3, 1949–January 3, 1993	44/0/0*
George H. Mahon D-TX	January 3, 1937–January 3, 1979	44/0/0*
Charles Melvin Price D-IL	January 3, 1945–April 22, 1988	43/4/0

* Tied.

Carl Trumbull Hayden (D-AZ) served a total of 56 years and 10 months in Congress, spending nearly 15 years in the House before spending seven consecutive terms in the Senate.

CONGRESSIONAL WIDOWS: Women Who Completed Their Late Husbands' Terms

Maryon Pittman Allen (D-AL, Senate)   Succeeded James Browning Allen, who died June 1, 1978

Elizabeth Bullock Andrews (D-AL, House)   Succeeded George William Andrews, who died December 25, 1971

Jean Spencer Ashbrook (R-OH, House)   Succeeded John Milan Ashbrook, who died April 24, 1982

Irene Bailey Baker (R-TN, House)   Succeeded Howard Henry Baker, who died January 7, 1964

Veronica Grace Boland (D-PA, House)   Succeeded Patrick Boland, who died May 18, 1942

Vera Cahalan Bushfield (R-SD, Senate)   Succeeded Harlan J. Bushfield, who died September 27, 1948

Katharine Edgar Byron (D-MD, House)   Succeeded William Devereux Byron, who died February 27, 1941

Lois Capps (D-CA, House)   Succeeded Walter Capps, who died October 28, 1997

Marian Williams Clarke (R-NY, House)   Succeeded John Davenport Clarke, who died November 5, 1933

Willa McCord Blake Eslick (D-TN, House)   Succeeded Edward Everett Eslick, who died June 14, 1932

Willa Lybrand Fulmer (D-SC, House)   Succeeded Hampton Pitts Fulmer, who died October 19, 1944

Elizabeth Hawley Gasque (D-SC, House)   Succeeded Allard H. Gasque, who died June 17, 1938

Florence Reville Gibbs (D-GA, House)   Succeeded Willis B. Gibbs, who died August 7, 1940

Muriel Buck Humphrey (D-MN, Senate)   Succeeded Hubert Humphrey, who died January 13, 1978

Catherine Small Long (D-LA, House)   Succeeded Gillis W. Long, who died January 20, 1985

Rose McConnell Long (D-LA, Senate)   Succeeded Huey Long, who died September 10, 1935

Clara Gooding McMillan (D-SC, House)   Succeeded Thomas Sanders McMillan, who died September 29, 1939

Mae Ella Nolan (R-CA, House)   Succeeded John I. Nolan, who died Novmber 18, 1922

Catherine Dorris Norrell (D-AR, House)   Succeeded William F. Norrell, who died February 15, 1961

Pearl Peden Oldfield (D-AR, House)   Succeeded William Oldfield, who died November 19, 1928

Louise Goff Reece (R-TN, House)   Succeeded B. Carroll Reece, who died March 19, 1961

Corrine Boyd Riley (D-SC, House)   Succeeded John Jacob Riley, who died January 1, 1962

Edna Oakes Simpson (R-IL, House)   Succeeded Sidney Simpson, who died October 26, 1958

Lera Millard Thomas (D-TX, House)   Succeeded Albert Thomas, who died February 15, 1966

CONGRESSIONAL WIDOWS:
Women Who Were Elected After Completing Their Late Husbands' Terms

The women on this list took their husbands' seats and made a congressional career for themselves.

Corinne "Lindy" Claiborne Boggs (D-LA, House, March 20, 1973–January 3, 1991)   Succeeded Hale Boggs Sr., whose plane disappeared October 16, 1972, and whose seat was declared vacant January 3, 1973

Frances Payne Bolton (R-OH, House, February 27, 1940–January 3, 1969)   Succeeded Chester Castle Bolton, who died October 29, 1939

Vera Daerr Buchanan (D-PA, House, July 24, 1951–November 26, 1955)* Succeeded Frank Buchanan, who died April 27, 1951

Sala Burton (D-CA, House, June 21, 1983–February 1, 1987)* Succeeded Phillip Burton, who died April 10, 1983

Beverly Barton Butcher Byron (D-MD, House, January 3, 1979–January 2, 1993) Succeeded Goodloe Edgar Byron, who died October 11, 1978

Hattie Ophelia Wyatt Caraway (D-AR, Senate, November 13, 1931–January 2, 1945) Succeeded Thaddeus H. Caraway, who died November 6, 1931

Marguerite Stitt Church (R-IL, House, January 3, 1951–January 3, 1963) Succeeded Ralph E. Church, who died March 21, 1950

Cardiss Collins (D-IL, House, June 5, 1973–January 2, 1997) Suceeded George Washington Collins, who died December 8, 1972

Jo Ann Emerson (I-MO, House, November 8, 1996–) Succeeded Bill Emerson, who died June 22, 1996

Mary Elizabeth Pruett Farrington (R-HI, House delegate, July 31, 1954–January 3, 1957) Succeeded Joseph Rider Farrington, who died June 19, 1954

Kathryn Elizabeth Granahan (D-PA, House, November 6, 1956–January 3, 1963) Succeeded William T. Granahan, who died May 25, 1956

Florence Prag Kahn (R-CA, House, March 4, 1925–January 3, 1937) Succeeded Julius Kahn, who died December 18, 1924

Maude Elizabeth Kee (D-WV, House, July 17, 1951–January 3, 1965) Succeeded John Kee, who died May 8, 1951

Maurine Brown Neuberger (D-OR, Senate, November 9, 1960–January 3, 1967) Succeeded Richard Lewis Neuberger, who died March 9, 1960

Shirley Neil Pettis (R-CA, House, April 29, 1975–January 3, 1979)   Succeeded Jerry L. Pettis, who died February 14, 1975

Charlotte Thompson Reid (R-IL, House, January 3, 1963–October 7, 1971)   Stood in for Frank R. Reid, who died in August 1962 while campaigning

Edith Nourse Rogers (R-MA, House, June 30, 1925–September 10, 1960)*   Succeeded John Jacob Rogers, who died March 28, 1925

Margaret Chase Smith (R-ME, House, June 3, 1940–January 3, 1949; Senate, 1949–1973)   Succeeded Clyde H. Smith, who died April 8, 1940

Leonor Kretzer Sullivan (D-MO, House, January 3, 1953–January 3, 1977)   Succeeded John B. Sullivan, who died January 29, 1951

Effiegene Locke Wingo (D-AR, House, November 4, 1930–March 3, 1933)   Succeeded Otis Theodore Wingo, who died October 21, 1930

---

* Died in office.

CONGRESSIONAL COUPLES

Congress is not the easiest place to find and keep a spouse. Although a married couple in Congress may share a place in DC, each partner must maintain a separate residence in his or her respective district or state.

Emily Taft Douglas (D-IL, House, 1945–1947) and **Paul Douglas** (D-IL, Senate, 1949–1967)

Nancy Landon Kassebaum (R-KS, Senate, 1979–1997) and **Howard Baker Jr.** (R-TN, Senate, 1967–1985)

Martha Elizabeth Keys (D-KS, House, 1975–1979) and **Andrew Jacobs Jr.** (D-IN, House, 1965–1973, 1975–1997)

Ruth Hanna McCormick  (R-IL, House, 1929–1931) and (1) **Joseph Medill McCormick** (R-IL, House, 1917–1919; Senate, 1919–1925); (2) **Albert Gallatin Simms** (R-NM, House, 1929–1931)

Susan Molinari (R-NY, House, 1990–1997) and **Bill Paxon** (R-NY, House, 1989–)

Olympia Snowe (R-ME, House, 1979–1994; Senate, 1994–) and **John Rettie McKernan Jr.** (R-ME, House, 1983–1987)

Only two couples married while both were in office: Keys-Jacobs and Paxon-Molinari. Keys and Jacobs later divorced.

FATHER-DAUGHTER PAIRS IN CONGRESS

Hundreds of sons have followed their fathers to Capitol Hill. There have been far fewer women in Congress and therefore far fewer father-daughter pairs. If enough congressmen celebrate Take Your Daughters to Work Day, their numbers may increase in future generations.

Albert E. Austin (R-CT, House, 1939–1941) and (stepdaughter) **Clare Boothe Luce** (R-CT, House, 1943–1947)

William Jennings Bryan (D-NE, House, 1891–1895) and **Ruth Bryan Owen** (D-FL, House, 1929–1933)

Thomas D'Alesandro Jr. (D-MD, House, 1939–1947) and **Nancy Pelosi** (D-CA, House, 1987–)

Guy Despard Goff (R-WV, Senate, 1925–1931) and **Louise Goff Reece** (R-TN, House, 1961–1963)

James Madison Gudger Jr. (D-NC, House, 1903–1907, 1911–1915) and **Katherine Gudger Langley** (R-KY, House, 1927–1931)

Mark Hanna (R-OH, Senate, 1897–1904) and **Ruth Hanna McCormick** (R-IL, House, 1929–1931)

Olin DeWitt Talmadge Johnston (D-SC, Senate, 1945–1965) and **Elizabeth J. Patterson** (D-SC, House, 1987–1993)

William E. Mason (R-IL, House, 1887–1891; Senate, 1897–1903; House, 1917–1921) and **Winnifred Spragus Mason Huck** (R-IL, House, 1922–1923)

Guy Molinari (R-NY, House, 1981–1990) and **Susan Molinari** (R-NY, House, 1990–1997)

Edward Roybal (D-CA, House, 1963–1993) and **Lucille Roybal-Allard** (D-CA, House, 1993–)

★ ★ ★

MEMBERS OF CONGRESS KNOWN OR BELIEVED TO BE OF AMERICAN INDIAN DESCENT

Senators and congressmen are listed along with their tribal affiliations.

Hiram Revels (R-MS, Senate, 1870–1871)   Lumbee

Richard Cain (R-SC, House, 1873–1875, 1877–1879)   Cherokee*

Matthew Stanley Quay (R-PA, Senate, 1887–1899, 1901–1904)   Abenaki, Seneca, or Delaware*

Charles Curtis (R-KS, House, 1893–1907; Senate, 1907–1913, 1915–1929)   Kaw-Osage†

Robert Latham Owen (D-OK, Senate, 1907–1925)   Cherokee

Charles D. Carter (D-OK, House, 1907–1927)   Chickasaw and Cherokee

William Wirt Hastings (D-OK, House, 1915–1921, 1923–1935)   Cherokee

Will Rogers Jr. (D-CA, House, 1943–1944)   Cherokee

William G. Stigler (D-OK, House, 1944–1952)   Choctaw

Benjamin Reifel (R-SD, House, 1961–1971)   Rosebud Sioux

Clem Rogers McSpadden (D-OK, House, 1972–1975)   Cherokee

Ben Nighthorse Campbell (D-CO, House, 1987–1993; D, R-CO, Senate, 1993–)   Northern Cheyenne

---

* Believed by biographers to be of Indian descent but either did not know of his heritage or chose not to publicize it.

† Also served as vice president, 1929–1933.

AFRICAN AMERICANS IN CONGRESS DURING RECONSTRUCTION

The period of Reconstruction saw a great many newly freed slaves entering voting booths and getting onto ballots. A wave of them—all Republicans, members of Abraham Lincoln's party— were elected to Congress. After Reconstruction ended, states began to employ poll taxes, literacy tests, and other tactics to keep blacks from participating in the electoral process.

Hiram Rhoades Revels   MS, Senate, 1870–1871

Jefferson Franklin Long   GA, House, 1870–1871

Joseph Hayne Rainey   SC, House, 1870–1879

Robert Carlos De Large   SC, House, 1871–1873

Robert Brown Elliott   SC, House, 1871–1875

Benjamin Sterling Turner   AL, House, 1871–1873

Josiah T. Walls   FL, House, 1871–1876

Pinckney Benton Stewart Pinchback   GA, House, 1872; Senate, 1873*

---

* Because of election irregularities, never seated.

Richard Harvey Cain   SC, House, 1873–1875, 1877–1879

John Roy Lynch   MS, House, 1873–1877, 1882–1883

Alonzo J. Ransier   SC, House, 1873–1875

James T. Rapier   AL, House, 1873–1875

Blanche Kelso Bruce   MS, Senate, 1875–1881

Jeremiah Haralson   AL, House, 1875–1877

John Adams Hyman   NC, House, 1875–1877

Charles E. Nash   LA, House, 1875–1877

Robert Smalls   SC, House, 1875–1879, 1881–1887

James E. O'Hara   NC, House, 1883–1887

Henry Plummer Cheatham   NC, House, 1889–1893

John Mercer Langston   VA, House, 1890–1891

Thomas E. Miller   SC, House, 1889–1891

George Washington Murray   SC, House, 1893–1897

George Henry White   NC, House, 1897–1901

ASIAN AMERICANS AND PACIFIC ISLANDERS IN CONGRESS

Jonah Kuhio Kalanianole   R-HI, House delegate, 1903–1922

Dalip Singh Saund   D-CA, House, 1957–1963

Hiram Leong Fong   R-HI, Senate, 1959–1977

Daniel Inouye   D-HI, House, 1959–1963; Senate, 1963–

Spark Masayuki Matsunaga   D-HI, House, 1963–1977; Senate, 1977–1990

Patsy Takemoto Mink   D-HI, House, 1965–1977, 1990–

Norman Mineta   D-CA, House, 1975–1995

Samuel Ichiye Hayakawa   R-CA, Senate, 1977–1983

Daniel K. Akaka   D-HI, House, 1977–1990; Senate, 1990–

Robert T. Matsui   D-CA, House, 1979–

Patricia Saiki   R-HI, House, 1987–1991

Jay C. Kim   R-CA, House, 1991–

> *Two states have elected Asian American governors, all Democrats: Washington (Gary Locke, 1997–) and Hawaii (George Ariyoshi, 1974–1986; John Waihee, 1986–1994; and Ben Cayetano, 1994–).*

POLISH AMERICANS IN CONGRESS

Though General Tadeusz Kościuszko participated in the American Revolution, Polish immigrants did not begin arriving in large numbers until after the Civil War. More than fifty Polish Americans have served in the Congress, most of them from midwestern states like Illinois and Michigan.

George Sea Shanklin (D-KY, House, 1865–1867)   The first Polish American member of Congress

Alvin E. O'Konski (R-WI, House, 1943–1973)   Urged Poles to abandon the Democrats after Roosevelt let the Soviets control postwar Poland

Clement Zablocki (D-WI, House, 1949–1983)   Chairman of the House Foreign Relations Committee and advocate of nuclear freeze

John D. Dingell (D-MI, House, 1955–)   Ranking minority member of the Commerce Committee; replaced his father, John Dingell, who served from 1933 to 1955

Edmund Muskie (D-ME, Senate, 1959–1980)   One-time presidential candidate; family's name originally Marciszewski

Dan Rostenkowski (D-IL, House, 1959–1995)   Powerful chairman of the House Ways and Means Committee until indicted in 1994 for embezzlement, fraud, and tampering with witnesses

David Bonior (D-MI, House, 1977–)   Minority whip since 1991

Barbara A. Mikulski (D-MD, House, 1977–1987; Senate, 1987–)
The first woman elected to the Senate without having first
served as a replacement for her husband

Frank H. Murkowski (R-AK, Senate, 1981–)   Active in pursu-
ing peace between North and South Korea

Marcy Kaptur (D-OH, House, 1983–)   Leading opponent of
NAFTA and polka fan

INFORMAL CONGRESSIONAL ORGANIZATIONS

*Members of Congress join with other members of one or both
houses to form groups based on geography, local industry, and
shared interests.*

Bicycle Caucus*
Concerned Senators for the Arts
Congressional Alcohol Fuels Caucus
Congressional Automotive Caucus
Congressional Bearing Caucus†
Congressional Footwear Caucus
Congressional Friends of Animals
Congressional Sportsmen's Caucus‡
Congressional Boating Caucus
House Trails Caucus
Interstate 69 Midcontinent Highway Caucus
Medical Technology Caucus
Minor League Baseball Caucus
Northeast Agricultural Caucus
Porkbusters Coalition
Senate Beef Caucus
Senate Textile Steering Committee

---

* For members who bicycle to Capitol Hill.
† For members with bearing manufacturers in their district.
‡ For promoting hunting, fishing, and other outdoor activities.

MEMBERS OF CONGRESS WHO WERE CONGRESSIONAL PAGES

Pages have been around since 1827. They deliver messages and run errands for members of Congress. The job was once reserved for young boys, but nowadays high school juniors spend a year in the page program.

Robert E. Bauman   R-MD, House, 1973–1981

Douglas H. Bosco   D-CA, House, 1983–1991

Jim Cooper   D-TN, House, 1983–1995

John D. Dingell Jr.   D-MI, House, 1955–

Bill Emerson   R-MO, House, 1981–1996

Christopher J. Dodd   D-CT, House, 1975–1981; Senate 1981–

Arthur Pue Gorman   D-MD, Senate, 1881–1889, 1903–1906

James William "Bill" Grant   D/R-FL, House, 1987–1991

William Dawson Gunter Jr.   D-FL, House, 1973–1975

Jon Clifton Hinson   R-MS, House, 1979–1981

Jed Joseph Johnson Jr.   D-OK, House, 1965–1967

Paul E. Kanjorski   D-PA, House, 1985–

Jim Kolbe   R-AZ, House, 1985–

Donald McLean   R-NJ, House, 1933–1945

William Neff Patman   D-TX, House, 1981–1985

David Hampton Pryor   D-AR, House, 1966–1973; Senate, 1979–1997

William Scott   D-PA, House, 1885–1889

Compton White Jr.   D-ID, House, 1963–1967

> *The fathers of several of these congressmen, including John Dingell and Chris Dodd, also served in Congress.*

★ ★ ★

OLD-BOY NETWORK:
Frat Boys in Congress

College fraternity rush chairmen brag about the distinguished careers alumni have pursued as they ply prospective members with liquor. It may be a comfort to know that many members of Congress have been through absurd and sometimes painful hazing rituals. What follows is a selection of prominent congressional fraternity brothers.

DKEs

More than 100 members of Congress have been members of the college fraternity Delta Kappa Epsilon.

James G. Blaine (R-ME)   House, 1863–1876; Senate, 1876–1881

George Bush (R-TX)   House, 1967–1970

John Hubbard Chafee (R-RI)   Senate, 1977–

Thomas Eagleton (D-MO)   Senate, 1968–1987

Gerald Ford (R-MI)   House 1949–1974

Rutherford Hayes (R-OH)   House, 1865–1867

William Randolph Hearst (D-NY)   House, 1903–1907

Henry Cabot Lodge (R-MA)   House, 1887–1893; Senate, 1893–1924

Russell Long (D-LA)   Senate, 1948–1987

Dan Quayle (R-IN)   House, 1977–1981; Senate, 1981–1989

Ted Stevens (R-AK)   Senate, 1968–

Phi Delta Thetas

Brockman "Brock" Adams (D-WA)   House, 1965–1977; Senate, 1987–1993

Dennis Webster DeConcini (D-AZ)   Senate, 1977–1995

Benjamin Harrison (R-IN)   Senate, 1881–1887

John Bennett Johnston Jr. (D-LA)   Senate, 1972–1997

Paul Norton "Pete" McCloskey Jr. (R-CA)   House, 1967–1983

Frederick Muhlenberg (R-PA)   House, 1789–1797

Samuel Augustus "Sam" Nunn (D-GA)   Senate, 1972–1997

Adlai Stevenson (D-IL)   House, 1875–1877, 1879–1881

> *Brock Adams withdrew from the 1992 Senate race after several women came forward and said that over the years he had forced himself on them sexually after drugging them with a reddish liquid.*

Alpha Phi Alphas

Alpha Phi Alpha is a leading African American fraternity.

Edward William Brooke III (R-MA)   House, 1967–1979

William Levi Dawson (D-IL)   House, 1943–1970

Ronald Vernie Dellums (D-CA)   House, 1971–

Julian Carey Dixon (D-CA)   House, 1979–

Harold E. Ford (D-TN)   House, 1975–1997

William Gray (D-PA)   House, 1979–1991

Charles B. Rangel (D-NY)   House, 1971–

CONGRESSIONAL FIRSTS

The first congressional act   "An Act to Regulate the Time and Manner of administering certain Oaths," signed into law by George Washington on June 1, 1789

The first congressional investigation   An investigation of the conduct of Major General Arthur St. Clair's defeat in an expedition along the Ohio-Indiana border, 1792

The first convicted felon elected to Congress   Matthew Lyon (R-VT); first served in the House in 1797; in October 1798 was convicted of violating the Sedition Act; after being sentenced to four months in jail, reelected from prison and served until 1801 and again from 1803 to 1811

The first pages in the House   Charles Chalmers, Edward Dunn, and John C. Burch, 1827

The first female reporter admitted to the Senate press gallery
Jane Gray Swisshelm, *New York Tribune*, April 17, 1850

The first brothers to serve in Congress simultaneously Israel
Washburn Jr. (Whig/R-ME), Elihu Benjamin Washburne
(Whig-IL), and Cadwallader Colden Washburn (R-WI), in
the 34th to 36th Congresses, 1855–1861. (A fourth brother,
William Drew Washburn, served after the Civil War.)

The first rabbi to lead the House in its opening prayer Morris
Jacob Raphall of Congregation B'nai Jeshurun of New York,
February 1, 1860

The first Speaker of the House to become vice president
Schuyler Colfax; Speaker from 1863 to 1868; elected vice
president in 1868

The first African American to deliver a speech on the House floor
John Willis Menard, in 1869. (His election was contested
and the seat declared vacant in February 1869.)

The first Speaker of the House to die in office Michael Kerr;
died August 19, 1876

The first Congress to appropriate a billion dollars The 52d
Congress, 1891–1893

The first doorkeeper of the House elected to Congress Walter
Preston Brownlow (R-TN); doorkeeper from 1881 to 1883;
served from 1897 to 1910

The first Socialist elected to the House Victor Berger (Socialist-WI); served from 1911 to 1913; barred from Congress for
anti–World War I writings even though elected in 1918 and
1920; then served from 1923 to 1929

The first senator to be elected directly* Blair Lee (D-MD), November 4, 1913

The first woman to serve in the House Jeannette Rankin (R-
MT); served from 1917 to 1919 and from 1941 to 1943

The first woman to head a congressional committee Mae Ella
Nolan (R-CA); headed the Committee on Expenditures in
the Post Office Department, 1923–1925

The first air-conditioned session of Congress The 75th Congress, 2d Session, which opened on November 15, 1937

The first member of Congress to vote against war twice Jeannette Rankin (R-MT), 1917 and 1941

The first reigning queen to address a joint session of Congress Wilhelmina of the Netherlands, August 4, 1942

The first Cabinet officer to address a joint session of Congress Secretary of State Cordell Hull, November 18, 1943

The first televised joint session of Congress January 3, 1947

The first female page in the House Gene Cox, daughter of Congressman Edward Eugene Cox (D-GA), January 3, 1949

The first senator elected as a write-in candidate Strom Thurmond (D-SC), November 3, 1954

The first African American woman elected to the House Shirley Chisholm (D-NY), 1968

The first Puerto Rican elected to the House Herman Badillo (D-NY), 1970

The first Roman Catholic priest elected to the House Robert F. Drinan (D-MA), 1970

The first majority whip elected Speaker of the House Carl Albert (D-OK); whip from 1955 to 1962; Speaker from 1971 to 1977

The first member of Congress granted maternity leave Yvonne Brathwaite Burke (D-CA), 1973

The first House minority leader to become president Gerald Ford (R-MI), 1974

---

* The 17th amendment, ratified in 1913, provided for popular election of senators rather than election by state legislatures.

CONGRESSIONAL EXCLUSIONS

Each house of Congress can decide not to seat a member if he or she does not meet the requirements for membership enumerated in Article I of the Constitution. Representatives must be at least 25 years old, U.S. citizens for 7 years, and residents of their states. Senators must be at least 30 years old, U.S. citizens for 9 years, and residents of their states.

Albert Gallatin (D-PA, Senate)   1793   Had been a citizen only eight years

John Bailey (no party–MA, House)   1823   Didn't live in the district he represented; returned to Massachusetts and was elected to fill his vacant spot

James Shields (D-IL, Senate)   1849   Was six months short of citizenship requirement; was reelected and began service nine years and one week after becoming a citizen

John Young Brown (D-KY, House)   1867   Was disloyal to the Union during the Civil War

Phillip F. Thomas (D-MD, Senate)   1867   Gave money to his son, a Confederate soldier, at the beginning of the Civil War

W. D. Simpson (I-SC, House)   1867   Was disloyal to the Union during the Civil War

John A. Wimpy (I-GA, House)   1867   Was disloyal to the Union during the Civil War

John D. Young (D-KY, House)   1867   Was disloyal to the Union during the Civil War

Benjamin Whittemore (R-SC, House)   1870   Sold placements at the U.S. Military Academy

George Quayle Cannon (R–Utah Territory, House)   1882   Practiced polygamy and elected by means of questionable procedure

Brigham D. Roberts (D-UT, House)   1900   Convicted of polygamy

Victor Louis Berger (Socialist-WI, House)   1919   Opposed the war in print, in violation of the Espionage Act of 1917

Adam Clayton Powell Jr. (D-NY, House) 1967 Accused of various forms of financial misconduct, including a no-show job for his wife and travel at government expense; sued, saying that Congress had no right to exclude any member for reasons other than violation of the enumerated constitutional requirements of age, citizenship, and residency; was re-elected to fill his vacant seat after the Supreme Court ruled in his favor

> *Two men who were elected to the Senate prior to their 30th birthdays were nevertheless allowed to join the Senate. Henry Clay (no party–KY, 1806) was not sworn in until after his birthday, and Rush Holt (D-WV, 1935) did not present his credentials for admission until he turned 30.*

CONGRESSIONAL EXPULSIONS

Members of Congress can be expelled by a two-thirds vote of the house they serve in. Attempts to expel members because they were corrupt (or even because they were Mormon) have not often succeeded.

William Blount (no party–TN, Senate) 1797 Conspired against the government

Thomas Bragg (D-NC, Senate) 1861 Supported the Confederacy

John C. Breckinridge (D-KY, Senate) 1861 Supported the Confederacy

Henry Cornelius Burnett (D-KY, House) 1861 Supported the Confederacy

James Chesnut Jr. (D-SC, Senate) 1861 Supported the Confederacy

John Bullock Clark (D-MO, House) 1861 Supported the Confederacy

Thomas Lanier Clingman (D-NC, Senate) 1861 Supported the Confederacy

John Hemphill (States Rights–TX, Senate) 1861 Supported the Confederacy

Robert Hunter (D-VA, Senate) 1861 Supported the Confederacy

James Murray Mason (D-VA, Senate) 1861 Supported the Confederacy

Charles Burton Mitchel (D-AR, Senate) 1861 Supported the Confederacy

Alfred Osborn Pope Nicholson (D-TN, Senate) 1861 Supported the Confederacy

John W. Reid (D-MO, House) 1861 Supported the Confederacy

William Sebastian (D-AR, Senate) 1861 Supported the Confederacy

Louis T. Wigfall (D-TX, Senate) 1861 Supported the Confederacy

Jesse D. Bright (D-IN, Senate) 1862 Supported the Confederacy

Waldo Porter Johnson (D-MO, Senate) 1862 Supported the Confederacy

Trusten Polk (D-MO, Senate) 1862 Supported the Confederacy

Ozzie Myers (D-PA, House) 1980 Corruption in Abscam

> *William Sebastian had remained loyal to the Union until his death in 1865, even though Arkansas joined the Confederacy during the Civil War. The Senate reversed Sebastian's expulsion posthumously and gave his back pay to his heirs.*

CONGRESSIONAL CENSURES

Censure is an option when members of Congress disapprove of the conduct of a fellow member but do not wish to expel him or her. Although censure carries no physical or financial punishments, it is a harsh rebuke and has often led members to leave Congress.

Timothy Pickering (Federalist-MA, Senate) 1811 Read aloud from secret Louisiana Purchase documents

William Stanbery (Anti-Jacksonian–OH, House) 1832 Insulted the Speaker of the House

Joshua Reed Giddings (Whig-OH, House) 1842 Defended slave mutiny

Benjamin Tappan (D-OH, Senate)   1844   Leaked to the press information about the Texas-annexation treaty

Laurence Massillon Keitt (D-SC, House)   1856   Was complicit in assault on Senator Charles Sumner

Benjamin G. Harris (D-MD, House)   1864   Made treasonous statements

Alexander Long (D-OH, House)   1864   Made treasonous statements

John Winthrop Chanler (D-NY, House)   1866   Insulted the House

Lovell Rousseau (R-KY, House)   1866   Assaulted Congressman Josiah Bushnell Grinnell

John Ward Hunter (I-NY, House)   1867   Insulted a fellow member

Edward Dexter Holbrook (D-ID, House delegate)   1868   Made offensive statements

Benjamin Whittemore (R-SC, House)   1870   Involved in corruption

Fernando Wood (D-NY, House)   1868   Made offensive statements

Roderick Randum Butler (R-TN, House)   1870   Involved in corruption

John T. Deweese (R-NC, House)   1870   Involved in corruption

Oakes Ames (R-MA, House)   1873   Involved in Crédit Mobilier scandal

James Brooks (D-NY, House)   1873   Involved in Crédit Mobilier scandal

John Y. Brown (D-KY, House)   1875   Insulted a fellow member

William Dallas Bynum (D-IN, House)   1890   Made offensive statements

John Lowndes McLaurin (D-SC, Senate)   1902   Involved in a brawl with Senator Tillman

Benjamin Ryan Tillman (D-SC, Senate)   1902   Involved in a brawl with Senator McLaurin

Thomas Lindsay Blanton (D-TX, House)   1921   Inserted obscene materials in *Congressional Record*

Hiram Bingham (R-CT, Senate)   1929   Hired manufacturing lobbyist to help with tariff legislation

Joseph Raymond McCarthy (R-WI, Senate)   1954   Insulted other senators and obstructed the investigation

Thomas Joseph Dodd (D-CT, Senate)   1966   Used campaign funds for personal benefit

Herman Talmadge (D-GA, Senate)   1979   Used campaign funds and official funds for personal benefit

Charles Coles Diggs Jr. (D-MI, House)   1979   Used staff funds for personal benefit

Charles H. Wilson (D-CA, House)   1983   Used campaign funds for personal benefit and took gifts from a person trying to influence legislation

Daniel Bever Crane (R-IL, House)   1990   Had sex with a 17-year-old female page

David F. Durenberger (R-MN, Senate)   1990   Made an improper book deal and claimed improper rent reimbursements

Gerry E. Studds (D-MA, House)   1990   Had sex with a 17-year-old male page

Senators Bingham and McCarthy were "condemned," and Senator Talmadge was "denounced," but both amount to a censure.

HOUSE REPRIMANDS

The only reason a reprimand, a fairly recent congressional innovation, is better than a censure is that the guilty party does not have to stand in the well of the House while the Speaker reads the resolution condemning him aloud.

Robert Sikes (D-FL)   1976   Failed to disclose finances, involved in conflict of interest

John McFall (D-CA)   1978   Failed to report campaign contributions from Korean businessman Tongsun Park

Edward Roybal (D-CA)   1978   Failed to report campaign contributions from Park

Charles Wilson (D-CA)   1978   Failed to report wedding gift of cash from Park

George Vernon Hansen (R-ID)   1984   Failed to make financial disclosures

Austin J. Murphy (D-PA)   1987   Had a no-show employee on his staff and gave government resources to his former law firm

Barney Frank (D-MA)   1990   Fixed parking tickets and wrote a misleading recommendation for a male prostitute

Newt Gingrich (R-GA)   1997   Put tax-exempt funds to political use and submitted false information to the Ethics committee

Newt Gingrich was the first Speaker of the House to receive a reprimand. None has been censured.

REAPPORTIONMENT WINNERS AND LOSERS: States That Have Gained or Lost Seats in the House Since 1910

In 1910, the House of Representatives grew to its current size of 435 members. Since then the United States has experienced a demographic shift, and Americans have abandoned the Northeast and the Midwest for the South and the West. As a result, the balance of power has changed in Congress and in the electoral college.

State	Number of Seats Gained	State	Number of Seats Lost
California	41	Pennsylvania	15
Florida	19	New York	12
Texas	12	Illinois	7
Arizona*	5	Missouri	7
Washington	4	Iowa	6
Michigan	3	Massachusetts	6
Colorado	2	Kentucky	5
Maryland	2	Kansas	4
New Mexico*	2	Alabama	3
North Carolina	2	Arkansas	3
Oregon	2	Indiana	3
Hawaii*	2	Mississippi	3
Connecticut	1	Nebraska	3
Nevada	1	Ohio	3
New Jersey	1	West Virginia	3
Utah	1	Maine	2
Virginia	1	Minnesota	2
Alaska*	1	North Dakota	2
		Oklahoma	2
		South Dakota	2
		Wisconsin	2
		Georgia	1
		Louisiana	1
		Montana	1
		Rhode Island	1
		South Carolina	1
		Tennessee	1
		Vermont	1

* Became a state after 1910.

WORST YEARLY CONGRESSIONAL ATTENDANCE RECORDS SINCE 1987

Attendance figures are based on the percentage of roll-call votes that a member of Congress cast a yea or nay vote in. The average current representative or senator is present for about 95% of all roll-call votes. Veteran lawmakers, like Congressman William Natcher (D-KY, 1953–1994), advise members to miss a roll-call vote early so they are not obsessed with keeping a perfect attendance record. Natcher never followed this advice; he cast the last of his 18,401 roll-call votes (excluding quorum calls) from a hospital gurney. He holds the record for casting the most consecutive roll-call votes.

Senate		Year	% of Votes Present	Reason for Absence
Joseph R. Biden Jr.	D-DE	1988	17	Running for president; recovering from aneurysm
Al Gore	D-TN	1987	42	Running for president
Paul Simon	D-IL	1987	42	Running for president
Al Gore	D-TN	1992	57	Running for vice president
Joseph Biden	D-DE	1987	62	Running for president
Jesse Helms	R-NC	1992	63	Recovering from heart-bypass surgery
David Kemp Karnes	R-NE	1988	70	Not reelected
Tom Harkin	D-IA	1992	74	Running for president
Tom Harkin	D-IA	1991	75	Running for president
Bob Kerrey	D-NE	1991	77	Running for president

House	Year	% of Votes Present	Reason for Absence
Eldon Beau Boulter R-TX	1988	15	Running for Senate
Richard Gephardt D-MO	1987	19	Running for president
James Joseph "Jim" Florio D-NJ	1989	19	Running for governor
Craig Washington D-TX	1994	20	None given
James Andrew "Jim" Courter R-NJ	1989	25	Running for governor
Buddy Roemer D-LA	1987	29	Running for governor
Buddy MacKay D-FL	1988	29	Running for Senate
Connie Mack R-FL	1988	31	Running for Senate
Jack Kemp R-NY	1987	33	Running for president
Daniel A. Mica D-FL	1988	34	Running for Senate
Larry Jones Hopkins R-KY	1991	38	Running for governor
Jack Kemp R-NY	1988	42	Running for president
Bill Nelson D-FL	1990	45	Running for governor
Dean A. Gallo R-NJ	1994	48	Ill (died in office)
Robert Garcia D-NY	1989	51	Involved in Wedtech corruption scandal
Bob Traxler D-MI	1992	51	Mugged on Capitol Hill
Joseph M. McDade R-PA	1996	51	On trial
Cardiss Collins D-IL	1989	52	Ill
W. J. "Billy" Tauzin D-LA	1987	52	Running for governor
Blanche Lambert Lincoln R-AR	1996	52	Gave birth to twins

★ ★ ★

WORST MIDTERM ELECTIONS SINCE THE CIVIL WAR

When an incumbent president is unpopular, great shifts can take place in Congress as voters replace members of the president's party with members of the opposition party.

President and Party	Year	Seats Lost House*	Senate	Total
Grover Cleveland (D)	1894	116	5	121
Ulysses Grant (R)	1874	96	8	104
Benjamin Harrison (R)	1890	85	0	85
Warren Harding (R)	1922	75	8	83
Franklin Roosevelt (D)	1938	71	6	77
William Howard Taft (R)	1910	57	10	67
Franklin Roosevelt (D)	1942	55	9	64
Dwight Eisenhower (R)	1958	48	13	61
Bill Clinton (D)	1994	52	9[†]	61
Herbert Hoover (R)	1930	49	8	57
Harry Truman (D)	1946	45	12	57
Woodrow Wilson (D)	1914	59	5	54

---

* Between 1890 and 1910, total was 357 seats; since 1910, it has been 435.

† Includes the seat held by Richard C. Shelby (AL), who switched to the Republican Party after the election.

CONGRESSIONAL SALARIES
SINCE 1789

The following are the years when members of Congress decided to raise (or, in a few cases, lower) their salaries.

	House Salary	Senate Salary
1789	$6.00*	$6.00*
1795	—	7.00*
1796	—	6.00*
1815	1,500.00	1,500.00
1817	8.00*	8.00*
1855	3,000.00	3,000.00
1865	5,000.00	5,000.00
1871	7,500.00	7,500.00
1873	5,000.00	5,000.00
1907	7,500.00	7,500.00
1925	10,000.00	10,000.00
1932	9,000.00	9,000.00
1933	8,500.00	8,500.00
1935	10,000.00	10,000.00
1947	12,000.00	12,000.00
1955	22,500.00	22,500.00
1965	30,000.00	30,000.00
1969	42,500.00	42,500.00
1975	44,600.00	44,600.00
1977	57,500.00	57,500.00
1979	60,662.50	60,662.50
1982	69,800.00	—
1983	—	69,800.00
1984	72,600.00	72,600.00
1985	75,100.00	75,100.00
1987[†]	77,400.00	77,400.00
1987[‡]	89,500.00	89,500.00
1990	96,500.00	98,400.00
1991[†]	125,100.00	101,900.00
1991[§]	—	125,100.00
1992	129,500.00	129,500.00
1993	133,600.00	133,600.00

* Per diem.   † January.   ‡ March.   § August.

CONGRESSIONAL SALARIES IN TERMS OF 1990 DOLLARS, AT TEN-YEAR INTERVALS

By applying the composite consumer price index, it is easy to see that congressional salaries have not grown as much as they seem to have, nor are members of Congress as well paid now as they have been at other times.

Year	House	Senate
1860	$46,890	$46,890
1870	49,777	49,777
1880	63,537	63,537
1890	71,697	71,697
1900	77,376	77,376
1910	102,829	102,829
1920	48,843	48,843
1930	78,150	78,150
1940	93,036	93,036
1950	65,125	65,125
1960	99,343	99,343
1970	143,162	143,162
1980	96,259	96,259
1990	96,500	98,400

LUTHER PATRICK'S RULES FOR A CONGRESSMAN, 1940

Luther Patrick (D-AL), served in the House from 1937 to 1943 and from 1945 to 1947.

1. Entertain with a smile constituents, their wives, their sons, sons' wives, etc. Go with them to the White House; show good reason why you are unable to personally have them meet the President; take daughters to meet midshipmen at Annapolis.

2. Explain what bill is up for debate; points for discussion; how it will be passed; how you will vote and why.

3. Attend to balcony and point out Speaker Bankhead, leaders Rayburn and Martin, Ham Fish, Dewey Short, that man Martin Dies,* and name each lady member of Congress.

4. Respond to worthy causes; make after-dinner speeches, before-dinner speeches; learn to eat anything, anywhere, any night—work all day, dictate all night, and be fresh as a rain-washed daisy for next day's duties.

5. Be a cultured gentleman, a teller of ribald stories, a profound philosopher, preserve a story of "Confucius say" gags, be a ladies' man, a man's man, a he-man, a diplomat, a Democrat with a Republican slant, a Republican with a Democratic viewpoint, an admirer of the old Roosevelt way, a hater of the New Deal, a new dealer, an older dealer, and a quick dealer.

6. Learn how to attend six to eight major functions, rushing home and back during each term on one round-trip travel.

7. Have the dope on hot spots in town, with choice telephone numbers for the gay boys back home, and help to contact all local moral organizations and uplift societies in Washington.

8. Learn to be expert guide. Keep car in tip-top shape.

9. Know names and dates related to all points of interest, and be able to explain and supply information regarding public buildings and statuary about Washington.

10. Be an authority on history, travel, psychology, philosophy, education, civics, finance, export trade, government printing, international relations, neckties, and fishing tackle.

---

* William Bankhead (D-AL) was Speaker of the House from 1936 to 1940. In 1940, Sam Rayburn (D-TX) and Joseph Martin (R-MA) were House majority leaders. Hamilton Fish (D-NY) had been in the House since 1920; Dewey Short (R-MO) had been in the House from 1929 to 1931 and since 1935; and Martin Dies (D-TX) was chairman of the House Un-American Affairs Committee.

NINE COMMANDMENTS OF HEALTH

Dr. George W. Calver, the Capitol Hill physician from 1928 to 1966, issued these recommendations for members of Congress in 1953.

I. Eat wisely.

II. Drink plentifully (of water).

III. Eliminate thoroughly.

IV. Exercise rationally.

V. Accept inevitables (don't worry).

VI. Play enthusiastically.

VII. Relax completely.

VIII. Sleep sufficiently.

IX. Check up occasionally.

TEN POSTTERM PERKS

The privileges of a member of Congress do not end once he or she has left office.

1. **Access to the floor**   Former members have access to the floor of the house they served in, with a couple of exceptions. Former members of the House employed as lobbyists and those with a personal or a pecuniary interest in a bill under discussion are barred from the House floor, and former senators are barred from lobbying on the Senate floor for one year after leaving office. Former senators have floor privileges in the House, and all former members have floor privileges at joint sessions of Congress.

2. **Right to purchase office furnishings**   Members of the House have the right to buy the standard congressional desk-and-chair set at the time of their retirement. Senators may buy their chamber chair and any office furnishings considered surplus.

3. **Extension of the right to frank**   House and Senate members may continue to frank official mail for 90 days after leaving office.

4. **Access to the *Congressional Record***   Former House and Senate members are allowed one free copy of the *Congressional Record* daily.

5. **Access to the Library of Congress and the House or the Senate Library**   Former members may keep their borrowing privileges.

6. **Priority in committee testimony**   Former House and Senate members may testify at congressional hearings before other witnesses testify.

7. **Access to parking**   Former senators may get a permit allowing them to use the outdoor Senate parking lots.

8. **Credit union membership**   Former House and Senate members may keep their memberships in the congressional credit unions.

9. **Access to the members' dining room**   Former members may continue to use the congressional dining room.

10. **Use of the House gym**   For a fee former members of the House may continue to work out in the House gymnasium.

CEMETERIES IN WHICH THE MOST MEMBERS OF CONGRESS ARE BURIED

Many former members of Congress are buried in their home districts. Some cemeteries in and around Washington, DC, and in populous states have especially high concentrations of congressional bones, however. Perhaps they are in special session in the next world. (In the breakdowns below, those who served in both houses of Congress are counted only as senators.)

Arlington National Cemetery, Arlington, VA

102 members of Congress: 27 senators, 75 representatives

Green-Wood Cemetery, Brooklyn, NY

100 members of Congress: 8 senators, 92 representatives

Congressional Cemetery, Washington, DC

76 members of Congress: 17 senators, 59 representatives

Spring Grove Cemetery, Cincinnati, OH

48 members of Congress: 7 senators, 41 representatives

Bellefontaine Cemetery, St. Louis, MO

47 members of Congress: 12 senators, 35 representatives

Woodlawn Cemetery, Bronx, NY

46 members of Congress: 4 senators, 42 representatives

Rock Creek Cemetery, Washington, DC

43 members of Congress: 10 senators, 33 representatives

Mount Auburn Cemetery, Cambridge, MA

41 members of Congress: 12 senators, 29 representatives

Calvary Cemetery, Queens, NY

33 members of Congress: 2 senators, 31 representatives

Crown Hill Cemetery, Indianapolis, IN

32 members of Congress: 14 senators, 18 representatives

EUGENE McCARTHY'S TEN COMMANDMENTS FOR NEW MEMBERS OF CONGRESS

I. Vote against anything introduced with "re-"—reforms, reorganizations, recodifications, and especially resolutions.

II. Do not have a perfect, or near-perfect, attendance record. If a new member has an attendance record better than 80%, there is reason to believe that he or she has been wasting time answering roll calls and quorum calls. A member who has been in office for several terms should work his attendance record down to 65 or 70%.

III. Do not worry too much about rules or procedures or

spend much time trying to learn them. The Senate rules are simple enough to be learned, but they are seldom honored in practice. The House rules are generally applied, but they are too complicated to be worth mastering. The parliamentarian is always available.

IV. Beware of a staff that is too efficient. Never trust a staff member who regularly gets to the office before you do and who stays after you leave.

V. Don't worry too much about intelligence. Remember that politics is much like coaching professional football—those who are most successful are just smart enough to understand the game, but not smart enough to lose interest.

VI. Don't knock the seniority system; you may have seniority sooner than you anticipate. Moreover, the practice of having senior members assume responsibility as committee chairpersons, although not a rational process, does, as Gilbert Chesterton observed of the ancient practice of having the oldest son of a king accede to the throne, "save a lot of trouble."

VII. Don't, unless the issue is overwhelming, be the only one, or one of a few, who is right about it, especially if it is an issue that will not go away. It is difficult to say to one's colleagues in Congress, "I am sorry I was right. Please forgive me." They won't.

VIII. Remember that the worst accidents occur in or near the middle of the road.

IX. Do not respond to the appeal of "party loyalty." This can be the last defense of political rascals. Remember that those who "go along" do not always "get along."

X. As Ed Leahy, noted reporter of the Chicago *Daily News,* said to me soon after I arrived in Congress thirty years ago, "Never trust the press."

CURRENT CONGRESSIONAL LISTS

THE 535 MEN AND WOMEN OF THE 105th Congress come from all sorts of backgrounds. Some members have ancestors who came to America when there were still 13 colonies and were elected to serve on Capitol Hill, and other members are themselves immigrants. Some come from backgrounds of privilege and attended fancy schools; others are self-made and never finished college. Before your local representative was elected, he may have been a veterinarian or an undertaker, a schoolteacher or an exterminator, or she may have owned a vineyard. Once they are elected, however, their past lives are sometimes forgotten, and they are remembered most for their service to their country.

CONGRESSIONAL LEGACIES IN THE 105TH CONGRESS

The United States is a democratic republic, not a hereditary oligarchy, but politics still runs in families.

Senate

Robert Foster Bennett (R-UT)   Son of Wallace Bennett (R-UT, Senate, 1951–1974)

Christopher Dodd (D-CT)   Son of Thomas Dodd (D-CT, House, 1953–1957; Senate, 1959–1971)

Edward M. Kennedy (D-MA)   Brother of John F. Kennedy (D-MA, House, 1947–1953; Senate, 1953–1960) and Robert Kennedy (D-NY, Senate, 1965–1968), grandson of John Francis Fitzgerald (D-MA, House, 1895–1901, March–October 1919), uncle of Joseph P. Kennedy II (D-MA, House, 1987–), and father of Patrick Kennedy (D-RI, House, 1995–)

Jon Llewellyn Kyl (R-AZ)   Son of Jon Henry Kyl (R-IA, House, 1959–1965, 1967–1973)

Carl Levin (D-MI)   Brother of Sander Levin (D-MI, House, 1983–)

Connie Mack (R-FL)   Grandson of Morris Sheppard (D-TX, House, 1902–1913; Senate, 1913–1941) and great-grandson of John Levi Sheppard (D-TX, House, 1899–1902)

John D. "Jay" Rockefeller IV (D-WV)   Great-grandson of Nelson Wilmarth Aldrich (R-RI, House, 1879–1881; Senate, 1881–1911), great-grandnephew of Richard Steere Aldrich (R-RI, House, 1923–1933), and son-in-law of Charles Harting Percy (R-IL, Senate, 1967–1985)

Olympia Snowe (R-ME)   Wife of John McKernan (R-ME, House, 1983–1987)

House

T. Cass Ballenger (R-NC)   Great-great-grandson of Lewis Cass (D-MI, Senate, 1845–1848, 1849–1857)

Charles Bass (R-NH)   Son of Perkins Bass (R-NH, House, 1955–1963)

Ken Bentsen (D-TX)   Nephew of Lloyd Bentsen (D-TX, House, 1948–1955; Senate, 1971–1993)

Lois Capps (D-CA)   Widow of Walter Capps (D-CA, House, 1997)

Philip Miller Crane (R-IL)   Brother of Daniel Crane (R-IL, House, 1979–1985)

John D. Dingell Jr. (D-MI)   Son of John D. Dingell (D-MI, House, 1933–1955)

John J. "Jimmy" Duncan Jr. (R-TN)   Son of John James Duncan (R-TN, House, 1965–1988)

Jo Ann Emerson (I-MO)   Widow of Bill Emerson (R-MO, House, 1980–1996)

Harold E. Ford Jr. (D-TN)   Son of Harold E. Ford (D-TN, House, 1975–1997)

Rodney Frelinghuysen (R-NJ)   Son of Peter Hood Ballantine Frelinghuysen Jr. (R-NJ, House, 1953–1975), nephew of Joseph Sherman Frelinghuysen (R-NJ, Senate, 1917–1923), great-great-grandson of Frederick Theodore Frelinghuysen (R-NJ, Senate, 1866–1869, 1871–1877), great-great-great-grandnephew of Theodore Frelinghuysen (R-NJ, Senate, 1829–1835), and great-great-great-great-grandson of Frederick Frelinghuysen (no party–NJ, Senate, 1793–1796)

William Goodling (R-PA)   Son of George Atlee Goodling (R-PA, House, 1961–1965, 1967–1975)

Amo Houghton (R-NY)   Grandson of Alanson Bigelow Houghton (R-NY, House, 1919–1922)

Asa Hutchinson (R-AR)   Brother of Tim Hutchinson (R-AR, House, 1993–1997; Senate, 1997–)

Walter Beaman Jones Jr. (R-NC)   Son of Walter Beaman Jones (D-NC, House, 1966–1992)

Joseph P. Kennedy II (D-MA)   Son of Robert Kennedy (D-NY, Senate, 1964–1968), nephew of John Kennedy (D-MA, House, 1947–1953; Senate, 1953–1960) and Edward Kennedy (D-MA, Senate 1962–), great-grandson of John Fitzgerald (D-MA, House, 1895–1901, March–October 1919), and cousin of Patrick Kennedy (D-RI, House, 1995–)

Patrick Kennedy (D-RI)   Son of Edward M. Kennedy (D-MA, Senate, 1962–), nephew of John Kennedy (D-MA, House, 1947–1953; Senate, 1953–1960) and Robert Kennedy (D-NY, Senate, 1964–1968), great-grandson of John Fitzgerald (D-MA, House, 1895–1901, March–October 1919), and cousin of Joseph Kennedy II (D-MA, House 1987–)

Tom Lantos (D-CA)   Father-in-law of Dick Swett (D-NH, House, 1991–1995)

Sander Levin (D-MI)   Brother of Carl Levin (D-MI, Senate, 1979–)

John L. Mica (R-FL)   Brother of Daniel Mica (D-FL, House, 1979–1989)

Alan Bowlby Mollohan (D-WV)   Son of Robert H. Mollohan (D-WV, House, 1953–1957, 1969–1983)

Nancy Pelosi (D-CA)   Daughter of Thomas D'Alesandro (D-MD, House, 1939–1947)

Bill Paxon (R-NY)   Husband of Susan Molinari (R-NY, House, 1990–1997) and son-in-law of Guy Molinari (R-NY, House, 1981–1990)

Tim Roemer (D-IN)   Son-in-law of J. Bennett Johnston (D-LA, Senate, 1972–1997)

Lucille Roybal-Allard (D-CA)   Daughter of Edward Roybal (D-CA, House, 1963–1993)

MEMBERS OF THE 105TH CONGRESS WHO HAVE NO COLLEGE DEGREE

Even today a college degree is not a requirement for success.

Senate

Conrad Burns R-MT
Lauch Faircloth R-NC
Rod Grams R-MN
Jim Ross Lightfoot R-IA

House

Brian P. Bilbray R-CA
Dan Burton R-IN
Sonny Callahan R-AL
Mac Collins R-GA
Terry Everett R-AL
Mark Foley R-FL
Elton Gallegly R-CA
William Hefner D-NC
William O. Lipinski D-IL
Matthew G. Martinez D-CA
Solomon Ortiz D-TX
Silvestre Reyes D-TX
Esteban E. Torres D-CA
Zach Wamp R-TN
C. W. Bill Young R-FL

HARVARD GRADUATES IN THE 105TH CONGRESS

These politicians received one degree or another—or, sometimes, more than one—from Harvard University.

Senate

Spencer Abraham (R-MI)   Law
Jeff Bingaman (D-NM)   BA
John Chafee (R-RI)   Law
Russell D. Feingold (D-WI)   BA
Bob Graham (D-FL)   Law
James M. Jeffords (R-VT)   Law
Ted Kennedy (D-MA)   BA
Herb Kohl (D-WI)   MBA
Carl Levin (D-MI)   Law
Jack Reed (D-RI)   MPP, law
Jay Rockefeller (D-WV)   BA
William V. Roth Jr. (R-DE)   Law, MBA
Ted Stevens (R-AK)   Law
Robert G. Torricelli (D-NJ)   MPA

House

Thomas Allen (D-ME)   Law
Doug Bereuter (R-NE)   MCP, MPA
Merrill Cook (R-UT)   MBA
Christopher Cox (R-CA)   Law, MBA
Michael D. Crapo (R-ID)   Law
Chet Edwards (D-TX)   MBA
Barney Frank (D-MA)   BA, law
Jane Harman (D-CA)   Law
Steve Horn (R-CA)   MPA
William Jefferson (D-LA)   Law
Nancy L. Johnson (R-CT)   BA
Ron Kind (D-WI)   BA
Sander Levin (D-MI)   Law
James H. Maloney (D-CT)   BA

Tom Petri (R-WI)   BA, law
Charles Schumer (D-NY)   BA, law
Robert C. "Bobby" Scott (D-VA)   BA
Brad Sherman (D-CA)   Law
John E. Sununu (R-NH)   MBA

YALE GRADUATES IN THE 105TH CONGRESS

These politicians received one or more degrees from Yale University.

Senate

John Ashcroft (R-MO)   BA, law
John Chafee (R-RI)   Law
Jim Jeffords (R-VT)   Law
John F. Kerry (D-MA)   BA
Joseph I. Lieberman (D-CT)   BA, law
Jay Rockefeller (D-WV)   BA
Arlen Specter (R-PA)   Law

House

Sherrod Brown (D-OH)   BA
Charles T. Canady (R-FL)   Law
Peter Deutsch (D-FL)   Law
Porter J. Goss (R-FL)   BA
Sheila Jackson-Lee (D-TX)   BA
David M. McIntosh (R-IN)   BA
Eleanor Holmes Norton (D-DC, delegate)   MA, law
David E. Price (D-NC)   PhD
David E. Skaggs (D-CO)   Law
Lamar Smith (R-TX)   BA
John M. Spratt Jr. (D-SC)   Law
Melvin Watt (D-NC)   Law

OVERQUALIFIED? PhDs IN THE 105TH CONGRESS

Senate

Phil Gramm (R-TX)   Economics
Daniel Patrick "Pat" Moynihan (D-NY)   International relations
Paul Wellstone (D-MN)   Political science

House

Neil Abercrombie (D-HI)   American studies
Dick Armey (R-TX)   Economics
Roscoe Bartlett (R-MD)   Engineering
Glen Browder (D-AL)   Political science
Philip Crane (R-IL)   American history
Danny K. Davis (D-IL)   Public administration
Vernon Ehlers (R-MI)   Physics
Bob Filner (D-CA)   History of science
Floyd Flake (D-NY)   Theology
Newt Gingrich (R-GA)   European history
Steve Horn (R-CA)   Political science
Tom Lantos (D-CA)   Economics
Dan Miller (R-FL)   Marketing
John Olver (D-MA)   Chemistry
Glenn Poshard (R-IL)   Education
David Price (D-NC)   Political science
Tim Roemer (D-IN)   International relations
Bud Shuster (R-PA)   Management and economics
Ted Strickland (D-OH)   Psychology
Sidney Yates (D-IL)   Jurisprudence

FORMER SCHOOLTEACHERS IN THE 105TH CONGRESS

Senate

Daniel Akaka   D-HI
Robert C. Smith   R-NH
Strom Thurmond   R-SC

House

Neil Abercrombie   D-HI
Gary Ackerman   D-NY
Herbert Bateman   R-VA
Steve Chabot   R-OH
James E. Clyburn   D-SC
Larry Combest   R-TX
Barbara Cubin   R-WY
Eliot Engel   D-NY
Wayne Gilchrest   R-MD
Bill Goodling   R-PA
Kay Granger   R-TX
Luis V. Gutierrez   D-IL
Dennis Hastert   R-IL
Darlene Hooley   D-OR
Dale Kildee   D-MI
Carolyn Cheeks Kilpatrick   D-MI
Ray LaHood   R-IL
Nick Lampson   D-TX
Karen McCarthy   D-MO

Jack Metcalf   R-WA
Constance Morella   R-MD
Mark Neumann   R-WI
Robert Ney   R-OH
Anne Meagher Northup   R-KY
William J. Pascrell Jr.   D-NJ
Ed Pastor   D-AZ
Donald M. Payne   D-NJ
Glenn Poshard   D-IL
Jack Quinn   R-NY
Ralph Regula   R-OH
Ileana Ros-Lehtinen   R-FL
Marge Roukema   R-NJ
Jim Saxton   R-NJ
John M. Shimkus   R-IL
Karen L. Thurman   D-FL
Edolphus Towns   D-NY
Bruce Vento   D-MN
Curt Weldon   R-PA

DOCTORS
IN THE 105TH CONGRESS

*If anyone asks, "Is there a doctor in the House?" the answer is
Yes. The only doctor in the Senate is Bill Frist (R-TN).*

Tom Coburn (R-OK) Obstetrician

John Cooksey (R-LA) Ophthalmologist

John Ensign (R-NV) Veterinarian

Greg Ganske (R-IA) Plastic surgeon

John Linder (R-GA) Dentist

Jim McDermott (D-WA) Psychiatrist

Charles Norwood (R-GA) Dentist

Ron Packard (R-CA) Dentist

Ron Paul (R-TX) Obstetrician/gynecologist

Vic Snyder (D-AR) Family practice

David Weldon (R-FL) Internist

TALKING HEADS:
Former Radio and Television
Broadcasters in the 105th
Congress

*Since the days of Father Charles E. Coughlin (1891–1979), radio and
television personalities have influenced American politics. Some broad-
casters have chosen to give up their microphones for lawmaking.*

Senate

Sam Brownback (R-KS) Radio broadcaster, 1978–1979

Conrad Burns (R-MT) Radio and TV broadcaster, 1968–1986

Rod Grams (R-MN) News anchor, 1976–1991

Jesse Helms (R-NC) Executive vice president, WRAL-TV and
Tobacco Radio Network, 1960–1972

Kay Bailey Hutchison (R-TX) Political and legal correspondent, 1967–1970

House

Henry Bonilla (R-TX)   TV reporter, 1976–1980; writer and producer, 1982–1985; assistant news director, 1985–1986; executive news producer, 1986–1989

J. D. Hayworth (R-AZ)   Sports reporter and anchor, 1980–1994

Ernest J. Istook (R-OK)   Political reporter, 1973–1976

Jay Johnson (D-WI)   Anchorman, 1987–1996

Ron Klink (D-PA)   Reporter and anchor, 1978–1992

Scott L. Klug (R-WI)   Investigative reporter, 1976–1988; news anchor, 1988–1990

Tom Lantos (D-CA)   TV commentator, 1955–1963

Dana Rohrabacher (R-CA)   Radio journalist, 1970–1980

ALAN SIMPSON'S DOZEN BEST POLITICAL JOURNALISTS

Simpson (R-WY, Senate, 1979–1997) articulated his frustrations with the Washington press corps in his book Right in the Old Gazoo *(1997). Here he singles out the journalists for whom he has the most respect and admiration.*

1. **Miles Benson**   Newhouse News Service
2. **David Broder**   *The Washington Post*
3. **Helen Dewar**   *The Washington Post*
4. **Sam Donaldson**   ABC News*
5. **Rowland Evans**   Syndicated columnist
6. **Meg Greenfield**   *Newsweek*
7. **Ted Koppel**   ABC News
8. **Jim Lehrer**   *The NewsHour with Jim Lehrer*
9. **Elaine Povich**   *Newsday*
10. **Mark Shields**   Syndicated columnist†
11. **Budge Sperling**   *The Christian Science Monitor*
12. **Karen Tumulty**   *Time*

---

* "A spirited, pesky rascal."
† "A good egg."

FARMERS AND RANCHERS IN THE 105TH CONGRESS

Senate

Ben Nighthorse Campbell (R-CO)   Rancher and horse trainer

Larry E. Craig (R-ID)   Rancher and farmer

Lauch Faircloth (R-NC)   Hog farmer

Charles E. "Chuck" Grassley (R-IA)   Farmer

House

Scotty Baesler (D-KY)   Tobacco farmer

Allen Boyd (D-FL)   Farmer

Larry Combest (R-TX)   Farmer

Calvin Dooley (D-CA)   Farmer

Greg Ganske (R-IA)   Farmer

Wally Herger (R-CA)   Rancher

William Jenkins (R-TN)   Farmer

Thomas Latham (R-IA)   Farmer

Frank D. Lucas (R-OK)   Farmer and rancher

Richard W. Pombo (R-CA)   Cattle rancher

George P. Radanovich (R-CA)   Farmer

Joe Skeen (R-NM)   Sheep rancher

Robert Smith (R-OR)   Rancher

Nick Smith (R-MI)   Farmer

Charles W. Stenholm (D-TX)   Farmer

Bob Stump (R-AZ)   Cotton and grain farmer

Jerry Weller (R-IL)   Farmer

★ ★ ★

MEMBERS OF THE 105TH CONGRESS WHO WERE IN THE INSURANCE BUSINESS

Senate

Wendell Ford (D-KY)   Insurance agent

House

William Barrett (R-NE)   Insurance company owner

Dan Burton (R-IN)   Founder of insurance agency

Jon Christensen (R-NE)   Marketing director of insurance company

William Clay (D-MO)   Life insurance agent

Michael Doyle (D-PA)   Insurance agent

Kay Granger (R-TX)   Insurance agent

J. D. Hayworth (R-AZ)   Insurance agent

Rich Hill (R-MT)   Owner of insurance company

Tim Holden (D-PA)   Insurance broker

Jack Kingston (R-GA)   Insurance agent

Joseph Knollenberg (R-MI)   Insurance agent

Tom Latham (R-IA)   Insurance agent

Jerry Lewis (R-CA)   Insurance executive

Donald Payne (D-NJ)   Insurance executive

John Spratt (D-SC)   President of insurance agency

LAW-ENFORCEMENT OFFICERS IN THE 105TH CONGRESS

All of the former law-enforcement agents in the 105th Congress are in the House.

Scott McInnis (R-CO)   Police officer

Solomon Ortiz (D-TX)   Sheriff

Michael Oxley (R-OH)   FBI agent

Frank D. Riggs (R-CA)   Police officer and deputy sheriff

Bart Stupak (D-MI)   Police officer

FOREIGN-BORN MEMBERS OF THE 105TH CONGRESS

All of the senators were born in the United States.

Lincoln Diaz-Balart (R-FL)   Born in Havana, Cuba

Elizabeth Furse (D-OR)   Born in Nairobi, Kenya

Samuel Gejdenson (D-CT)   Born in Eschwege, Germany

Peter Hoekstra (R-MI)   Born in Groningen, the Netherlands

Jay Kim (R-CA)   Born in Seoul, South Korea

Tom Lantos (D-CA)   Born in Budapest, Hungary

Ileana Ros-Lehtinen (R-FL)   Born in Havana, Cuba

RESTAURATEURS IN THE 105TH CONGRESS

Senate

Bob Kerrey (D-NE)   An owner of Grandmother's restaurants, a Nebraska chain (three in Omaha, one in Lincoln)

House

John Elias Baldacci (D-ME)   Family runs Momma Baldacci's restaurant in Bangor

Ken Calvert (R-CA)   Owned The Jolly Fox in Corona

Jay Dickey (R-AR)   Owned Taco Bell and Baskin-Robbins franchises

Mark Foley (R-FL)   Owned the Lettuce Patch in Lake Worth

David L. Hobson (R-OH)   Founder and member of the board of directors of the Cooker Bar and Grill chain, with restaurants in the Midwest and the Southeast

Ron Klink (D-PA)   Owner of Dagwood's in Pittsburgh

Dan Miller (R-FL)   Owns Memorial Pier restaurant in Bradenton

David R. Obey (D-WI)   Family owned the Gaslite Supper Club and Motel in Madison

Clifford B. Stearns (R-FL)   Owns T.V. Sports Bar in Gainesville and a Howard Johnson and the Stage Stop, both in Silver Springs

The late Sonny Bono (R-CA) was the owner of Bono restaurants in West Hollywood, Palm Springs, and Houston.

MEMBERS OF THE 105TH CONGRESS WITH UNIQUE OCCUPATIONS

Senate

Ben Nighthorse Campbell (R-CO)   Horse trainer and jewelry designer

John Glenn (D-OH)   Astronaut

Kay Bailey Hutchison (R-TX)   Former owner of McCraw Candies

House

Michael Bilirakis (R-FL)   Steelworker

Tom DeLay (R-TX)   Owner of Albo Pest Control

Elizabeth Furse (D-OR)   Owner of Helvetia Vineyards

Gil Gutknecht (R-MN)   Real estate auctioneer

Maurice Hinchey (D-NY)   Former thruway toll collector

Sue Kelly (R-NY)   Owner of building-renovating business and a flower shop

Ron Lewis (R-KY)   Owner of Alpha Christian Bookstore

Howard P. "Buck" McKeon (R-CA)   Co-owner of Howard and Phil's Western Wear

John P. Murtha (D-PA)   Owner of Johnstown Minute Car Wash

Major Owens (D-NY)   Librarian

George Radanovich (R-CA)   Owner of Radanovich Winery

Lynn Woolsey (D-CA)   Former owner of personnel service

Lynn Woolsey was also once on welfare.

FEMALE MEMBERS OF THE 105TH CONGRESS NOT ENDORSED BY THE NATIONAL WOMEN'S POLITICAL CAUCUS

The NWPC describes itself as "a national, grassroots organization dedicated to increasing the number of women in elected and appointed office at all levels of government, regardless of party affiliation." Despite that description, it did not see fit to endorse all the women running in the 1996 elections.

Senate

Kay Bailey Hutchison   R-TX

House

Helen Chenoweth   R-ID
Barbara Cubin   R-WY
Pat "Patsy Ann" Danner   D-MO

Jennifer Dunn   R-WA
Jo Ann Emerson   I-MO
Tillie Fowler   R-FL
Kay Granger   R-TX
Marcy Kaptur   D-OH
Susan Molinari   R-NY
Sue Myrick   R-NC
Anne Northup   R-KY
Deborah Pryce   R-OH
Ileana Ros-Lehtinen   R-FL
Linda Smith   R-WA
Karen Thurman   D-FL

TEN COMMENTS BY H. L. MENCKEN ON DEMOCRACY

Henry Louis Mencken (1880–1956) was a writer, editor, and critic for Baltimore newspapers and one of America's wisest, wittiest, and most opinionated political commentators.

1. Democracy is the theory that intelligence is dangerous. It assumes that no idea can be safe until those who can't understand it have approved it. (1913)
2. [Democracy is] the theory that two thieves will steal less than one. (1913)
3. It is a bit hoggish, but it might be worse. It will be centuries before we are ready for anything better. (1920)
4. It is dirty, it is dishonest, it is incompetent, it is at war with every clean and noble impulse of man—and yet the eunuchs who write our books and profess in our colleges go on assuming that it is not only immortal, but also impeccable—that to propose mopping it up by *force majeure,* as smallpox and yellow fever have been mopped up, is a sin against the Holy Ghost. (1921)
5. The principal virtue of democracy is that it makes a good show—one incomparably bizarre, amazing, shocking, obscene. (1921)
6. Democracy is the liberty of the have-nots. Its aim is to destroy the liberty of the haves. (1922)
7. Democracy is a sort of laughing gas. It will not cure anything, perhaps, but it unquestionably stops the pain. (1925)
8. We are dependent on whatever good flows out of democracy upon men who do not believe in democracy. (1926)
9. The Fathers who invented it, if they could return from Hell, would never recognize it. It was conceived as a free government of free men; it has become simply a

battle of charlatans for the votes of idiots. The way to save it is not to try to put down the charlatans, for turning one out only lets another and worse one in; the way is to take the vote away from the idiots. (1937)

10. It was unquestionably a more or less noble experiment, but it simply failed to work. (1940)

SUPREME COURT LISTS

Richard Nixon remarked that "our chief justices have probably had more profound and lasting influence on their times and the direction of the nation than most presidents." Nixon may be an unintentional exception to his own statement, since Watergate has altered the political climate. But the Supreme Court has shaped our political history through its rulings and often has the final say on the political issues of the day.

CHIEF JUSTICES
OF THE UNITED STATES

John Jay	NY, 1789–1795
Oliver Ellsworth	CT, 1796–1800
John Marshall	VA, 1801–1835
Roger Taney	MD, 1836–1864
Salmon Portland Chase	OH, 1864–1873
Morrison R. Waite	OH, 1874–1888
Melville W. Fuller	IL, 1888–1910
Edward Douglass White	LA, 1910–1921
William Howard Taft	CT, 1921–1930
Charles Evans Hughes	NY, 1930–1941

Harlan F. Stone	NY, 1941–1946
Frederick M. Vinson	KY, 1946–1953
Earl Warren	CA, 1953–1969
Warren E. Burger	VA, 1969–1986
William H. Rehnquist	AZ, 1986–

★ ★ ★

LONGEST-SERVING SUPREME COURT JUSTICES

The post of Supreme Court justice, unlikely the highest-level job in the executive and legislative branches of the government, is a lifetime appointment, and many justices have spent the better part of their lives on the Court.

Justice	President Who Made Appointment	Years/Months/Days
William O. Douglas	Franklin Roosevelt	36/7/8
Stephen J. Field	Abraham Lincoln	34/8/22
John Marshall	John Adams	34/5/9*
Hugo L. Black	FDR	34/1/0
John M. Harlan	Rutherford Hayes	33/10/16*
Joseph Story	James Madison	33/9/23*
James Moore Wayne	Andrew Jackson	32/5/26*
John McLean	Jackson	32/0/28*
Byron R. White	John Kennedy	31/2/18
Bushrod Washington	John Adams	30/11/6*
William Johnson	Thomas Jefferson	30/4/11*
William J. Brennan Jr.	Dwight Eisenhower	30/4/2*

* Died in office.

SHORTEST-SERVING SUPREME COURT JUSTICES

Justice	President Who Made Appointment	Years/Months/Days
Edwin McMasters Stanton	Ulysses Grant	0/0/4*
James Francis Byrnes	Franklin Roosevelt	1/3/22
Thomas Johnson	George Washington	1/3/26
John Rutledge	Washington	1/5/9
Robert Trimble	John Quincy Adams	2/3/16†
Howell E. Jackson	Benjamin Harrison	2/5/18
Arthur J. Goldberg	John Kennedy	2/10/0
Abe Fortas	Lyndon Johnson	3/9/3
William Henry Moody	Theodore Roosevelt	3/11/8
Alfred Moore	John Adams	4/1/16
Horace H. Lurton	William Howard Taft	4/6/22

* Confirmed by the Senate but died before serving.
† Died in office.

SUPREME COURT NOMINATIONS REJECTED BY THE FULL SENATE

Senators have chosen to reject Supreme Court candidates for reasons political and jurisprudential.

John Rutledge   George Washington's nominee for promotion to chief justice, 1795; rejected 14–10

Alexander Wolcott   James Madison's nominee, 1811; rejected 24–9

John Spencer   John Tyler's nominee, 1844; rejected 26–21

George W. Woodward   James Polk's nominee, 1845; rejected 29–20

Jeremiah Sullivan Black   James Buchanan's nominee, 1861; rejected 26–25

Ebenezer Rockwood Hoar   Ulysses Grant's nominee, 1869; rejected 33–24

William B. Hornblower   Grover Cleveland's nominee, 1893; rejected 30–24

Wheeler H. Peckham   Grover Cleveland's nominee, 1894; rejected 41–32

John J. Parker   Herbert Hoover's nominee, 1930; rejected 41–39

Clement F. Haynsworth   Richard Nixon's nominee, 1969; rejected 55–45

G. Harrold Carswell   Richard Nixon's nominee, 1970; rejected 51–45

Robert Bork   Ronald Reagan's nominee, 1987; rejected 58–42

SUPREME COURT NOMINATIONS WITHDRAWN BY THE PRESIDENT

William Paterson   George Washington's proposed nominee, 1793

Reuben H. Walworth   John Tyler's proposed nominee, 1844

Edward King   John Tyler's proposed nominee, 1844

George Williams   Ulysses Grant's proposed nominee, 1873

Caleb Cushing   Ulysses Grant's proposed nominee, 1874

Abe Fortas   Lyndon Johnson's proposed nominee for chief justice, 1968

Douglas Ginsburg   Ronald Reagan's proposed nominee, 1987 (nomination never formally submitted)

SUPREME COURT NOMINATIONS POSTPONED

John Jordan Crittenden   John Quincy Adams's nominee, 1828

Roger Taney   Andrew Jackson's nominee, 1835 (later confirmed as chief justice)

Edward King   John Tyler's nominee, 1844, later withdrawn

George E. Badger   Millard Fillmore's nominee, 1853

SUPREME COURT NOMINATIONS NOT ACTED ON BY THE SENATE

John M. Read   John Tyler's nominee, 1845

Edward Bradford   Millard Fillmore's nominee, 1852

William Micou   Fillmore's nominee, 1853

Henry Stanbery   Andrew Johnson's nominee, 1866 (reappointed by James Garfield and confirmed)

Stanley Matthews   Rutherford Hayes's nominee, 1881

Homer Thornberry   Lyndon Johnson's nominee, 1968

SUPREME COURT NOMINATIONS CONFIRMED BY THE SENATE BUT DECLINED BY THE APPOINTEE

In these times nobody would be foolish enough to submit to the scrutiny involved in the confirmation process only to decline a place in the Supreme Court after winning approval. But in the past, presidents sent their nominations to the Senate without the nominee's knowledge.

Robert Harrison George Washington's nominee, 1789

William Cushing Washington's nominee for chief justice, 1796

John Jay John Adams's nominee for chief justice, 1800

Levi Lincoln James Madison's nominee, 1811

John Quincy Adams Madison's nominee, 1811

William Smith Martin Van Buren's nominee, 1837

Roscoe Conkling Chester Arthur's nominee, 1882

William Cushing, already an associate justice, kept the title of chief justice for a week and even attended a dinner party celebrating his new position before he turned down the honor, on the grounds of his "infirm and declining state of health.

SUPREME COURT APPOINTMENTS BY PRESIDENT

President		President	
George Washington	10	Rutherford Hayes	2
Franklin Roosevelt	9	Chester Arthur	2
Andrew Jackson	6	John Kennedy	2
William Howard Taft	6	Lyndon Johnson	2
Abraham Lincoln	5	George Bush	2
Dwight Eisenhower	5	Bill Clinton	2
Ulysses Grant	4	James Monroe	1
Grover Cleveland	4	John Quincy Adams	1
Benjamin Harrison	4	John Tyler	1
Warren Harding	4	Millard Fillmore	1
Harry Truman	4	Franklin Pierce	1
Richard Nixon	4	James Buchanan	1
Ronald Reagan	4	James Garfield	1
John Adams	3	William McKinley	1
Thomas Jefferson	3	Calvin Coolidge	1
Theodore Roosevelt	3	Gerald Ford	1
Woodrow Wilson	3	William Henry Harrison	0
Herbert Hoover	3	Zachary Taylor	0
James Madison	2	Andrew Johnson	0
Martin Van Buren	2	Jimmy Carter	0
James Polk	2		

In 1937, Franklin Roosevelt tried to overcome Supreme Court opposition to the New Deal by adding six more seats to the Court and installing sympathetic justices. He was unable to get Congress to approve his Court-packing plan, but he nevertheless filled seven vacancies in the next four years.

SUPREME COURT JUSTICES APPOINTED ACROSS PARTY LINES

Samuel Nelson (D)   1845, by John Tyler (Whig)

Stephen J. Field (D)   1865, by Abraham Lincoln (R)

Howell E. Jackson (D)   1893, by Benjamin Harrison (R)

Horace H. Lurton (D)   1909, by William Howard Taft (R)

Joseph R. Lamar (D)   1910, by Taft (R)

Louis Brandeis (R)   1916, by Woodrow Wilson (D)

Pierce Butler (D)   1922, by Warren Harding (R)

Benjamin Cardozo (D)   1932, by Herbert Hoover (R)

Felix Frankfurter (I)   1939, by Franklin Roosevelt (D)

Harold Burton (R)   1945, by Harry Truman (D)

William J. Brennan Jr. (D)   1956, by Dwight Eisenhower (R)

Lewis F. Powell Jr. (D)   1971, by Richard Nixon (R)

> *Edward D. White (D) and Harlan F. Stone (R) were promoted from associate justice to chief justice under presidents of the opposite party.*

SUPREME COURT JUSTICES WHO WERE CABINET MEMBERS

John Marshall   John Adams's secretary of State, 1800–1801; chief justice, 1801–1835

John McLean   James Monroe's and John Quincy Adams's postmaster general, 1823–1829; associate justice, 1830–1861

Roger Taney   Andrew Jackson's attorney general, 1831–1833; acting secretary of the Treasury, 1833–1834; chief justice, 1836–1864

Levi Woodbury   Jackson's secretary of the Navy, 1831–1834; Jackson's and Martin Van Buren's secretary of the Treasury, 1834–1841; associate justice, 1845–1851

Nathan Clifford   James Polk's attorney general, 1846–1848; associate justice, 1858–1881

Salmon Chase Abraham Lincoln's secretary of the Treasury, 1861–1864; chief justice, 1864–1873

Lucius Quintus Cincinnatus Lamar Grover Cleveland's secretary of the Interior, 1885–1888; associate justice, 1888–1893

Joseph McKenna William McKinley's attorney general, 1897–1898; associate justice, 1898–1925

William R. Day William McKinley's secretary of State, 1898; associate justice, 1903–1922

William Moody Theodore Roosevelt's secretary of the Navy, 1902–1904; attorney general, 1904–1906; associate justice, 1906–1910

James C. McReynolds Woodrow Wilson's attorney general, 1913–1914; associate justice, 1914–1941

William Howard Taft TR's secretary of War, 1804–1808; chief justice, 1921–1930

Charles Hughes Associate justice, 1910–1916; Warren Harding's and Calvin Coolidge's secretary of State, 1921–1925; chief justice, 1930–1941

Harlan Stone   Coolidge's attorney general, 1924–1925; associate justice, 1925–1941; chief justice, 1941–1946

James Byrnes   Associate justice, 1941–1942; Harry Truman's secretary of State, 1945–1947

Robert H. Jackson   Franklin Roosevelt's attorney general, 1940–1941; associate justice, 1941–1954

Frederick Vinson   Truman's secretary of the Treasury, 1945–1946; chief justice, 1946–1953

Thomas C. Clark   Truman's attorney general, 1945–1949; associate justice, 1949–1967

Arthur Goldberg   John Kennedy's secretary of Labor, 1961–1962; associate justice, 1962–1965

> *James Byrnes is the only justice to serve in the Cabinet after his time on the Supreme Court.*

SUPREME COURT JUSTICES WHO WERE CONGRESSMEN

Henry Baldwin	D-CT, 1817–1822
Philip Barbour	R-VA, 1814–1825
James Byrnes	D-SC, 1911–1925
Nathan Clifford	D-ME, 1839–1843
Gabriel Duvall	No party–MD, 1794–1796
Lucius Lamar	D-MS, 1857–1860, 1873–1877
John Marshall	Federalist-PA, 1799–1800, 1801–1835
Joseph McKenna	R-CA, 1885–1892
John McKinley	D-VA, 1833–1835
John McLean	D-OH, 1813–1816
William Henry Moody	R-MA, 1895–1902
Mahlon Pitney	R-NJ, 1895–1899
Joseph Story	Democratic Republican-MA, 1808–1809
William Strong	D-PA, 1847–1851
George Sutherland	R-UT, 1901–1903
Frederick Vinson	D-KY, 1924–1929, 1931–1938
James Wayne	D-GA, 1829–1835

CAMPAIGN LISTS

T HE FIRST MODERN PRESIDENTIAL campaign took place in 1840, when the wealthy war hero William Henry Harrison beat the incumbent, Martin Van Buren, by posing as a log-cabin-dwelling, hard-cider-swilling man of the people. Nowadays politicians always seem to be running for office even when elections are several years away. Their behavior makes some sense. As Everett Dirksen once said, "During a political campaign, everyone is concerned with what a candidate will do on this or that question if he is elected. Except the candidate—he's too busy wondering what he'll do if he isn't elected."

EUGENE MCCARTHY'S FIVE SUBTLE SIGNS OF DEMAGOGUERY

Eugene McCarthy (D-MN) was a congressman (1949–1959) and a senator (1959–1971). Running on an anti–Vietnam War platform, he sought the Democratic presidential nomination in 1968 and ran as an independent in the 1976 election, when he won less than 1% of the popular vote. He was also known for his humorous political writings.

1. Does the candidate reserve the first seats in the second-class section of an airplane, thus being in position to greet and be seen by the tourist or second-class passengers on boarding but also to slip through the curtain to work the first-class section and even be invited by airline personnel to move up?

2. Does the candidate now—or has he in a past campaign—call himself, for example, William (Bill) or Robert (Bob) or Patrick/Patricia (Pat)? Or does the candidate, known previously as John III or IV, drop the III or IV for the campaign, thus in effect repudiating father, grandfather, and possibly great grandfather?

3. Is the candidate so heavily into physical fitness (e.g., jogging) that he reports his time for the mile or two-mile run, or for longer distances? In the presidential campaign, does the candidate walk or bicycle across a state? These actions are marginally acceptable in campaigns for governor, but not for the presidency or even the Senate.

4. Does the candidate cry easily and often in public? What brings on the crying? Does the candidate cry out of the inner corner of the eye, the outer, or straight down the center of the lower lid, as Bette Davis did? Or do the eyes just well up?

5. Does the candidate take credit for—or has he or she been credited with strength of character because of—a primitive experience without protesting such attribution? Jimmy Carter was given a high mark by *Newsweek* in 1976 because he had used an outdoor toilet, and Senator Muskie had his character formed and strengthened early in life because he was bathed in a washtub. I have had both of these experiences without realizing what they have done for my character.

LOSING MAJOR-PARTY PRESIDENTIAL CANDIDATES

Thomas Jefferson 1796

Aaron Burr 1800

Charles Pinckney 1804, 1808

DeWitt Clinton 1812

Rufus King 1816

John Quincy Adams 1820

Andrew Jackson, Henry Clay, and **William Crawford** 1824

John Quincy Adams 1828

Henry Clay 1832

William Henry Harrison 1836

Martin Van Buren 1840

Henry Clay 1844

Lewis Cass and **Martin Van Buren** 1848

Winfield Scott 1852

John Frémont and **Millard Fillmore** 1856

Stephen Douglas, John Breckinridge, and **John Bell** 1860

George McClellan 1864

Horatio Seymour 1868

Horace Greeley 1872

Samuel Tilden 1876

Winfield Scott Hancock 1880

James Blaine 1884

Grover Cleveland 1888

Benjamin Harrison 1892

William Jennings Bryan ☞ 1896, 1900, 1908

Alton Parker 1904

William Howard Taft and **Theodore Roosevelt** 1912

Charles Hughes 1916

James Cox 1920

John Davis and **Robert La Follette** 1924

Alfred Smith 1928

Herbert Hoover 1932

Alfred Landon 1936

Wendell Willkie   1940
Thomas Dewey   1944
Thomas Dewey, Strom Thurmond, and **Henry Wallace**   1948
Adlai Ewing Stevenson   1952, 1956
Richard Nixon   1960
Barry Goldwater   1964
Hubert Humphrey and **George Wallace**   1968
George McGovern   1972
Gerald Ford   1976
Jimmy Carter and **John B. Anderson**   1980
Walter Mondale   1984
Michael Dukakis   1988
George Bush and **H. Ross Perot**   1992
Bob Dole and **H. Ross Perot**   1996

> *Winfield Scott Hancock, the Democratic nominee for president in 1880, was named for General Winfield Scott, the Whig nominee in 1852.*

ELECTIONS BILL CLINTON LOST

Vice presidential nomination   Boys Nation, mock government group, 1963
Senior class secretary   Hot Springs High School, 1963
Student council president   Georgetown University, 1967
Congressman   3d Congressional District, Arkansas, 1974
Governor   Arkansas, 1980

MARIO CUOMO'S
BEST AMERICAN POLITICIANS
WHO NEVER RAN FOR PRESIDENT

Mario Cuomo, governor of New York State from 1982 to 1994, flirted repeatedly with the notion of running for president.

Alexander Hamilton

John Marshall

Fiorello La Guardia

Oliver Wendell Holmes

Benjamin Franklin

Douglas MacArthur

John Jay

Eleanor Roosevelt

PRESIDENTIAL CANDIDATES WHO WERE ON THE NATIONAL BALLOT AT LEAST THREE TIMES AND NEVER WON

George Clinton   Democratic-Republican, 1789, 1792, 1796; Independent-Republican, 1808

Charles Pinckney   Federalist   1800, 1804, 1808

Henry Clay   No party, 1824; National Republican, 1832; Whig, 1844

Gerrit Smith   National Liberty; 1848, 1852, 1856

William Jennings Bryan   Democrat; 1896, 1900, 1908

Eugene Victor Debs Socialist, 1900, 1904, 1908, 1912, 1920

John Zahnd   National Independent (Greenback), 1924, 1928, 1932, 1936, 1940

Norman Mattoon Thomas   Socialist, 1928, 1932, 1936, 1940, 1944, 1948

Farrell Dobbs   Socialist Workers, 1948, 1952, 1956, 1960

Eric Hass   Socialist Labor, 1952, 1956, 1960, 1964

Earle Harold Munn   Prohibition, 1964, 1968, 1972

Gus Hall   Communist, 1972, 1976, 1980, 1984

Lyndon LaRouche   U.S. Labor/Independent, 1976, 1984, 1988

> *Harold Stassen sought the Republican presidential nomination nine times between 1944 and 1992.*

WOMEN WHO RAN FOR PRESIDENT BUT COULDN'T VOTE FOR THEMSELVES

The 19th Amendment, ratified in 1920, gave women the right to vote. Before that, only men voted in presidential elections.

Victoria Claflin Woodhull ☞
(NY)   National Radical Reform (Equal Rights), 1872

Belva Ann Bennett Lockwood
(Washington, DC)
National Equal Rights, 1884, 1888

AFRICAN AMERICANS WHO RAN FOR PRESIDENT

Frederick Douglass   Threw his hat into the ring at the Republican National Convention, 1888; received one delegate's vote

Eldridge Cleaver   Peace and Freedom candidate, 1968; received 36,385 votes

Dick Gregory   New Party candidate, 1968; received 47,097 votes

Charlene Mitchell   Communist candidate, 1968; received fewer than 1,000 votes

Shirley Chisholm   Sought Democratic nomination, 1972; did not receive significant support

Angela Davis   Communist candidate, 1980; received 43,871 votes

Larry Holmes   Workers World candidate, 1984; received 15,329 votes

Jesse Jackson   Sought Democratic nomination twice: in 1984, came in third; in 1988, placed second

Ron Daniels   Independent candidate, 1992; received 27,575 votes

Lenora Fulani   New Alliance candidate, 1992; received 73,707 votes

Douglas Wilder   Sought Democratic nomination, 1992; dropped out of the race before the New Hampshire primary

Alan Keyes   Sought Republican nomination, 1996; stayed in the race through the convention

Monica Moorehead   Workers World candidate, 1996; received 29,082 votes

STATES THAT MOST OFTEN AND LEAST OFTEN VOTED FOR THE WINNING PRESIDENTIAL CANDIDATE, 1804–1996

"As Maine goes, so goes the nation" became common wisdom in the 1888 presidential campaign, but the evidence does not support the statement. Maine isn't even in the top ten. The figures below show the percentage of elections in which the state gave the majority of its electoral votes to the winning and losing candidates. The first four presidential elections are excluded because before the 12th Amendment was ratified in 1804, each elector had two votes.

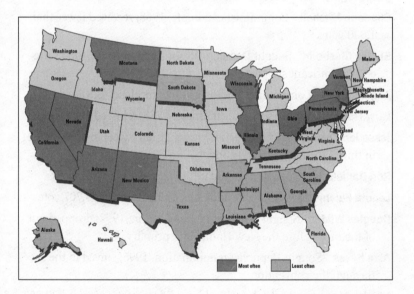

States That Most Often Chose the Winner

New Mexico	95.5%	(21 out of 22 elections)
Illinois	86.7	(39 out of 45)
California	86.5	(32 out of 37)
New York	83.6	(41 out of 49)
Pennsylvania	83.6	(41 out of 49)
Arizona	81.8	(18 out of 22)
Ohio	81.6	(40 out of 49)
Nevada	79.4	(27 out of 34)
Wisconsin	78.9	(30 out of 38)
Montana	77.8	(21 out of 27)

States That Least Often Chose the Winner

Mississippi	51.2%	(22 out of 43 elections)
Alabama	54.6	(24 out of 44)
Georgia	56.3	(27 out of 48)
South Carolina	56.3	(27 out of 48)
Texas	58.3	(21 out of 36)
Arkansas	59.0	(23 out of 39)
South Dakota	59.3	(16 out of 27)
Alaska	60.0	(6 out of 10)
Kentucky	61.2	(30 out of 49)
Louisiana	62.2	(28 out of 45)

After Franklin Roosevelt carried every state but Maine and Vermont in his 1936 landslide victory over Alf Landon, FDR's campaign manager, James Farley, rewrote the adage—"As Maine goes, so goes Vermont."

STATES THAT HAVE MOST OFTEN SUPPORTED REPUBLICAN OR DEMOCRATIC PRESIDENTIAL CANDIDATES

Since 1860, when Republicans and Democrats became the two major political parties, Republicans have won 21 of 35, or 60%, of the presidential elections. Party names have remained constant, but party principles have changed. Southern states like Florida that were once solidly Democrat have become reliably Republican, whereas once staunchly Republican states like Massachusetts and Illinois have gravitated toward the Democrats. The figures below show the percentage of elections in which the state gave the majority of its electoral votes to one party's candidate.

States That Most Often Voted for Republican Presidential Candidates

Vermont	91.4%	(33 out of 35 elections)
Alaska	90.0	(9 out of 10)
Maine	85.7	(30 out of 35)
South Dakota	81.5	(22 out of 27)
Indiana	80.0	(28 out of 35)
Kansas	79.4	(27 out of 34)
Nebraska	78.8	(26 out of 33)
North Dakota	77.8	(21 out of 27)
Iowa	77.1	(27 out of 35)
New Hampshire	77.1	(27 out of 35)

States That Most Often Voted for Democratic Presidential Candidates

Hawaii	80.0%	(8 out of 10 elections)
Georgia	79.4	(27 out of 34)
Arkansas	76.4	(26 out of 33)
Texas	69.7	(23 out of 33)
North Carolina	67.7	(23 out of 34)
Alabama	64.7	(22 out of 34)
Tennessee	64.7	(22 out of 34)
Mississippi	63.6	(21 out of 33)
Missouri	62.9	(22 out of 35)
South Carolina	61.8	(21 out of 34)

STATES WITH THE HIGHEST AND LOWEST VOTER TURNOUT, 1996

The United States has an embarrassingly low voter-turnout rate as compared with that of other democratic nations. About half of all eligible Americans vote in presidential elections, and local primaries can draw as little as 10% of voters.

States with the Highest Voter-Turnout Rates

Maine	64.53%	**Vermont**	58.61
Minnesota	64.26	**Idaho**	58.19
Montana	62.92	**New Hampshire**	58.03
South Dakota	61.10	**Iowa**	57.72
Wyoming	60.11	**Oregon**	57.50

States with the Lowest Voter-Turnout Rates

Nevada	39.35%	**California**	43.31
Hawaii	40.83	**West Virginia**	45.01
Texas	41.20	**Arizona**	45.39
South Carolina	41.46	**Mississippi**	45.58
Georgia	42.60	**North Carolina**	45.75

The voter-turnout rate of Washington, DC, was 42.70.

STATES THAT COULD GUARANTEE THE PRESIDENCY IN THE YEAR 2000

A winning presidential candidate must receive a majority of votes in the electoral college—at least 270 of 538. Since the winner takes all of each state's electoral votes, a successful candidate could lose every vote in 39 states as long as he or she wins the other 11.

California	54 electoral votes	**Ohio**	21
New York	33	**Michigan**	18
Texas	32	**New Jersey**	15
Florida	25	**North Carolina**	14
Pennsylvania	23	**Georgia**	13*
Illinois	22	**Virginia**	13*

* Either one of these two could be the eleventh state.

STATES THAT COULD HAVE GUARANTEED THE PRESIDENCY, 1900

There were 447 votes in the electoral college in 1900, and the winning candidate had to receive 244 of them to win. This list ranks the most populous states in 1900 by the number of electoral votes they cast. In addition to the states named here, one more state with at least 8 electoral votes would have had to have voted for the winner.

New York	36	**Indiana**	15
Pennsylvania	32	**Massachusetts**	15
Illinois	24	**Michigan**	14
Ohio	23	**Iowa**	13*
Missouri	17	**Georgia**	13*
Texas	15	**Kentucky**	13*

* Any two of these three could account for the eleventh and twelfth states.

FAITHLESS ELECTORS

Faithless electors are members of the electoral college who are pledged to vote for one candidate but in fact vote for another.

Name, State, and Year		Pledged To	Voted For
Samuel Miles	PA, 1796	John Adams	Thomas Jefferson

Name, State, and Year		Pledged To	Voted For
Preston Parks	TN, 1948	Harry Truman	Strom Thurmond
W. F. Turner	AL, 1956	Adlai Stevenson	Walter B. Jones*
Henry Irwin	OK, 1960	Richard Nixon	Harry F. Byrd†
Lloyd Bailey	NC, 1968	Nixon	George Wallace
Roger MacBride	VA, 1972	Nixon	John Hospers‡
Mike Padden	WA, 1976	Gerald Ford	Ronald Reagan
Margaret Leach	WV, 1988	Michael Dukakis	Lloyd Bentsen

> *Theodora Nathan, the Libertarian candidate for vice president in 1972, was the first woman to receive an electoral vote, thanks to faithless elector Roger MacBride.*

---

* An Alabama judge.
† Democratic senator from Virginia.
‡ Libertarian candidate.

★ ★ ★

MANCHESTER UNION-LEADER ENDORSEMENTS IN THE NEW HAMPSHIRE REPUBLICAN PRESIDENTIAL PRIMARY SINCE 1948

The New Hampshire primary is the earliest in the campaign-season calendar, and so the Republican-dominated state has a disproportionately loud voice in determining the eventual nominee. Ever since William Loeb became president and publisher of the Manchester Union-Leader *in 1946, Republican presidential candidates have actively courted the newspaper's editors and sought its endorsement. Nackey Scripps Loeb, William Loeb's widow, now runs the paper.*

Year	Candidate Endorsed	Primary Winner	Presidential Nominee
1948	Thomas Dewey	—*	Dewey
1952	Robert Taft	Dwight Eisenhower	Eisenhower
1956	—†	Dwight Eisenhower	Eisenhower
1960	Richard Nixon	Nixon	Nixon
1964	Barry Goldwater	Henry Cabot Lodge	Goldwater
1968	Richard Nixon	Nixon	Nixon
1972	John Ashbrook	Richard Nixon	Nixon
1976	Ronald Reagan	Gerald Ford	Ford
1980	Ronald Reagan	Reagan	Reagan
1984	Ronald Reagan	Reagan	Reagan
1988	Pete du Pont	George Bush	Bush
1992	Pat Buchanan	George Bush	Bush
1996	Pat Buchanan	Buchanan	Bob Dole

---

* Unpledged at-large delegates were elected.

† No candidate was endorsed.

★ ★ ★

SUPER TUESDAY STATES, 1988

The first Super Tuesday, a coordinated regional primary intended to give southern states a greater say in the nominating process, was held in 1988. Massachusetts and Rhode Island also held primaries on that day, and four western states—Hawaii, Idaho, Nevada, and Washington—held Democratic Party caucuses on Super Tuesday.

Alabama	Mississippi
Arkansas	Missouri
Florida	North Carolina
Georgia	Oklahoma
Kentucky	Tennessee
Louisiana	Texas
Maryland	Virginia

SUPER TUESDAY STATES, 1996

Florida	Oregon
Louisiana	Tennessee
Mississippi	Texas
Oklahoma	

OTHER NAMES CONSIDERED FOR THE REGIONAL PRIMARY BEFORE SUPER TUESDAY WAS CHOSEN

Awesome Tuesday	Super-Duper Tuesday
Hyper Tuesday	Super-Grits
Mega Tuesday	Titanic Tuesday
Mega-Super Tuesday	

MOST BALLOTS REQUIRED AT NATIONAL PARTY CONVENTIONS

Since World War II, candidates for president have usually been anointed long before the party convention, and the vote taken by the delegates has been a mere formality. For much of the country's history, however, nominees were chosen at party conventions, and as often as not the favored candidate at the beginning of the convention did not receive the nomination. Negotiations and deals took place between ballots, and the balloting process resembled a horse race, with candidates jockeying for position and pulling ahead of one another.

Democratic Convention, 1924   **Ballots:** 103   **Leader after first ballot:** William McAdoo   **Nominee:** John Davis

From its first national convention in 1832 until 1936, the Democratic Party required a two-thirds vote to approve its presidential nominee. For the first 99 ballots no candidate received even a simple majority. The party was split along city-country lines, with Governor Alfred Smith (NY) favored by urban delegates and William McAdoo (CA) preferred by rural ones. John Davis (also NY) received less than 3% of the delegates' support in the first ballot but came on strong after McAdoo released his delegates for a round 100. This was the longest party convention in the nation's history, lasting 17 days gavel to gavel.

Democratic Convention, 1860   **Ballots:** 59   **Leader after first ballot:** Stephen Douglas   **Nominee:** Stephen Douglas

Debate over the Democrats' position on slavery led 45 southern delegates to walk out of the convention. On the first ballot, Stephen Douglas had the votes of two thirds of the remaining delegates, but it was decided that the eventual nominee must have the support of two thirds of all 303 delegates. After 57 ballots the convention was adjourned. Another walkout ensued after the Democrats reconvened two months later, and this time less than two thirds of the delegates remained. After two more ballots, the Democrats anointed Douglas.

Whig Convention, 1852   **Ballots:** 53   **Leader after first ballot:** Millard Fillmore   **Nominee:** Winfield Scott

The final Whig nominating convention was a three-way battle among the incumbent president, Millard Fillmore; war hero Winfield Scott; and party stalwart Daniel Webster. Fillmore and Scott were almost even, but Webster's supporters prevented either one from gaining the majority required for nomination. Attempts at a Fillmore-Webster alliance failed, leading to Scott's victory.

Democratic Convention, 1852   **Ballots:** 49   **Leader after first ballot:** Lewis Cass   **Nominee:** Franklin Pierce

In 1852, four men were considered serious contenders: Senator Lewis Cass (MI), William Learned Marcy (NY), James Buchanan, and Stephen Douglas. At one point or another in the balloting, each held the lead. Franklin Pierce, a former senator with a negligible national reputation who had retired to a private law practice, first received support on the 35th ballot and won the nomination on the 49th, after two frantic days of politicking.

Democratic Convention, 1912   **Ballots:** 46   **Leader after first ballot:** Champ Clark   **Nominee:** Woodrow Wilson

House Speaker Champ Clark (MO) led the field in the first ten ballots. He had the votes of a majority of the delegates, but that support started to erode. William Jennings Bryan announced that he would not support the same candidate Tammany Hall was backing, and he switched to Woodrow Wilson. Wilson took the lead after 30 ballots and won with a two-thirds majority on the 46th.

Democratic Convention, 1920   **Ballots:** 44   **Leader after first ballot:** William McAdoo   **Nominee:** James Cox

The stroke-stricken incumbent president, Woodrow Wilson, did not endorse a successor, and some two dozen presidential hopefuls won votes on the first ballot. William McAdoo, who was married to Wilson's daughter and had served in his Cabinet, emerged as an early leader even though prior to the convention he had officially withdrawn from the race. For three days, McAdoo and Governor James Cox (OH) traded the first-place position until Cox won on the 44th ballot.

Republican Convention, 1880 **Ballots:** 36 **Leader after first ballot:** Ulysses Grant **Nominee:** James Garfield
Many prominent Republicans, most notably boss Roscoe Conkling (NY), wanted to give the incumbent president, Ulysses Grant, a shot at a third term. Grant had more votes on the first 34 ballots than any of his competitors, including 1884 nominee James Blaine and John Sherman, secretary of the Treasury. Congressman James Garfield won some support on the 34th ballot, and his protest that he was not in the running fell on deaf ears.

Democratic Convention, 1868 **Ballots:** 22 **Leader after first ballot:** G. H. Pendleton **Nominee:** Horatio Seymour
At first the pack was led by G. H. Pendleton (OH), the Democrats' 1864 vice presidential nominee. He was trailed by the nearly removed Republican President, Andrew Johnson. When Pendleton's and Johnson's support faded, Civil War general Winfield Hancock and then Senator Thomas Hendricks (IN) became front-running candidates. On the 22nd ballot, the Ohio delegation backed former governor Horatio Seymour (NY), who was not seeking the nomination. After the roll call, every Democratic delegate shifted his vote to Seymour, and he became the unanimous nominee.

Democratic Convention, 1856 **Ballots:** 17 **Leader after first ballot:** James Buchanan **Nominee:** James Buchanan
On the first ballot—a three-way race among the incumbent president, Franklin Pierce; Stephen Douglas; and James Buchanan, then Pierce's ambassador to Great Britain— Pierce placed second. Buchanan and Douglas surged as Pierce faded. Wishing to avoid a deadlock, Douglas withdrew after the 16th ballot.

Republican Convention, 1920 **Ballots:** 10 **Leader after first ballot:** Leonard Wood **Nominee:** Warren Harding
Governor Frank Lowden (IL), Senator Hiram Johnson (CA),

and Major General Leonard Wood entered the convention as the three front-runners, but none emerged as the likely nominee in the first day's balloting. According to legend, party leaders called Warren Harding into a smoke-filled room; Harding avoided mentioning his extramarital affairs and won the blessing of the bosses. He won in the next day's balloting.

KEYNOTE SPEAKERS AT NATIONAL PARTY CONVENTIONS

Keynote speeches give Republicans and Democrats the opportunity to showcase rising stars, introducing them to the delegates as well as to the public at large. After the nomination speech and the nominee's acceptance speech, the keynote speech, in which the speaker lays out the party's vision, is the highlight of the convention.

Republicans

Henry Cabot Lodge (MA senator)   1920
Frederick Steiwer (OR senator)   1936
Harold Stassen (MN governor)   1940
Earl Warren (CA governor)   1944
Dwight Green (IL governor)   1948
Douglas MacArthur (five-star terminated general)   1952
Arthur Langlie (WA governor)   1956
Walter H. Judd (MN congressman)   1960
Mark Hatfield (OR governor)   1964
Daniel Evans (WA governor)   1968
Richard Lugar (Indianapolis mayor)   1972
Howard Baker Jr. (TN senator)   1976
Guy Vander Jagt (MI congressman)   1980
Katherine Ortega (treasurer of the United States)   1984
Thomas Kean (NJ governor)   1988
Phil Gramm (TX senator)   1992
Susan Molinari (NY congresswoman)   1996

Democrats

Alben Barkley (KY senator)   1936
William Bankhead (AL congressman
and Speaker of the House)   1940
Robert S. Kerr (OK governor)   1944
Alben Barkley (KY senator)   1948
Paul Dever (MA governor)   1952
Frank Clement (TN governor)   1956
Frank Forrester Church (ID senator)   1960
John Pastore (RI senator)   1964
Daniel Inouye (HI senator)   1968
Reubin Askew (FL governor)   1972
John Glenn (OH senator)
and **Barbara C. Jordan** (TX congresswoman)   1976
Morris Udall (AZ congressman)   1980
Mario M. Cuomo (NY governor)   1984
Ann W. Richards (TX state treasurer)   1988
Bill Bradley (NJ senator)   1992
Evan Bayh (IN governor)   1996

Though many keynote speakers have run for president, none has ever been elected to the highest office.

CITIES THAT HAVE HOSTED MORE THAN ONE MAJOR-PARTY CONVENTION

Cities vie to host political conventions because they add to the local economy as well as to the city's prestige. The major parties favored Chicago as a convention site until 1968, when protesters and police clashed during the Democratic National Convention. In 1996, the Democrats were brave enough to return to the Windy City.

CHICAGO   25

Democratic   11   1864, 1884, 1892, 1896, 1932, 1940, 1944, 1952, 1956, 1968, 1996

Republican **14** 1860, 1868, 1880, 1884, 1888, 1904, 1908, 1912, 1916, 1920, 1932, 1944, 1952, 1960

BALTIMORE 12

Democratic **9** 1832, 1836, 1840, 1844, 1848, 1852, 1860, 1872, 1912

Republican **1** 1864

Whig **2** 1844, 1852

PHILADELPHIA 8

Democratic **2** 1936, 1948

Republican **5** 1856, 1872, 1900, 1940, 1948

Whig **1** 1848

ST. LOUIS 5

Democratic **4** 1876, 1888, 1904, 1916

Republican **1** 1896

NEW YORK 5

Democratic **5** 1868, 1924, 1976, 1980, 1992

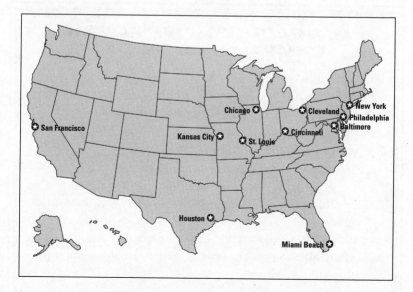

SAN FRANCISCO 4

　Democratic　2　1920, 1984

　Republican　2　1956, 1964

CINCINNATI　3

　Democratic　2　1856, 1880

　Republican　1　1876

KANSAS CITY, MO　3

　Democratic　1　1900

　Republican　2　1928, 1976

MIAMI BEACH　3

　Democratic　1　1972

　Republican　2　1968, 1972

CLEVELAND　2

　Republican　2　1924, 1936

HOUSTON　2

　Democratic　1　1928

　Republican　1　1992

BILL BRADLEY'S FIVE FAVORITE CAMPAIGN ACTIVITIES

Bill Bradley was a Rhodes Scholar, a member of the New York Knicks, and a senator (D-NJ, 1979–1997). It is unclear whether his campaigning days are behind him.

1. Listening to people's stories
2. Walking the Jersey shore in the summer
3. Walking down the movable ramp to get on a plane for another flight to another campaign stop
4. Speaking to an audience with a speech you have confidence in
5. Blowing up balloons and handing them to children along a July Fourth parade route and then waving to their parents

TEN RARE CAMPAIGN BADGES

Campaign buttons have evolved from metal objects sewn on to clothing to the pin-back celluloid models of today. Political badges originate as cheap or free merchandise, but with collecting a popular hobby, rare ones have become quite expensive. This list was assembled by Ted Hake, the author of the three-volume Encyclopedia of Political Buttons *and proprietor of Hake's Americana and Collectibles, York, PA.*

1. **James Cox–Franklin Roosevelt** (1920) 1¼-in celluloid button with portraits of both candidates $50,000 (estimated value)

2. **Abraham Lincoln–Andrew Johnson** (1864) Shield-shaped brass pin with tin portraits of both candidates, each at the center of a U.S. flag $20,000

3. **Woodrow Wilson–Thomas Marshall** (1912) 1¼-in celluloid button with both candidates shown as passengers in a rowboat and the slogan "I Wood-Row Wilson and Marshall to Victory" $15,000

4. **Theodore Roosevelt** (1904) 1¾-in celluloid button with a cartoon of Roosevelt outweighing opponent Alton Parker on a set of scales held by Uncle Sam $12,000

5. **John Davis–Charles Bryan** (1924) 1¼-in celluloid button with portraits of both candidates facing center $10,000

6. **William McKinley–Garret Hobart** (1896) 1¼-in celluloid button showing the two candidates riding a tandem bicycle toward the White House $8,000

7. **Anti–Harry Truman** (1948) 1½-in lithographed tin button resembling an eight ball, with Truman's photo under the 8 $8,000

8. **William Jennings Bryan–John Kern** (1908) 1¾-in celluloid button with the Statue of Liberty beaming light onto portraits of both candidates $5,000

9. **George Washington** (1789) Brass coat button celebrating Washington's inauguration, with his initials at center and the slogan "Long Live the President" $4,000

10. **John Kennedy–Lyndon Johnson** (1960) 3½-in celluloid button with slogan " 'Kennedettes': Girls for Kennedy and Johnson" $3,500

The five most prized campaign buttons are from Cox's 1920 campaign.

14 MEMORABLE CAMPAIGN-SONG STANZAS

Since William Henry Harrison's campaign victory in 1840, campaign songs have been one of the best methods of rallying supporters and undermining opponents. Some of America's greatest popular songwriters have penned or adapted tunes for favored candidates.

1. Andrew Jackson v. John Quincy Adams (1828) "The Hickory Tree"

While Jonny was lounging on crimson and down
And stuffing both pockets with pelf
Brave Andrew was pulling John Bull's colors down
And paying his army himself.

2. Martin Van Buren v. William Henry Harrison (1840) Sung to "Rock-a-Bye Baby"

Hush-a-bye baby, Daddy's a Whig
Before he comes home hard cider he'll swig
Then he'll be tipsy and over he'll fall
Down will come Daddy, Tip, Tyler, and all.

3. Henry Clay v. James Polk (1844) "Clay and Freylinghuysen"

No doubt they'd rather hear us groan
But that we'll leave to them alone
For with good Clay and Freylinghuysen
The way we'll beat them is surprisin'.

4. Van Buren v. Lewis Cass and Zachary Taylor (1848) "Martin Van of Kinderhook"

He who'd vote for Zacky Taylor
Needs a keeper or a jailer
And he who still for Cass can be,
He is a Cass without a C;
The man on whom we love to look
Is Martin Van of Kinderhook.

5. John Bell v. John Breckinridge, Abraham Lincoln, and Stephen Douglas (1860) "Get out of the Way"

There's a bell in Independence Hall
Which in seventy-six rang for us all
There's another Bell whose mighty tongue
Speaks "The Union" now wherever it's rung.

6. Grover Cleveland v. Benjamin Harrison (1888) "His Grandfather's Hat"

His grandfather's hat is too big for his head
But Ben tries it on just the same
It fits him too quick which has oft times been said
With regard to his grandfather's fame
It was bought long ago and it made a pretty show
In that jolly hard cider campaign
But it doesn't fit even a little bit
on Benjamin Harrison's brain.

7. Theodore Roosevelt v. Alton Parker (1904) "Who Is Parker?"

Oh, I know our Billy Bryan, I went crazy for him twice
And yellow Billy Hearst, he's the man who has the price
I remember Grover Cleveland, too, with Wall Street for a
barker
But what I really want to know is—Who is Parker?

8. William Howard Taft v. William Jennings Bryan (1908) "Get on the Raft with Taft"

Get on the raft with Taft, boys
Get in the winning boat
The man worthwhile with the big glad smile
Will get the honest vote
We'll save the country sure, boys
From Bryan, Hearst and graft
So all join in, we're sure to win
Get on the raft with Taft.

9. Woodrow Wilson
v. Charles Hughes (1916)
"Be Sure That Woodrow Wilson
Leads the Band"

We're going to celebrate the end of the war in ragtime
Ev'ry nation soon will sing in rag rhyme
England, France and Germany,
even folks from Italy
The aristocrats and the diplomats,
Marching arm in arm, see them tip their hats
To a raggy melody.

10. Warren Harding
v. James Cox (1920)
"Harding, You're the Man for Us"
by Al Jolson

We know we'll always find him
With Coolidge right behind him
And Coolidge never fails you must agree
We know he will be guarding
The Nation just like Harding
When they are both in Washington, D.C.
Harding, Coolidge is your mate
Harding, lead the ship of state
You'll get the people's vote
And you'll also get the donkey's goat!

11. Alfred Smith
v. Herbert Hoover (1928)
"Better Times with Al"
by Irving Berlin

Good times with Hoover
Better times with Al
Blue skies with Hoover
Bluer skies with Al
Prosperity does not depend on who's in the chair
We're bound to have prosperity no matter who's there.

12. Alfred Landon v. Franklin Roosevelt (1936) "Happy Landin' with Landon"

Take a trip on a safety ship
And make a happy landin' with Landon
Cast your vote, strike a better note
And make a happy landin' with Landon
He is the man we should all foller
Plain folks like you and me
He knows a dime from a dollar
And how to use it with economy.

13. Harry Truman v. Thomas Dewey (1948) "I'm Just Wild About Harry" by Noble Sissle and Eubie Blake

F.D.R. had his New Deal
And Truman now will follow through
My country's wild about Harry
And Harry's wild about
Cannot do without
Both my country and me.

14. Dwight Eisenhower v. Adlai Stevenson (1952 and 1956) "I Like Ike" by Irving Berlin

I like Ike
I'll shout it over a mike
Or a phone
Or from the highest steeple
I like Ike
And Ike is easy to like
Stands alone
The choice of We the People.

Composers and lyricists are not always pleased when politicians appropriate their songs for campaigns. Bruce Springsteen demanded that Ronald Reagan stop playing "Born in the U.S.A." at campaign appearances, and Isaac Hayes sicced his lawyers on Bob Dole after he transformed "Soul Man" into "Dole Man."

PRESIDENTIAL CAMPAIGN SLOGANS

To praise their candidates or bash their opponents, campaign managers and speechwriters make up slogans with all sorts of mnemonic devices, including rhymes, puns, and alliteration in the hope that catchy slogans stay with people as they enter the voting booth.

Rhyming Slogans

LORD, HOW THE FEDERALISTS WILL STARE/AT JEFFERSON IN ADAMS' CHAIR   Thomas Jefferson, 1800

WITH TIP AND TYLER WE'LL BUST VAN'S BILER
William Henry Harrison, 1840

VAN, VAN, VAN/VAN IS A USED-UP MAN
William Henry Harrison, 1840

HOORAY FOR CLAY   Henry Clay, 1844

HURRAH FOR HAYES AND HONEST WAYS   Rutherford Hayes, 1876

MA MA, WHERE'S MY PA? GONE TO THE WHITE HOUSE, HA HA HA
James Blaine, 1884

BLAINE, BLAINE, JAMES G. BLAINE, THE CONTINENTAL LIAR
FROM THE STATE OF MAINE   Grover Cleveland, 1884

GROVER, GROVER, FOUR MORE YEARS OF GROVER/OUT THEY GO,
IN WE GO, THEN WE'LL BE IN CLOVER   Cleveland, 1892

LET EVERY HONEST FELLOW FROM MAINE TO OREGON/LET EVERY
HONEST FELLOW UNLESS HE'S A SON-OF-A-GUN/BE SURE AND VOTE
FOR BENJAMIN HARRISON   Benjamin Harrison, 1892

IN GOD WE TRUST, IN BRYAN WE BUST   William McKinley, 1896

WE'RE READY FOR TEDDY AGAIN   Theodore Roosevelt, 1912

THE MOOSE IS LOOSE   TR, 1912

IN HOOVER WE TRUSTED, NOW WE ARE BUSTED
Franklin Roosevelt, 1932

HARRY, HENRY, DEWEY, PHOOEY   Strom Thurmond, 1948

I LIKE IKE   Dwight Eisenhower, 1952

WE'RE MADLY FOR ADLAI   Adlai Stevenson, 1956

KENNEDY IS THE REMEDY   John Kennedy, 1960

ALL THE WAY WITH LBJ   Lyndon Johnson, 1964

RON TURNS US ON   Ronald Reagan, 1980

Punning Slogans

WE POLKED 'EM IN '44, WE'LL PIERCE 'EM IN '52
Franklin Pierce, 1852

FREE SOIL, FREE SPEECH, AND FRÉMONT   John Frémont, 1856

GRANT US ANOTHER TERM   Ulysses Grant, 1872

KEEP COOL WITH COOLIDGE   Calvin Coolidge, 1924

EVERYTHING WILL BE ROSY WITH ROOSEVELT
Franklin Roosevelt, 1932

LAND A JOB WITH LANDON   Alfred Landon, 1936

Alliterative Slogans

RUM, ROMANISM, AND REBELLION   Grover Cleveland, 1884

ROMANISM, ROOSEVELT, AND ROCKEFELLER
William Jennings Bryan, 1908

CATHOLICISM, COMMERCIALISM, AND COERCION
William Howard Taft, 1908

CAUTIOUS CAL AND CHARGING CHARLIE   Calvin Coolidge, 1924*

HOOVER, HYDE, HELL, AND HARD TIMES:
THE REPUBLICAN FOUR-H CLUB   Franklin Roosevelt, 1932†

LIFE, LIBERTY, AND LANDON   Alfred Landon, 1936

BOSSES, BOODLE, BUNCOMBE, AND BLARNEY
Anti–Harry Truman, 1948

HELP HUSTLE HARRY HOME   Truman, 1948

CRIME, CORRUPTION, COMMUNISM, KOREA
Dwight Eisenhower, 1952

PEACE, PROGRESS, PROSPERITY   Eisenhower, 1956

DUMB, DANGEROUS, AND DECEPTIVE   Ronald Reagan, 1980

---

* Charlie was Charles Dawes, Coolidge's running mate.
† Hyde was Arthur M. Hyde, Hoover's secretary of Agriculture.

*In his 1932 primary campaign, Democratic candidate William
Murray used the slogan BREAD, BUTTER, BACON, AND BEANS.*

Slogans Promising Prosperity

Many Americans vote with their wallets and their pocketbooks, so presidential candidates appeal to the desire for upward economic mobility. Presidents use prosperity as a way to keep their jobs; both Bill Clinton and Ronald Reagan were reelected after financially rosy first terms.

HARRISON, TWO DOLLARS A DAY AND ROAST BEEF
William Henry Harrison, 1840

LAND FOR THE LANDLESS   Abraham Lincoln, 1860

FORTY ACRES AND A MULE   Ulysses Grant, 1868

THREE ACRES AND A COW   James B. Weaver (Populist), 1884

WE'LL ALL HAVE OUR POCKETS LINED WITH SILVER
William Jennings Bryan, 1896

FOUR MORE YEARS OF THE FULL DINNER PAIL
William McKinley, 1900

A CHICKEN IN EVERY POT AND TWO CARS IN EVERY GARAGE
Herbert Hoover, 1928

PROSPERITY IS JUST AROUND THE CORNER   Hoover, 1929

JOBS AND FOOD FOR ALL   Hubert Humphrey, 1968

Anti-FDR Slogans, 1940

NO ROOSEVELT DYNASTY

WE WANT ROOSEVELT TO ABDICATE

NO FRANKLIN THE FIRST

WPA—WORST PUBLIC ADMINISTRATION

1ST TERM GOOD, 2ND TERM GOOD ENOUGH,
3RD TERM GOOD FOR NOTHING

NO THIRD INTERNATIONALE, THIRD REICH, THIRD TERM

OUT STEALING THIRD

TWO GOOD TERMS DESERVE A PAROLE

NO MAN IS GOOD THREE TIMES

Anti-Reagan Slogans, 1984

SEND HIM BACK TO HOLLYWOOD

JANE WYMAN WAS RIGHT

IMPEACH THE LEECH, PUT THE BUTTON
OUT OF HIS REACH

OUT THE DOOR IN '84

LET THEM EAT JELLY BEANS

POT IS AN HERB, REAGAN'S A DOPE

RON REAGAN HAS DONE FOR AMERICA
WHAT PANTY HOSE DID FOR FINGER FUCKING

PRESIDENTIAL CANDIDATE SOBRIQUETS

Candidates often have positive and negative nicknames attached to them as the campaigns wear on.

The Red Fox of Kinderhook   Martin Van Buren, 1840

Napoleon of the Stump   James Polk, 1844

The Fainting General   Franklin Pierce, 1852

The Great Decliner   Horatio Seymour, 1868

The Galena Tanner   Ulysses Grant, 1872

Old White Hat   Horace Greeley, 1872

His Fraudulency   Rutherford Hayes, 1876

The Beast of Buffalo   Grover Cleveland, 1884

The Boy Orator of the Platte   William Jennings Bryan, 1896

Uncle Jumbo   William Howard Taft, 1908

The Happy Hooligan   Warren Harding, 1920

Silent Cal   Calvin Coolidge, 1924

The Hermit Author of Palo Alto   Herbert Hoover, 1928

The Man of Independence   Harry Truman, 1948

Fearless Fosdick   Richard Nixon, 1968

The Great Communicator   Ronald Reagan, 1980

Slick Willie   Bill Clinton, 1992

ROBERT BRYANT HAYNES'S POLITICAL PLATFORM

Haynes was 16 when he ran for president as an independent in 1988. His running mate, Dale Darnell, was 14.

1. I would decrease income tax rate by 50%
2. Favor a return to the GOLD STANDARD
3. Believe in a national legalization of lotteries and gambling casinos
4. Would pay off the national debt by taking the necessary money from the U.S. Treasury
5. Call for 25% reduction of all elected federal officials
6. Support the implementation of the Strategic Defense Initiative
7. Support the abolition of the National Security Council
8. Oppose any effort to cut the defense budget
9. Believe in the abolition of plea-bargaining
10. Believe in direct court sentences without a parole chance
11. Believe in capital punishment
12. Believe in statehood for Puerto Rico
13. Support the quarantining of AIDS victims
14. Support the testing of AIDS in marriage license
15. Believe the Electoral College should be banned and replaced by a national popular vote
16. Work towards colonization of Mars
17. Support Equal Rights Amendment
18. Believe in the restoration of school prayer
19. Against abortion
20. Believe in the Constitution and the capitalist economy

BOB DOLE'S TEN NICEST THINGS ABOUT NOT BEING AN ELECTED OFFICIAL

Bob Dole (R-KS) has been in public service for most of his life. He served in the House from 1961 to 1969 and then in the Senate until 1996. He sought the Republican presidential nomination several times and lost the general election to Bill Clinton in 1996.

1. More time to attend Brooklyn Dodgers games.
2. Can fall off a stage in peace and quiet.
3. Easier to balance household budget than federal budget.
4. No longer have to refer to senators as "distinguished colleagues."
5. Don't have to work at Lincoln Bedroom check-in desk.
6. Content knowing won more votes than anyone else named Bob in American history.
7. No need to prepare bothersome inaugural address.
8. No longer face ridicule for saying, "I'm from the government and I'm here to help you."
9. Favorite TV shows no longer interrupted by own campaign ads.
10. New slogan: "A Better Tan for a Better America!"

THIRD-PARTY LISTS

SMALL PARTIES HAVE IT ROUGH—THEY have never elected a president or controlled Congress—but they have made a difference in American life. They have brought about changes in the law and even amendments to the Constitution, and their concentration on single issues has motivated the two major parties to react, sometimes by co-opting their plans and sometimes by persecuting their members. The presence of third parties continually challenges and improves the two-party system.

SIGNIFICANT THIRD PARTIES

Anti-Mason Party (1827–1836)   Founded as a result of the mysterious disappearance of William Morgan, a former Freemason from upstate New York who threatened to publish an exposé of the Masonic movement. The party was built on a fear that the Masons and other secret societies posed a threat to democracy and Christianity. The national party weakened after the 1832 elections, when it carried Vermont, although it retained influence in parts of the Northeast.

Liberty Party (1839–1848)   A one-issue abolitionist party. Though its presidential candidate fared poorly in 1840 and 1844, his supporters in 1844 may well have cost Henry Clay the presidency.

Free-Soil Party (1847–1854)   An antislavery movement (incorporating the Liberty Party) that opposed extending slavery to any new territories or states. The party put forward Martin Van Buren in 1848 and elected Salmon Chase to the Senate. Its membership was folded into the nascent Republican Party.

American Party (1849–1860)   Nicknamed Know-Nothings by Horace Greeley because it obscured its ties to its supporters, the American Party was a popular nativist and, specifically, anti-Catholic movement. In the 1850s, the party elected half a dozen governors and played a major role in more than a dozen state legislatures.

Constitutional Union Party and **Southern Democratic Party** (1860)   Two splinter parties that formed as the country headed for civil war. Southern Democrats supported slavery and therefore split from the Democratic Party. The Constitutional Unionists, a collection of former Whigs and Know-Nothings, were devoted solely to the preservation of the Union at all costs.

Prohibition Party (1869–)   In addition to its advocacy of temperance and the 18th Amendment, the Prohibition Party has advocated women's suffrage, silver and paper coinage, cuts in military spending, balancing the federal budget, and permitting school prayer. Its heyday was 1884–1920.

Liberal Republican Party (1870–1872)   A faction of the Republican

Party opposed to high tariffs, radical Reconstrution, and corruption in Ulysses Grant's administration. After a successful partnership with the Democrats in 1870 in Missouri, the Liberal Republicans' nominees and platform were adopted by the Democratic Party in 1872.

National Party (1874–1888)   Also known as the Greenbacks because of their opposition to a return to the gold standard after the Civil War; a left-wing party with its base of support among farmers. Nationals ran as fusion candidates with Republicans in the South and with Democrats elsewhere. They were early supporters of regulated interstate commerce and women's suffrage.

People's Party (1891–1903)   A populist movement that opposed monopolies and supported direct election of senators, equal rights, nationalized railroad and telephone systems, a progressive income tax, and the free coinage of silver as well as gold. The People's Party, with support among black as well as white southern farmers and workers, elected governors in more than 11 states in the 1890s. Frank Baum's 1900 novel *The Wonderful Wizard of Oz* is thought to be a populist political allegory.

Socialist Party (1901–)   Opposed war and supported class struggle. Led by Eugene Debs and Norman Thomas, the Socialist Party lost most of its support after World War II.

Progressive Party (1912)   Formed after the Republicans chose incumbent president William Howard Taft over former president Theodore Roosevelt as its nominee; known as the Bull Moose Party because TR declared himself to be "as fit as a bull moose" when nominated. Progressives supported reforms that were meant to improve the lot of workers, women, and children.

Progressive Party (1924)   Led by Senator Robert La Follette (WI), the Progressives were opposed to the influence of big business in U.S. government in general, monopolies in particular, and conscription; they promoted farm relief and public ownership of railroads and sought to bring farmers and workers together.

Union Party (1936–1939)   Led by radio demagogue Father Charles Coughlin and Congressman William "Liberty Bill" Lemke (ND). The Union Party combined the "Share the

Wealth" slogans of Senator Huey Long (LA) and Coughlin's anti-Communist, anti–New Deal, anti-Semitic program.

Progressive Party (1948–1952)   A broad but unsteady coalition of left-wing groups. These Progressives were led by former vice president Henry Wallace in 1948 and Vincent W. Hallinan in 1952.

States' Rights Party (1948–1951)   A segregationist, white supremacist movement; also known as Dixiecrats. Governor Strom Thurmond (SC) and his supporters split from the Democratic Party when its platform incorporated such civil rights reforms as federal antilynching laws and abolition of the poll tax.

American Independent Party (1968–1976)   The segregationist movement of former governor George Wallace (AL) that used phrases like "law and order" and "tough on crime" as euphemisms for the rejection of the changes taking place in America in the 1960s. Four years after the party's founding, Wallace was shot during an appearance in a Maryland mall, and the party never fared well under other leaders.

Peace and Freedom Party (1967–)   A coalition of Black Panthers and other new-left groups that supported black liberation and an end to the war in Vietnam. Some of its supporters backed the People's Party in 1972 and the independent candidacy of Senator Eugene J. McCarthy (D-MN) in 1976. The party is still active, mainly in California.

Libertarian Party (1971–)   Supports giving precedence to the rights of individuals over those of the state. Platform planks have included legalization of marijuana, gay rights, and abolition of public education, social services, the draft, mandatory jury duty, and the national census.

Reform Party (1995–)   Founded by H. Ross Perot and his supporters as a way of institutionalizing the platform from his 1992 protest candidacy: term limits, campaign finance reform, and fiscal and ethical responsibility. In 1996, Ross Perot defeated former Colorado governor Richard Lamm for the party's presidential nomination, and Reform candidates ran in local elections around the country.

THE TEN MOST POPULAR THIRD-PARTY AND INDEPENDENT PRESIDENTIAL CANDIDATES

1. **Theodore Roosevelt** (1912)   TR became president following William McKinley's assassination. He won reelection in 1904 but decided not to seek a third term in 1908. He chose his successor, William Howard Taft, who easily won the Republican nomination and defeated Democrat William Jennings Bryan. Displeased by the conservative tendencies of the Taft administration, TR proclaimed his progressive New Nationalism agenda and challenged Taft for the party nomination. After the Republicans chose Taft, TR's supporters organized the Progressive (Bull Moose) convention. Roosevelt won 27.4% of the vote and outpolled Taft.

2. **Millard Fillmore** ☛ (1856) Fillmore, who finished Zachary Taylor's term in office, was denied renomination by the Whigs in 1852 but was nominated by the American (Know-Nothing) Party. Fillmore was nominated in absentia, while on a year-long European tour (and despite his having met the Pope while in Rome). Fillmore received 21.5% of the vote, finishing third, behind James Buchanan and John Frémont.

3. **H. Ross Perot** ☛ (1992, 1996) Perot, a self-made Texas billionaire, capitalized on frustration with the two-party system and the inefficiency and enormity of the federal government. In speeches and in infomercials that

he paid for out of his own pocket, he pledged to run the government more like a successful business. In 1992, Perot won 18.9% of the vote as an independent candidate and might have done even better had he not suspended his candidacy in mid-July and reentered the race just more than a month before election day. In 1996, he was coy about his desire to seek the presidency again, but United We Stand, his national organization, nominated the big-eared Texan at its convention. Perot's appeal was diminished, but he finished with 9% of the popular vote.

4. **John Breckinridge** (1860)   The last presidential election before the Civil War revealed deep regional divisions. Democrats from the South unsuccessfully lobbied for a plank in the party platform in defense of slavery. Proslavery delegates walked out of an April convention and were locked out of another meeting in June. These delegates and others nominated John Breckinridge as their candidate, who ran on the Southern Democratic ticket. He came in third in a four-way race, receiving 18.1% of the total popular vote. More than half the voters in the eleven southern states that would secede from the Union cast a ballot for Breckinridge.

5. **Robert La Follette** (1924)   Senator La Follette (R-WI) supported many of President Woodrow Wilson's domestic reforms but opposed U.S. participation in World War I and the League of Nations. La Follette, running on the Progressive Party ticket, took on the unelected incumbent, Calvin Coolidge. Perennial Socialist Party nominee Eugene Debs chose not to run, so La Follette also ran on the Socialist ticket. He won 16.6% of the vote in an underfunded campaign.

6. **George Wallace** (1968)   In 1958, having received endorsements from the NAACP and Alabama's Jewish community, Wallace lost his first gubernatorial election, a primary runoff, to a race-baiting fellow Democrat. Later, in the governor's seat, Wallace became a national poster boy for segregation. As the American Independent Party's presidential candidate, he sup-

ported law and order and opposed civil rights and the antiwar movement. Wallace won 13.5% of the vote and captured five states in the Deep South. His campaign taught Richard Nixon and future presidential candidates how to pander to working-class white southern voters.

7. **John Bell** (1860) A former Speaker of the House, War secretary, and senator from Tennessee, Bell was the candidate of the Constitutional Union Party. With his strongest support coming from urban centers and big-property owners, Bell placed fourth behind Abraham Lincoln, Stephen Douglas, and John Breckinridge, winning 12.7% of the vote.

8. **Martin Van Buren** ☞ (1848) Van Buren won the presidency in 1836 but in 1840 was defeated by William Henry Harrison. Eight years later the Free-Soil Party chose Van Buren as its presidential nominee. The party was not on the ballot south of Maryland, and the former president won only 10.1% of the vote.

9. **James Weaver** (1892) Former congressman Weaver (National-IA) won 3.3% of the vote in 1880 when he first ran for president on the National Party ticket. Twelve years later the People's Party fielded Weaver as its candidate. He received 8.5% of the popular vote and placed first in five states west of the Mississippi.

10. **William Wirt** (1832) In 1832, both major-party candidates, Andrew Jackson and Henry Clay, were Masons. Oddly enough, so was Wirt, the Anti-Mason Party's nominee. Nevertheless, he won 7.8% of the popular vote and carried Vermont.

THIRD-PARTY PRESIDENTIAL CANDIDATES WHO RECEIVED ELECTORAL VOTES

The number of electoral votes these candidates received is listed in the right-hand column.

William Wirt (Anti-Mason) 1832	7
Millard Fillmore (American) 1856	8
John Breckinridge (Southern Democrat) 1860	72
John Bell (Constitutional Union) 1860	39
James Weaver (People's) 1892	22
Theodore Roosevelt (Progressive) 1912	88
Robert La Follette Sr. (Progressive) 1924	13
Strom Thurmond (States' Rights) 1948	39
Harry Byrd (no party) 1960	15
George Wallace (American Independent) 1968	46
John Hospers (Libertarian) 1972	1

Senator Harry Byrd (D-VA) is the only one of these candidates who did not participate in the general election. Fourteen un- pledged electors from Alabama and Mississippi and one faith- less elector from Oklahoma (who was pledged to Richard Nixon) voted for him.

THIRD-PARTY ISSUES THAT CHANGED AMERICA

Many significant changes in American social conditions and political life began as third-party ideas. Eventually these ideas were co-opted by one or both major parties and became part of the mainstream political debate.

Prohibition   Advocated by the Prohibition Party from the late 19th century; led to the 18th Amendment (ratified 1919; repealed by the 21st Amendment, 1933)

Women's suffrage   Advocated by the Prohibition and Socialist parties from the late 19th century and supported by both major parties in 1916; led to the 19th Amendment (ratified 1920)

Direct election of senators   Advocated by the Prohibition and Populist parties in the late 19th century; led to the 17th Amendment (ratified 1913)

Immigration restrictions   Advocated by the Populist Party from 1892 and adopted by the Democrats in 1896; led to the Immigration Act (1924)

Progressive income tax   Advocated by the Populist and Socialist parties from 1892; led to the 16th Amendment (ratified 1913)

Shorter working hours   Advocated by the Populist and Socialist parties from 1892; led to state laws and the Fair Labor Standards Act (1938)

Prohibition of child labor   Advocated by the Socialist Party from 1904 to 1912; led to the Keating-Owen Act (1916)

Public works programs to employ the unemployed   Advocated by the Socialist Party from 1928; led to New Deal public-works programs

Unemployment insurance   Advocated by the Socialist Party from 1928; led to the Social Security Act (1935)

Getting "tough on crime"   Advocated by the American Independent Party in 1968 and co-opted by the Republicans; led to Omnibus Crime Control and Safe Streets Act (1968) and other laws

THIRD PARTIES WITH "QUALIFIED" BALLOT STATUS FOR 1998

Minor parties that win a significant percentage of the vote qualify for a line on the ballot in the next major election, alongside the Democrats and the Republicans. Minor parties that have not qualified for a line on the ballot must collect a much larger number of signatures to win a place on the ballot.

Reform Party   32 states   AK, AZ, AR, CA, CT, GA, ID, IL, IA, KS, KY, LA, ME, MA, MI, MN, MS, MO, MT, NB, NV, NM, NY, OH, OK, OR, SC, UT, VT, VA, WA, WI

Libertarian Party   22 states   AZ, CA, DE, GA, ID, IN, KS, MI, MS, MO, MT, NV, NM, OR, SC, SD, TX, UT, VT, WV, WI, WY

U.S. Taxpayers' Party   10 states   CA, CT, DE, ID, MS, MO, NV, NY, SC, WI

Green Party   9 states   AK, CA, CT, ME, NV, NM, OR, VT, WI

Natural Law Party   9 states   CA, DE, ID, MS, MT, NV, OR, SC, VT

A Connecticut Party   1 state   CT

Alaska Independence Party   1 state   AK

Conservative Party   1 state   NY

Cool Moose Party   1 state   RI

Freedom Party   1 state   NY

Grassroots Party   1 state   VT

Liberal Party   1 state   NY

Liberty Union Party   1 state   VT

New Progressive Party   1 state   WI

Patriot Party   1 state   SC

Peace and Freedom Party   1 state   CA

Socialist Party   1 state   OR

Statehood Party   DC

Umoja Party   DC

STATE-BALLOT ACCESS FOR MINOR-PARTY CANDIDATES

The ease of getting on the ballot varies from state to state. State laws determine the number or the percentage of voter signatures required to place a candidate affiliated with an unestablished party on the ballot.

States with the Easiest Ballot Access for the 1998 Senate Races

State	Number of Signatures Needed	% of All Registered Voters
Mississippi	0	—
Vermont	0	—
New Jersey	800	0.02
Utah	300	0.03
Colorado	1,000	0.04
Delaware	200*	0.05
Wisconsin	2,000	0.06
Minnesota	2,000	0.07
Iowa	1,500	0.09
New York	15,000	0.15

* Estimated.

States with the Most Difficult Ballot Access for the 1998 Senate Races

State	Number of Signatures Needed	% of All Registered Voters
Louisiana	128,000*	5.00
Wyoming	8,000	3.32
Oklahoma	60,336	3.05
Florida	242,337	3.00
Maryland	78,000*	3.00
Arkansas	26,528	1.94
Montana	10,097	1.71
North Dakota	7,000	1.48
Idaho	9,835	1.40
Alabama	35,973	1.32
Tennessee	37,179	1.30

* Estimated.

GREENS ON CITY COUNCILS, 1997

*The environmentalist-reformist Green Party has elected repre-
sentatives to city councils around the country, either on its own
or with the support of one of the major parties.*

Stephan Miller Fayetteville, AR

Alva d'Orgeix Bisbee, AZ

Norm Wallen Flagstaff, AZ

Jenifer Hanan Arcata, CA

Jason Kirkpatrick Arcata, CA

Bob Ornelas Arcata, CA

Bruce Mast Albany, CA

Dona Spring Berkeley, CA

Dave Nakamura Blue Lake, CA

Julie Partansky Davis, CA

Steven Schmidt Menlo Park, CA

Mike Feinstein Santa Monica, CA

Alan Drusys Yucaipa, CA

Krista Paradise Carbondale, CO

Karen Mayo Bowdoinham, ME

George Lehigh Eastport, ME

Debra Orton Hermantown, MN

Matt Harline Columbia, MO

Cris Moore Santa Fe, NM

Joyce Brown Chapel Hill, NC

Dan Herber La Crosse, WI

Linda Bruce Superior, WI

*The Douglas County, Wisconsin, legislature has three Green
Party members.*

THE TEN STATES IN WHICH RALPH NADER DID THE BEST IN 1996

Ralph Nader was the Green Party candidate for president. This list shows the the percentage of the popular vote he received in the states in which he received the most votes.

1. **Oregon** 4.1
2. **Alaska** 3.2
3. **Hawaii** 2.9
4. **Washington** 2.7
5. **Maine** 2.5

6. **New Mexico** 2.4
7. **California** 2.4
8. **Vermont** 2.2
9. **Colorado** 1.7
10. **Rhode Island** 1.5

JOHN ANDERSON'S FIVE REFORMS MOST NECESSARY TO PRESERVE AMERICAN DEMOCRACY

Anderson (R-IL, House, 1961–1981) ran as an independent candidate for president in 1980. He now teaches at the Washington School of Law, American University.

1. Create a multiparty political system capable of providing a generally competitive political environment. America needs a new progressivism that is lacking in our present system.
2. Eliminate private money from American political campaigns altogether, substituting a public-financing system and adopting proportional representation.
3. Establish as a clear national goal and priority American leadership in the reform, restructuring, and empowerment of the present United Nations in order to lay the foundation for a democratic world federation based upon the rule of law.
4. Promote a world government capable of sharing the defense costs now borne by the United States; this should allow us to reduce those costs by more than one half.
5. Direct the resulting savings to the twin goals of eliminating a permanent underclass and creating a society that is less economically stratified.

STATE AND LOCAL LISTS

ALL POLITICS ARE LOCAL, BUT SOME politics are more local than others. States, counties, cities, towns, and villages all have their own political systems, and each locale takes a different approach so it can tend to its own needs. Alaska is a big state with a small legislature, and New Hampshire is a small state but has more than 400 state representatives in its two houses. But big or small, they all have something in common, perhaps because most politicians acting on the national stage honed their craft serving on school boards and working out of the neighborhood clubhouses of their political party.

THE BEST-PAID GOVERNORS

Yearly salaries quoted here are as of January 1996.

New York	$130,000	Illinois	119,439
Michigan	121,164	Ohio	115,762
Washington	121,000	Minnesota	114,506
California	120,000	South Carolina	106,078
Maryland	120,000	Pennsylvania	105,000

THE WORST-PAID GOVERNORS

Montana	$59,310	Colorado	70,000
Arkansas	60,000	Oklahoma	70,000
Nebraska	65,000	West Virginia	72,000
North Dakota	65,648	Louisiana	73,440
Maine	69,992	Arizona	75,000

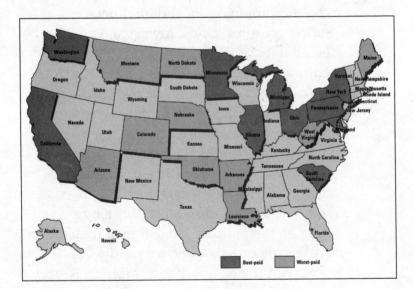

FEMALE GOVERNORS

Only 15 women have led the 50 states.

Nellie Tayloe Ross (D-WY, 1925–1927)   Replaced her husband, who died in office

Miriam Amanda "Ma" Ferguson (D-TX, 1925–1927, 1933–1935)   Replaced her husband, who was impeached

Lurleen Wallace (D-AL, 1967–1968)   Succeeded her husband*; died in office

Ella Grasso (D-CT, 1975–1980)   Elected in her own right

Dixie Lee Ray (D-WA, 1977–1981)   Elected in her own right

Martha Layne Collins (D-KY, 1983–1987)   Elected in her own right

Madeleine M. Kunin (D-VT, 1985–1991)   Elected in her own right

Kay A. Orr (R-NE, 1987–1991)   Elected in her own right

Rose Mofford (D-AZ, 1988–1991)   As the state's secretary of State, replaced Evan Mecham, who was impeached

Joan Finney (D-KS, 1991–1995)   Elected in her own right

Barbara Roberts (D-OR, 1991–1995)   Elected in her own right

Ann Richards (D-TX, 1991–1995)   Elected in her own right

Christine Todd Whitman (R-NJ, 1994–)   Elected in her own right

Jeanne Shaheen (D-NH, 1997–)   Elected in her own right

Jane Dee Hull (R-AZ, 1997–)   As the state's secretary of State, replaced Fife Symington, who resigned after he was convicted of fraud.

---

* George Wallace could not run for reelection. He served as a one-dollar-a-year "special assistant" to Lurleen and made many important decisions during her term.

★ ★ ★

STATES THAT HAVE REWRITTEN THEIR CONSTITUTIONS MOST OFTEN

The United States has existed for more than two hundred years under the same Constitution, but some of the states have not been as stable. The Civil War is one of the events that led states to scrap their old constitutions and start from scratch.

Louisiana   11 versions   1812, 1845, 1852, 1861, 1864, 1868, 1879, 1898, 1913, 1921, 1974

Georgia   10 versions   1777, 1789, 1798, 1861, 1865, 1868, 1877, 1945, 1976, 1982

South Carolina   7 versions   1776, 1778, 1790, 1861, 1865, 1868, 1895

Alabama   6 versions   1819, 1861, 1865, 1868, 1875, 1901

Florida   6 versions   1839, 1861, 1865, 1868, 1886, 1968

Virginia   6 versions   1776, 1830, 1851, 1869, 1902, 1970

Arkansas   5 versions   1836, 1861, 1864, 1868, 1874

Pennsylvania   5 versions   1776, 1790, 1838, 1873, 1968

Texas   5 versions   1845, 1861, 1866, 1869, 1876

STATE CONSTITUTIONS WITH THE MOST AMENDMENTS, AS OF JANUARY 1, 1996

Some states choose to amend their constitutions when ordinary legislation would have been sufficient to accomplish their goals.

Alabama	582	**Maine**	164
California	491	**Ohio**	157
South Carolina	465	**Oklahoma**	151
Texas	364	**New Hampshire**	143
New York	215	**North Dakota**	132
Maryland	207	**Wisconsin**	129
Oregon	201	**New Mexico**	127
Nebraska	198		

THE PROFESSIONALISM OF STATE LEGISLATURES

State legislatures differ as to how professional they are. California legislators and their staffs work all year, with lawmakers earning more than $60,000. New Hampshire state legislators, on the other hand, make only $100 yearly, with a six-month legislative session every other year. Still, it's hard to compare salaries since compensation for special sessions, committee work, and per diem expenses vary from state to state. The states on the first list are in session almost 10 months every year, whereas the ones on the second list spend less than 3 months a year in session.

States with Full-Time, Well-Staffed, Well-Paid Legislatures

California
Florida
Illinois
Massachusetts
Michigan

New Jersey
New York
Ohio
Pennsylvania
Wisconsin

States with Part-Time, Small-Staffed, Low-Paid Legislatures

Arkansas
Georgia
Idaho
Indiana
Maine
Mississippi
Montana
Nevada
New Hampshire

New Mexico
North Dakota
Rhode Island
South Dakota
Utah
Vermont
West Virginia
Wyoming

THE SIZE OF STATE LEGISLATURES
States with the Most Legislators

New Hampshire	424 legislators: 400 representatives, 24 senators
Pennsylvania	253 legislators: 203 representatives, 50 senators
Georgia	236 legislators: 180 representatives, 56 senators
New York	211 legislators: 150 representatives, 61 senators
Minnesota	201 legislators: 134 representatives, 67 senators
Massachusetts	200 legislators: 160 representatives, 40 senators

States with the Fewest Legislators

Nebraska	49 legislators
Alaska	60 legislators: 40 representatives, 20 senators
Delaware	62 legislators: 41 representatives, 21 senators
Nevada	63 legislators: 42 representatives, 21 senators
Hawaii	76 legislators: 51 representatives, 25 senators

Nebraska is the only state with a unicameral legislature. Every other state has both an upper and a lower house.

STATES WITH THE MOST UNCONTESTED SEATS IN THEIR LEGISLATURES, 1996

In only two thirds of all state legislative contests do both the Democratic Party and the Republican Party field candidates. In the remainder of elections, the one major-party candidate is virtually assured victory. Here are the ten states with the highest percentage of uncontested legislative elections in 1996. (Seven states did not elect legislators in 1996.)

Arkansas	67.5	**Florida**	50.7
Texas	60.2	**Rhode Island**	49.3
Massachusetts	58.5	**Wyoming**	48.0
Georgia	56.4	**Tennessee**	47.8
South Carolina	54.1	**Arizona**	47.8

STATES WITH TERM LIMITS ON THEIR LEGISLATORS

In the 1990s, nearly half of the states have voted to limit the number of times their legislators could run for reelection. Some states, such as Alabama and New Jersey, already had gubernatorial term limits.

State	Maximum Number of Years in House	Maximum Number of Years in Senate	Year Term Limits Passed
Arizona	8	8	1992
Arkansas	6	8	1992
California	6	8	1990
Colorado	8	8	1990
Florida	8	8	1992
Idaho	8	8	1994
Louisiana	12	12	1995
Maine	8	8	1993
Massachusetts	8	8	1994
Michigan	6	8	1992
Missouri	8	8	1992
Montana	8	8	1992
Nevada	12	12	1994
Ohio	8	8	1992
Oklahoma	12*	12*	1990
Oregon	6	8	1992
South Dakota	8	8	1992
Utah	12	12	1994
Washington	6	8	1992
Wyoming	6	12	1992

Twenty-three states have voted to limit the number of terms members of Congress from those states could serve, but the Supreme Court has found these limits to be unconstitutional.

---

* A total of 12 years may be served in the state legislature.

STATES WITH INITIATIVE

Initiative is the power of citizens to petition the state to propose a new law, which then is voted on in a statewide election. Indirect initiative means that the state legislature must approve a proposal before it is sent to the electorate; direct initiative does not require that intermediate step. Unless noted otherwise, the states have direct initiative.

Alaska	Nebraska
Arizona	Nevada*
Arkansas	North Dakota
California	Ohio
Colorado	Oklahoma
Idaho	Oregon
Maine*	South Dakota
Massachusetts*	Utah†
Michigan*	Washington†
Missouri	Wyoming
Montana	

* Indirect initiative.
† Direct and indirect initiative.

STATES WITH RECALL

Recall is the power of the electorate to remove officials from office in a statewide plebiscite. Some states do not allow the recall of judges.

Alaska	Michigan
Arizona	Montana
California	Nevada
Colorado	North Dakota
Georgia	Oregon
Idaho	Washington
Kansas	Wisconsin
Louisiana	

STATES WITH OPTIONAL CAMPAIGN-FINANCING FUNDS

Federal tax forms offer taxpayers the option of devoting $1 of their tax payment to a federal election-financing fund. Only 13% of taxpayers check that box even though doing so does not increase their tax burden. Some states also offer the option to finance state elections. The figures below reflect the most recent data, which in most cases come from the 1995 tax year. (In some states the amount may be doubled on joint returns.)

State	Amount	% of Returns Contributing
Hawaii	$2.00	19.0
Idaho	1.00	6.2
Iowa	1.50	7.3
Kentucky	2.00	5.2
Massachusetts	1.00	8.3
Michigan	3.00	7.4
Minnesota	5.00	13.0
New Jersey	1.00	21.9
New Mexico	2.00	—*
North Carolina	1.00	7.7
Ohio	1.00	10.4
Rhode Island	5.00	7.6
Utah	1.00	16.1
Wisconsin	1.00	8.4

---

* Only taxpayers who receive a refund can opt to contribute to the fund. New Mexico collected a total of $2,940 in donations to its campaign-financing fund in the 1995 tax year.

★ ★ ★

THE HIGHEST-PAID MAYORS OF CITIES WITH MORE THAN 100,000 RESIDENTS

City	Population	Mayoral Salary
Chicago, IL	2,732,000	$175,000
Houston, TX	1,702,000	133,552
New York, NY	7,333,000	130,000
San Francisco, CA	735,000	129,356
Detroit, MI	992,000	117,000
Jacksonville, FL	665,000	110,922
Newark, NJ	259,000	110,455
Philadelphia, PA	1,524,000	110,000
Boston, MA	548,000	110,000
Tampa, FL	286,000	110,000
Memphis, TN	614,000	108,000
Seattle, WA	521,000	105,850
Milwaukee, WI	617,000	102,543
Yonkers, NY	183,000	102,000
Atlanta, GA	396,000	100,000
Honolulu, HI	386,000	100,000
St. Petersburg, FL	239,000	100,000

UNPAID MAYORS OF CITIES WITH MORE THAN 100,000 RESIDENTS

The mayors of these 14 cities receive no salaries.

City	Population	City	Population
Sacramento, CA	374,000	Lancaster, CA	119,000
Montgomery, AL	195,000	Eugene, OR	118,000
Columbus, GA	186,000	Salem, OR	116,000
Providence, RI	151,000	Rancho Cucamonga, CA	115,000
Paterson, NJ	138,000	Independence, MO	112,000
Irvine, CA	126,000	Waco, TX	106,000
Overland Park, KS	125,000	Green Bay, WI	103,000

Mayor Richard Riordan of Los Angeles (population 3,449,000), a self-made businessman, opted to draw a yearly salary of only $1.

AFRICAN AMERICAN MAYORS BEFORE 1965

Before the passage of the Voting Rights Act of 1965, official and unofficial policies—poll taxes, literacy tests, and corrupt election boards—made it difficult for blacks to vote, let alone win an election, even in cities where blacks were in the majority.

Victor Blanco   San Antonio, TX, elected 1809

Robert H. Wood   Natchez, MS, 1890

T. B. Armstrong   Boley, OK, 1905

R. R. Ringe   Grambling, OK, 1908

Benjamin A. Green   Mound Bayou, MS, 1940

Mollie Robinson   Easton, TX, 1948

Bennie T. Woodward   Grambling, LA, 1953

Willie B. Hamilton   Howardville, MO, 1960

Hilliard T. Moore Sr.   Lawnside, NJ, 1961

William Steele Sr.   Lincolnville, SC, 1961

George Raymond Thomas   Brooklyn, IL, 1961

Lommie Lane   Wilson City, MO, 1962

Nathaniel Vereen Sr.   Eatonville, FL, 1962

Sam Wilcots   Boley, OK, 1962

George D. Carroll   Richmond, CA, 1964

Clyde Foster   Triana, AL, 1964

TEN LARGEST CITIES THAT NEVER HAVE ELECTED AN AFRICAN AMERICAN MAYOR

As white Americans fled to suburbia, urban voters elected black mayors by the dozens, including such legendary figures as Cleveland's Carl Stokes (1967–1971), Los Angeles's Tom Bradley (1973–1993), and Detroit's Coleman Young (1974–1993).

San Diego, CA

Phoenix, AZ

San Jose, CA

Indianapolis, IN

Jacksonville, FL

Columbus, OH

Milwaukee, WI

Boston, MA

El Paso, TX

Nashville, TN

Houston, the fourth-largest American city, elected its first African American mayor, Lee Brown, in 1997.

CITIES THAT ONCE HAD PREFERENCE VOTING

Preference voting was introduced during the Progressive Era as a way to defeat political machines and open up city councils to third parties. With preference voting, instead of choosing one candidate, voters rank several candidates in order of preference. If their first-choice candidate does not receive a winning share of support, their vote is transferred to their second choice, and so on until a winner is declared. Many preference voting schemes were repealed after World War II because they are slow and costly and because conservative voters opposed the election of minorities—Communists in New York, for example, and African Americans in Cincinnati. Cambridge, Massachusetts, is the only city that still uses preference voting.

Ashtabula, OH	1915–1931	**Yonkers, NY**	1938–1949
Boulder, CO	1917–1949	**Lowell, MA**	1942–1958
Kalamazoo, MI	1918–1921	**Long Beach, NY**	1943–1949
Sacramento, CA	1920–1923	**Coos Bay, OR**	1944–1949
West Hartford, CT	1921–1923	**Oak Ridge, TN**	1948–1958
Cleveland, OH	1921–1933	**Saugus, MA**	1947–1951
Cincinnati, OH	1924–1957	**Medford, MA**	1947–1952
Hamilton, OH	1926–1960	**Quincy, MA**	1947–1952
Toledo, OH	1934–1951	**Revere, MA**	1947–1952
Wheeling, WV	1935–1951	**Worcester, MA**	1947–1960
Norris, TN	1936–1947	**Hopkins, MN**	1949–1961
New York, NY	1936–1949		

NOBODY'S A WINNER

Since 1975, Nevada has given its citizens the option of voting for "None of These Candidates" in national and statewide elections. Nevada's most persistent candidate, None of These Candidates, won more votes than George Bush in the 1980 presidential primary and more than Ralph Nader in the 1996 general election. The following are elections in which None of These Candidates placed first (in these cases, the second-place candidate won the election).

1976 Republican congressional primary

1978 Republican congressional primary

1978 Republican primary for Nevada secretary of State

1986 Democratic primary for Nevada treasurer

THE GOOD, THE BAD, AND THE IMPEACHABLE

This chapter points out American politicians who won the Nobel Peace Prize and members of Congress who tried to kill each other. There are pioneering political figures from different backgrounds and ignominious perpetrators of professional and personal scandals. Politicians, in fact, are better at setting high ethical standards than they are at following them, but, as some of the lists in this chapter show, scandals don't always have dire consequences. The list of politicians who survived embarrassing sexual disclosures is nearly as long as the list of politicians ruined by them. (For now, President Clinton is counted among the survivors.)

U.S. WINNERS
OF THE NOBEL PEACE PRIZE

Theodore Roosevelt (1906)   TR's mediation of the New Hampshire peace conference ending the Russian-Japanese War, as well as his intervention in a conflict between Germany and France over Morocco, won him the prize.

Elihu Root (1912)   Roosevelt's secretary of State signed the Root-Takahira agreement guaranteeing peace in the Pacific.

Woodrow Wilson (1919)   The idealistic Wilson took pains to negotiate a just and lasting peace to World War I, "The War to End All Wars."

Frank B. Kellogg (1929)   The secretary of State under Calvin Coolidge sponsored the Kellogg-Briand pact, an agreement eventually ratified by 62 countries to solve conflicts peacefully.

Jane Addams and **Nicholas Murray Butler** (1931)   Addams found Chicago's Hull House, an internationally famous settlement house, and was an advocate of women's suffrage and peace. Butler wrote extensively about international peace.

Cordell Hull (1945)   During World War II, Hull envisioned an international organization that could maintain peaceful relations between countries. This vision led to the establishment of the United Nations.

Emily Greene Balch and **John R. Mott** (1946)   Balch helped to found the Women's International League for Peace and Freedom. Wellesley College, where she had taught economics and social science, denied her reappointment because of her pacificism. Mott was awarded the prize for his humanitarian acts in wartime, his leading role in establishing five world missionary movements, and his role in inspiring young people.

The American Friends Service Committee (1947)   The Quakers' relief organization received the award for providing food, clothing, ambulance service, and medical care during and after World War II. (The award was shared with their British counterpart, the Friends Service Council.)

Ralph J. Bunche (1950)   On behalf of the United Nations, Bunche mediated the conflict between Israel, Egypt, Jordan, Syria, and Lebanon following the UN's 1947 planned partition of Palestine.

George C. Marshall (1953)   As secretary of State, General Marshall promoted peace after World War II and developed the Marshall Plan to promote economic development and democracy in Europe.

Linus C. Pauling (1962)   Pauling, who won the Nobel Prize for chemistry in 1954, was an advocate of nuclear disarmament.

Martin Luther King Jr. (1964)   King was given the award for his nonviolent approach to racial integration.

Norman E. Borlaug (1970)   Borlaug, a plant pathologist and geneticist, discovered a high-yield, disease-resistant strain of wheat that helped alleviate world hunger.

Henry Kissinger (1973)   Kissinger, Richard Nixon's national security adviser and, later, secretary of State, shared the prize with North Vietnamese counterpart Le Duc Tho for negotiating a cease-fire in Vietnam. (Tho declined the award.)

International Physicians for the Prevention of Nuclear War (1985)   On the eve of a US-USSR summit, this Boston-based organization was given the prize for increasing public awareness of the catastrophic consequences of nuclear warfare.

Elie Wiesel (1986)   Wiesel, a Holocaust survivor and author of books about human suffering and the necessity for peace, was born in Romania; he became a U.S. citizen in 1963.

Jody Williams (1997)   Williams, the head of the International Campaign to Ban Landmines, shared the prize with her organization.

CODE OF ETHICS FOR GOVERNMENT SERVICE

These rules, the first ethics guidelines adopted by Congress, were passed in 1958. They still apply.

Any person in Government service should:

I. Put loyalty to the highest moral principles and to country above loyalty to persons, party, or Government department.

II. Uphold the Constitutions, laws, and regulations of the United States and of all governments therein and never be a party to their evasion.

III. Give a full day's labor for a full day's pay, giving earnest effort and best thought to performance of duties.

IV. Seek to find and employ more efficient and economical ways of getting tasks accomplished.

V. Never discriminate unfairly by the dispensing of special favors or privileges to anyone, whether for remuneration or not; and never accept, for himself or herself or family members, favors or benefits under circumstances which might be construed by reasonable persons as influencing the performance of government duties.

VI. Make no private promise of any kind binding upon the duties of the office, since a Government employee has no private word which can be binding on public duty.

VII. Engage in no business with the Government, either directly or indirectly, which is inconsistent with the conscientious performance of governmental duties.

VIII. Never use any information gained confidentially in the performance of governmental duties as a means of making private profit.

IX. Expose corruption wherever discovered.

X. Uphold these principles, ever conscious that public office is a public trust.

A SAMPLING OF GEORGE WASHINGTON'S *RULES OF CIVILITY & DECENT BEHAVIOUR IN COMPANY AND CONVERSATION*

At age 15, as part of his education, Washington copied 110 points from a popular etiquette book. The highlights appear here.

2. When in Company, put not your Hands to any Part of the Body, not usually Discovered.

5. If You Cough, Sneeze, Sigh, or Yawn, do it not Loud but Privately; and Speak not in your Yawning, but put Your Handkerchief or Hand before your face and turn aside.

13. Kill no Vermin as Fleas, lice, ticks &c in the Sight of Others, if you See any filth or thick Spittle put your foot Dexteriously upon it if it be upon the Cloths of your Companions, Put it off privately, and if it be on your own Cloths return Thanks to him who puts it off.

15. Keep your Nails clean and Short, also your Hands and Teeth Clean, yet without Shewing any great Concern for them.

23. When you see a Crime punished, you may be inwardly Pleased; but always shew Pity to the Suffering Offender.

26. In Pulling off your Hat to Persons of Distinction, as Nobleman, Justices, Churchmen &c make a Reverence, bowing more or less according to the Custom of the Better Bred, and Quality of the Person. Amongst your equals expect not always that they Should begin with you first, but to Pull off the Hat when there is no need is Affectation, in the Manner of Saluting and resaluting in words keep to the most usual Custom.

48. Wherein you reprove Another be unblameable yourself; for example is more prevalent than Precepts.

53. Run not in the Streets, neither go to slowly nor with Mouth open, go not Shaking y^r Arms, kick not the earth with y^r feet, go not upon the Toes, nor in a Dancing fashion.

54. Play not the Peacock, looking every where about you, to See if you be well Deck't, if your Shoes fit well, if your Stockings Sit neatly, and Cloths handsomely.

56. Associate yourself with Men of good Quality if you Esteem your own Reputation; for 'tis better to be alone than in bad Company.

80. Be not Tedious in Discourse or in reading unles you find the Company pleased therewith.

94. If you Soak bread in the Sauce let it be no more than what you put in your Mouth at a time and blow not your broth at Table but Stay till Cools of it Self.

100. Cleanse not your teeth with the Table Cloth Napkin Fork or Knife but if Others do let it be done wᵗ a Pick Tooth.

110. Labour to keep alive in your Breast that Little Spark of Celestial fire Called Conscience.

IMPEACHMENTS
OF FEDERAL OFFICIALS

Article I of the Constitution gives the House of Representatives the power of impeachment and the Senate the power of trying impeachments, for which a two-thirds majority is required to convict.

William Blount (no party–TN, Senate)   Charges dismissed January 14, 1799. Blount was accused by President John Adams of working with the British to wrest Florida and Louisiana from the Spanish. He was expelled from the Senate and then brought up on five articles of impeachment by the House. The Senate decided it no longer had jurisdiction and dismissed the charges.

John Pickering ☛ (U.S. District Court judge, NH)   Convicted March 12, 1804. Pickering, chief justice of New Hampshire before becoming a federal judge, was alcoholic and mentally unbalanced. He was impeached for "wickedly, meaning and intending to injure the revenues of the

United States." During his Senate trial, he challenged President Jefferson to a duel. After a debate over whether the insane could be tried, Pickering was convicted on all counts.

Samuel Chase (associate justice of the Supreme Court)   Acquitted March 1, 1805. Chase was a Federalist and a merciless Federalist partisan. Despite his anti-Republican animus, some Republicans did not vote to convict, and Chase was acquitted. The trial was a humbling experience for Chase, and he was much less bold afterward.

James H. Peck (U.S. District Court judge, MO)   Acquitted January 31, 1831. Charged with confining a lawyer on contempt charges, but his impeachment was related to concerns that he had exceeded his authority in rulings in land-grant cases.

West Hughes Humphreys (U.S. District Court judge, TN)   Convicted June 26, 1862. Humphreys accepted an appointment in the Confederate judiciary without resigning his U.S. judgeship. He was impeached on charges of rebellion and inciting revolt and convicted in a one-day trial.

Andrew Johnson (president)   Acquitted May 26, 1868. Johnson was impeached for violating the Tenure of Office Act, a law requiring Senate approval to remove Senate-confirmed officials appointed by the president. He escaped conviction by one vote.

William Belknap (secretary of War)   Acquitted August 1, 1876. Belknap resigned from the Cabinet after admitting to taking a kickback for granting an Indian trading-post concession. He was impeached, but the Senate no longer had jurisdiction over him.

Charles Swayne (U.S. District Court judge, FL)   Acquitted February 27, 1905. Swayne's impeachment charges included living outside his district and wrongly jailing lawyers for contempt of court. He was acquitted by the Senate, which felt his wrongs (some of which he owned up to) were not high crimes and misdemeanors.

Robert W. Archbald (associate judge of the U.S. Commerce

Court)   Convicted January 13, 1913. Archbald was convicted on five charges of using his position to gain free foreign travel and participating in questionable business deals.

Harold Louderback (U.S. District Court judge, CA)   Acquitted May 24, 1933. Louderback was charged with conspiracy in appointing bankruptcy receiverships. He was acquitted in a trial during the Hundred Days, the special session of Congress called by Franklin Roosevelt to enact New Deal legislation. Some Democrats believed the trial was meant to disrupt FDR's legislative program.

Halsted L. Ritter (U.S. District Court judge, FL)   Convicted April 17, 1936. Impeached on charges of practicing law while on the bench, income tax fraud, misconduct, and extortion. Although none of Ritter's misdeeds in itself was considered an impeachable offense, the Senate decided to convict him on one article, which said that his wrongs, taken altogether, merited his removal from the bench.

Harry E. Claiborne (U.S. District Court judge, NV)   Convicted October 9, 1986. Claiborne had already been convicted of tax evasion in criminal court, and he was impeached and removed from the bench while in prison.

Alcee L. Hastings (U.S. District Court judge, FL)   Convicted October 20, 1989. Impeached for leaking wiretaps, lying under oath, and allegations of bribery, Hastings had already been acquitted by a jury, but the Senate convicted him on eight of the eleven articles of impeachment. Hastings (D-FL) was elected to the House of Representatives in 1992 and still serves in the body that impeached him.

Walter L. Nixon Jr. (U.S. District Court judge, MS)   Convicted November 3, 1989. Nixon was serving a five-year prison sentence for perjury when the Senate convicted him on perjury charges.

★ ★ ★

AMERICA'S BEST POLITICAL SCANDALS

Printing (1820s–1850s)   For many years government printing contracts were considered a prime opportunity for dispensing political patronage. Beginning in 1819, the House elected its official printers. In 1852, to combat absurdly padded bills and other schemes for bilking the Treasury, the government created the position of Supervisor of Public Printing. The supervisor's office became a source of graft, and the government bought its own printing facility in 1860. The Government Printing Office is currently the biggest publisher in America.

The Peggy Eaton affair (1831)   While her husband was at sea, Margaret "Peggy" O'Neale Timberlake spent enough time with Senator John H. Eaton (D-TN) to raise eyebrows in Washington. After her husband died, she married the senator, and when Eaton joined Andrew Jackson's Cabinet as secretary of War, his wife was ostracized by other Washington wives, who were led by Floride Calhoun, wife of the vice president. Few people, among them the widowed president and the widowed secretary of State, Martin Van Buren, were willing to socialize with the Eatons publicly, and the spat led to a purge of the Jackson Cabinet. When Jackson ran for a second term, the loyal Van Buren replaced Calhoun on the Democratic ticket. (After John Eaton died, his widow married a Neapolitan dancing teacher who was less than half her age; he ran off with her granddaughter and her fortune.)

Crédit Mobilier (1868–1872)   Named for a corporation owned by Oakes Ames (R-MA, House) and his brother Oliver that was involved in the construction of the Union Pacific Railroad and drained the railroad's endowment. When a Senate investigation seemed likely, Ames distributed shares of Crédit Mobilier stock to members of Congress. Finally, in the run-up to the 1872 presidential election, the House and the Senate investigated. Among those who accepted shares of stock were Vice President Schuyler Colfax and future president James Garfield.

Whiskey Ring (1875)   Ulysses Grant's secretary of the Treasury, Benjamin H. Bristow, brought about the indictment of more than 200 people involved in a conspiracy whereby whiskey distillers bribed Internal Revenue officials in order to avoid paying taxes on the liquor they produced. Grant's personal secretary, Orville E. Babcock, was implicated but acquitted of criminal wrongdoing.

Teapot Dome (1921–1923)   Drilling leases on government oil reserves in Teapot Dome, Wyoming, and elsewhere were distributed to political cronies of Albert Fall, Warren Harding's secretary of the Interior, and others in the administration. Fall received kickbacks in exchange for the contracts, which were never bid on. By the time the Senate completed its investigation, Harding was dead and Fall had resigned. Fall was eventually convicted of accepting a bribe and served time in prison.

Watergate (1972–1974)   Named after the building in which the Democratic National Committee had its headquarters, which was broken into twice. The Watergate break-ins were found to be part of a larger Republican program of intelligence gathering and sabotage in the 1972 presidential campaign. Newspaper and congressional investigations uncovered numerous cover-ups and led to the dismissal and conviction of White House staffers and, in 1974, to the resignation of President Nixon himself.

Koreagate (1978)   South Korean rice broker Tongsun Park admitted that he had distributed approximately $850,000 to more than 30 congressmen between 1967 and 1976. Three House members were reprimanded for not reporting their gifts, and another, Richard T. Hanna (D-CA), pleaded guilty to conspiracy to defraud the government and served one year of a 30-month sentence. Park had thrown two birthday parties for House Speaker Tip O'Neill, but O'Neill suffered no punitive consequences for accepting Park's generosity.

Abscam (1980)   FBI agents invented an Arab sheikh who offered money to members of Congress in exchange for political favors. Six congressmen and one senator were video-taped or witnessed accepting money from "Sheikh Kambir Abdul Rahman," and all spent time in prison for their deeds. In the wake of Abscam, Rita Jenrette, the wife of one of the convicted congressmen, posed nude for *Playboy* and admitted that she and her husband, John Wilson Jenrette Jr. (D-SC), had had sex on the steps of the Capitol.

Iran-contra (1986–1991)   Ronald Reagan's administration secretly and illegally sold arms to Iran in exchange for the release of U.S. hostages held in Lebanon, and the government used the profits to finance the right-wing contra movement fighting the Communist government of Nicaragua. John Poindexter, former national security adviser, was sent to prison for lying to Congress in an attempt to cover up the affair, and several other officials received probation. Charges against Poindexter's underling, Oliver North, were eventually dropped; North became a popular hero and an attractive political candidate.

Whitewater (1992–)   In 1978, Bill and Hillary Clinton invested in a 200-acre real estate venture along Arkansas's White River. Their partners in Whitewater Development Corp., Jim and Susan McDougal, made the bulk of payments on the unsuccessful investment. During Clinton's first campaign for president, several questions were raised about the propriety of Whitewater, including conflicts of interest for Bill Clinton as governor and Hillary Clinton as a partner in the Rose Law Firm of Little Rock, in dealing with Madison Guaranty, Jim McDougal's insolvent savings-and-loan bank. An independent counsel's investigation has thus far led to several convictions, including those of Jim and Susan McDougal and former Arkansas governor Jim Guy Tucker, as well as a prison term for Susan McDougal for refusing to answer the counsel's questions. The independent counsel has also looked into the difficulties in the White House travel office, the suicide of Clinton aide Vincent Foster, the president's alleged extramarital affairs, and other matters tangentially related to Whitewater.

DUELS, FLOOR FIGHTS, AND OTHER VIOLENT INCIDENTS INVOLVING GOVERNMENT OFFICIALS

Members of Congress have not always settled matters in a gentlemanly fashion. Then again, duels were considered gentlemanly in the 18th and 19th centuries.

Roger Griswold v. **Matthew Lyon** (1798)   Lyon (R-VT) spat in the face of Griswold (Federalist-CT) after Griswold mocked him for alleged cowardly behavior during the Revolution. Two weeks later the first intracongressional brawl began. Griswold hit Lyon with a hickory cane; Lyon fought back with a pair of fireplace tongs. The next day the House passed a resolution asking Griswold and Lyon to take a pledge of nonviolence, which settled the matter.

Alexander Hamilton v. **Aaron Burr** (1804)   Former Treasury secretary Hamilton and Vice President Burr had a longstanding hatred of each other. Burr challenged Hamilton to a duel after Hamilton worked to defeat Burr in his bid for the governorship of New York and reportedly had described Burr as "a dangerous man, and one who ought not to be trusted with the reins of government." Most historians believe Hamilton shot first in the duel in Weehawken, New Jersey, but intentionally missed his target. Burr shot next and hit Hamilton, who died thirty hours later.

DEATH OF ALEX. HAMILTON.

George Campbell v. **Barent Gardenier** (1808)   The first intracongressional duel took place as a result of the passage of the Em-
bargo Act of 1807, which prohibited almost all commerce with
Britain, France, and other foreign countries in an effort to
bring an end to war in Europe. Gardenier (Federalist-NY)
railed against Congress for passing the act, claiming that it was
a measure in support of and inspired by Napoleon. Campbell
(D-TN) responded to Gardenier's speech with a vicious ad
hominem attack. Gardenier challenged Campbell to a duel, and
Campbell shot and seriously wounded Gardenier.

Henry Clay v. **John Randolph** (1824)   In the presidential election of
1824, Clay, who came in fourth in electoral votes, gave John
Quincy Adams his support. He became Adams's secretary of
State, and though they denied it, many saw the Clay appointment as the completion of a deal between the two. Among
those who denounced the Adams-Clay "corrupt bargain" was
Congressman John Randolph (no party–VA), who referred to
Clay as a "blackleg," a dishonest gambler. Clay challenged Randolph to a duel, which they fought on the banks of the Potomac
one April afternoon. Two pairs of shots were fired before the
duel was called off; the only damage done was to Randolph's
white coat.

John Adams II v. **Russell Jarvis** (1828)   Adams, the second son of
John Quincy Adams and his father's private secretary, said
some nasty things about Jarvis, an editorial writer for the
Washington Daily Telegraph, a paper opposed to President
Adams. Jarvis attacked John II in the rotunda of the Capitol.
The pressman was censured by the Congress after a House in-
vestigation.

William Jordan Graves v. **Jonathan Cilley** (1838)   Congressman Cilley (D-ME) criticized New York newspaper publisher James
Watson Webb on the House floor. Webb asked his second, Congressman Graves (Whig-KY), to issue a challenge to Cilley on
his behalf. Cilley refused to fight, insisting that any remarks
made in the House were constitutionally protected outside the
House. Graves himself then challenged Cilley because accord-

ing to dueling etiquette, refusal to accept a challenge consti-
tutes an insult to the second. Graves shot Cilley dead in the
duel even though the only grievance he had against him was a
formality.

Henry Stuart Foote ☞
v. **Thomas Hart Benton**
(1850)   The proposed
Compromise of 1850,
which involved the ad-
mission of California as a
free state, an end to slavery in Washington, DC,
and stricter fugitive slave
laws, provoked heated de-
bate in Congress. An ar-
gument between two
senators, Foote (D-MS)
and Benton (D-MO), es-
calated after Foote in-
sulted Benton. Benton
threatened Foote as he
moved toward him; Foote
pulled a pistol on Benton.
Other senators defused
the crisis, and neither
man was punished.

Preston Smith Brooks v. **Charles Sumner** (1856)   In his famous
"Crime Against Kansas" speech, a two-day attack on slavery,
Senator Sumner (R-MA) made ad hominem comments about
Senator Andrew Pickens Butler (States' Rights–SC) and several
other colleagues. Three days later Congressman Brooks (D-SC),
Butler's nephew, entered the Senate chamber and violently beat
Sumner with a gutta-percha cane until it broke. Sumner spent
more than three years in recovery before he could resume his
Senate duties. Brooks resigned, but South Carolinians elected

him to fill his vacant seat, and he returned to Washington two weeks later. Most members of Congress were appalled, but Brooks's constituents presented him with commemorative canes bearing the engraved message HIT HIM AGAIN.

Laurence Keitt v. **Galusha Grow** (1858)   Congressman Keitt (D-SC) called Congressman Grow (R-PA) a "black Republican puppy" in the midst of a debate over admitting Kansas to the Union. The two men traded words and then began a brawl on the floor of the House. One of them grabbed the other's wig, made a joke about having scalped his opponent, and laughter diffused the tension and ended the fight.

Lovell Rousseau v. **Josiah Grinnell** (1866)   In a House speech, Congressman Grinnell (R-IA) accused Congressman Rousseau (R-KY) of cowardice. A few weeks later Rousseau attacked Grinnell with a cane on a portico at the Capitol. Rousseau was censured by the House even though he had already sent a letter of resignation to the governor of Kentucky.

Benjamin Tillman v. **John McLaurin** (1902)   Senator Tillman (D-SC) and Senator McLaurin (D-SC) briefly scuffled on the Senate floor. The fight broke out after Tillman, in a discussion of the fate of the Philippines, assailed McLaurin's integrity. Tillman hit McLaurin over the eye; McLaurin popped Tillman in the nose. Several senators and the doorkeeper separated them. Both men were found in contempt of the Senate and were censured.

★ ★ ★

SEX SCANDALS THAT ENDED POLITICAL CAREERS

William Sharon (R-NE, Senate)   1880–1885   Sharon, a wealthy
widower, was nearly 60 when he met the 20-something Sarah
Althea Hill in 1880. He offered to make Hill his paid mistress,
but she wanted to marry the senator. While in California they
secretly signed papers stating that they were married, which in
that state constituted a wedding. When Sharon broke off the relationship, Hill sought revenge, first trying voodoo spells and
then legal remedies. She sued for divorce on grounds of adul-
tery, and Sharon countersued, claiming the marriage documents were fraudulent. She won the divorce, and Sharon died
in 1885 on the day the countersuit was to be decided.

Charles W. Jones (D-FL, Senate)   1885–1886   After ten years in
the Senate, Jones disappeared in late 1885. He was located the
next year in Detroit, where he had moved to woo a nondescript
35-year-old woman named Clothilde Palms. He did not return
to the Senate before his term expired but lived on the street and
in an asylum until he died ten years later.

William Preston Taulbee (D-KY, House)   1889   Taulbee, a former
minister, was caught having sex with a patent clerk in a Capitol
stairwell. His frolick was exposed by correspondent Charles E.
Kincaid in the *Louisville Times* in 1889, and Taulbee decided
not to seek reelection. The next year, Taulbee saw Kincaid on
the street and pounced on him. Two hours later Kincaid found
Taulbee at the Capitol and shot him dead. Kincaid, who
claimed it was self-defense, was acquitted of first-degree murder.

William Campbell Preston Breckinridge (D-KY, House)   1893   In
1884, Congressman Breckinridge, who was married and the
father of five, was giving a lecture to a group of young women
at the Sayre Institute in his home state. While inveighing
against "useless handshaking, promiscuous kissing, needless
touches, and all exposures" he met 17-year-old Madeline Pollard. He seduced Pollard, moved her to Washington, recom-

mended her for a government job, and impregnated her several times. He promised to marry her when his wife died, but in 1893 he married someone else instead, and Pollard sued him for breach of promise. Breckinridge's blame-the-temptress courtroom strategy backfired, and Pollard won. When Breckinridge ran for reelection in 1894, Kentucky women helped to defeat him even though they did not have the right to vote.

Arthur Brown (R-UT, Senate)   1897   One of the first two senators to be elected from Utah after its admission to the Union in 1896, Brown was married to his second wife, Isabel, when he began an affair with Anna Addison Bradley, a Republican committeewoman. Anna bore Brown a son a year later, and the two ran off to Idaho. Isabel Brown died in 1905, and the senator promised to marry Bradley. But he kept putting her off, and in 1906, when she discovered he had another mistress, she shot him. She was acquitted.

Walter Jenkins (D)   1964   An aide to Lyndon Johnson, Jenkins was arrested in 1964 in the men's room of a YMCA one block from the White House and charged with having sex with a man. Jenkins, who had been arrested in 1959 on the same charge, resigned his position.

Wilbur Mills (D-AR, House)   1974   Head of the House Ways and Means Committee, Mills was a well-respected congressman with an eye on the White House and a drinking problem. One evening in October 1974, police stopped him on a bridge for driving too fast and without headlights. His passenger, Fanne Foxe, a 38-year-old stripper, bolted out of the car and jumped into the Tidal Basin. Mills was reelected in November despite the nighttime drive with Foxe. In December, Foxe appeared at the Boston Burlesque Theater, and Mills joined her onstage. Mills was removed as chairman of the Ways and Means Committee and did not run for reelection.

Wayne Hays (D-OH, House)   1976   Hays, the unpopular head of the House Appropriations Committee, was discovered to be having an affair with a former Miss Virginia, Elizabeth Ray. He had arranged for a $14,000-a-year Capitol Hill job for her, and she boasted about her lack of qualifications: "I can't type. I can't file. I can't even answer the phone." After a failed suicide attempt, Hays resigned his chairmanship and did not seek reelection. (Ray said she had slept with other members of Congress, including Hubert Humphrey, but nothing came of these claims.)

Allan Turner Howe (D-UT, House)   1976   Howe was arrested for soliciting two undercover policewomen in Salt Lake City. The freshman congressman did not seek another term.

Jon Hinson (R-MS, House)   1980   At a press conference in August 1980, Hinson came out of the closet in order to preempt the report of an obscenity arrest in an Arlington, VA, park. Hinson was reelected, but the next April he was caught having sex in a House office building. He pleaded no contest to a charge of attempted oral sodomy and resigned his seat.

Robert Bauman (R-MD, House)   1980   Bauman, who had been president of the American Conservative Union and had cosponsored anti–gay rights legislation, was arrested for soliciting a 16-year-old male dancer four weeks before the 1980 election. Bauman blamed his behavior on drunkenness and lost the election. In 1986, he published *The Gentleman from Maryland: The Conscience of a Gay Conservative,* an account of his reconciling his homosexuality and his conservative politics.

Gary Hart (D-CO, Senate)   1987   A promising candidate for the 1988 Democratic presidential nomination, the twice-separated but still-married former Colorado senator dared the press to investigate rumors of his extramarital escapades. "If anybody wants to put a tail on me, go ahead. They'd be very bored," he said. *The Miami Herald* followed Hart and reported that he had had an overnight guest at his Washington home and had cruised to Bimini on the aptly named yacht *Monkey Business* with Donna Rice, a 29-year-old actress-model. Hart withdrew from the presidential race in May 1987 only to reenter it just before primary season. He fared poorly and dropped out for good.

Mike Pappas (D)   1988   Chief congressional aide to Royden P. Dyson (D-MD, House), Pappas was accused in 1988 of asking a male staffer to perform a striptease and using sex to recruit male employees. When the story became public, Pappas committed suicide by jumping from a New York hotel roof.

Donald E. "Buz" Lukens (R-OH, House)   1989   The mother of a 16-year-old girl whom Lukens had allegedly had sex with wore a wire and recorded his offer of a government job to hush up the charges. He was convicted and served nine days of a 30-day sentence. He lost the 1990 primary and resigned in the face of an ethics investigation.

John Tower (R-TX)   1989   A former senator, Tower was nominated by George Bush as his secretary of Defense. The Senate rejected the nomination in part because Tower had been accused of fondling a flight-crew member on a military base and chasing a secretary around a desk.

Daniel Crane (R-IL, House)   1983   Crane was found to have had an affair with a 17-year-old female page. A congressional investigation recommended a reprimand, but Congressman Newt Gingrich pushed for censure. Crane was defeated in his next election.

Brock Adams (D-WA, Senate)   1992   Former aide Kari Tupper first made accusations in 1988 that Adams drugged her in order to have sex with her. A 1992 *Seattle Times* article reported that eight women said Adams had forced himself on them sexually; some said Adams had used a red liquid to subdue them. After the article appeared, Adams ended his reelection bid.

Bob Packwood (R-OR, Senate)   1995   A long congressional ethics investigation looked into charges that Packwood had made many unwelcome sexual advances over the years. He was finally charged with 18 counts of sexual harassment as well as improper efforts to secure a job for his ex-wife and thereby reduce his alimony payments. He resigned in 1995 before the House had a chance to vote on his expulsion.

Mel Reynolds (D-IL, House)   1995   Reynolds was convicted of having sex with an underage campaign volunteer and sentenced to five years in prison. He has also been convicted on 15 counts of bank fraud. (Reynolds took over his seat from Gus Savage, who was found by a congressional investigation to have propositioned a Peace Corps volunteer.)

SEX SCANDALS THAT DIDN'T END POLITICAL CAREERS

George Washington (president)   1789–1797   As president, Washington survived all sorts of false rumors of sexual liaisons and illegitimate children.

Alexander Hamilton  (Federalist, secretary of the Treasury)   1792 Maria Reynolds came to Hamilton to request financial assistance. Though both were married, Hamilton observed, "It was quickly apparent that other than pecuniary consolation would be acceptable." Maria's husband, James Reynolds, tried to blackmail Hamilton, and when James was imprisoned for fraud, he pressured Hamilton to have him released. Hamilton confessed his sins, saying "There is nothing worse in the affair than an irregular and indelicate amour. For this, I bow to the just censure which it merits. I have paid pretty severely for the folly, and can never recollect it without disgust." He kept his position as secretary of the Treasury.

Thomas Jefferson (Democratic Republican, president)   1805   For several years, Jefferson tried to seduce Betsey Walker, the wife of an acquaintance. Though he was unsuccessful, an article was published in 1805 saying that he had cuckolded John Walker. Walker was goaded into challenging Jefferson to a duel. The president wrote a letter to Attorney General Levi Lincoln in which he admitted the extent of his wrongdoing: "You will perceive that while I plead guilty to one of the charges, that while young and single I offered love to a handsome lady, I acknowledge its incorrectness." His confession put an end to the trouble. Allegations of an affair with Sally Hemings were also published during Jefferson's political career, but without serious effect.

Andrew Jackson (D, presidential candidate) 1828 Jackson's wife, Rachel Donelson Robards Jackson (), had been married before, and though she believed herself to be divorced when she married Jackson, she was not. Consequently, she was slandered during the 1828 campaign. Jackson's bid was successful, but his wife died shortly after the election.

Richard Johnson (D, vice presidential candidate) 1836 Johnson, a War of 1812 hero and Martin Van Buren's running mate, had two children by an African American mistress, Julia Chinn. She had died by the time of the election, and he was supporting their children. The love affair was publicly known, yet Van Buren stood behind Johnson, and the candidates were elected. Afterward Johnson had several more black mistresses and brought one of them to Washington social events.

Daniel Edgar Sickles (D-NY, House) 1859 Sickles received anonymous letters stating that his wife, Teresa, was having an affair with Philip Barton Key, U.S. attorney of Washington, DC, and son of Francis Scott Key. Sickles, who was then keeping a prostitute as his mistress, shot Key three times, the last time from point-blank range. James Buchanan was a friend of Sickles's and he appointed a sympathetic replacement as U.S. attorney. Sickles pleaded temporary insanity, a novel defense, and was acquitted of murder.

Grover Cleveland (D, presidential candidate) 1884 Cleveland's first opponent for the presidency, James Blaine, made much out of Cleveland's illegitimate son by Maria Halpin. Nevertheless, Cleveland won the election and won a second term eight years later. (Blaine was a hypocrite on this matter; his first child was born fewer than nine months after his marriage. Cleveland did not publicize Blaine's shotgun wedding but word of it got around.)

Ted Kennedy (D-MA, Senate)   1969   In July 1969, Kennedy was intoxicated when he drove his car off the bridge linking Martha's Vineyard to Chappaquiddick Island. The senator survived, but his companion, Mary Jo Kopechne, drowned. Although Kennedy says he tried to save her, he did not report the incident for ten hours. He pleaded guilty to leaving the scene of an accident. Though he has held on to his Senate seat, his presidential aspirations were dashed at Chappaquiddick.

Donald Riegle (D-MI, House; senatorial candidate)   1976   Riegle was campaigning for the Senate when a former staffer gave the Detroit newspapers audiotapes that made clear that the two were sexually involved. (At one point, Riegle says to her, "I, God, feel such super love for you. By the way, the newsletter should start arriving.") Riegle won the election and remained in the Senate through 1994.

Marion Barry (D, mayor, Washington, DC)   1990   The FBI caught Barry smoking crack cocaine in a Washington hotel room with a woman who was not his wife. Barry spent six months in prison and in 1994 was reelected for the fourth time, running on a platform of forgiveness and redemption for himself and for his city.

Barney Frank (D-MA, House)   1990   Frank wrote a memo recommending that probation for Steve Gobie, a convicted male prostitute who lived with him for several years, be ended. Gobie continued to work as a prostitute, using Frank's apartment as a base of operations, and Frank denied knowledge of this. He received a reprimand from the House and remains in the Congress.

Gerry Studds (D-MA, House)   1990   Studds acknowledged having had an affair with a 17-year-old male page in 1983. He was officially censured by the House but was reelected until he retired in 1996.

Clarence Thomas (nominee for associate justice of the Supreme Court)   1991   Thomas was confirmed despite accusations that he had sexually harassed Anita Hill when both worked for the Equal Employment Opportunity Commission. Republican senators on the Judiciary Committee attacked Hill's character during her three days of testimony.

Bill Clinton (D, presidential candidate) 1992– In January 1992, Gennifer Flowers, a sometime lounge singer, told a supermarket tabloid about a 12-year affair she supposedly had with Clinton, the leading contender for the Democratic presidential nomination. Clinton weathered the scandal and was elected in 1992 with the help of female voters. Another former Arkanas state employee, Paula Jones, has since accused Clinton of sexual harassment and sued him for violating her constitutional rights. In the course of that suit, White House volunteer Kathleen Willey claimed Clinton propositioned her, and it was widely reported that Monica Lewinsky, a former White House intern, had an affair with the president. Clinton has denied sexual involvement with Jones, Willey, and Lewinsky.

George Bush (R, presidential candidate) 1992 After Clinton's alleged infidelity became a campaign issue, reporters began to explore rumors linking Bush to longtime aide Jenifer Fitzgerald. Bush and Fitzgerald issued denials and the stories had little impact on the 1992 campaign.

CONGRESSMEN WHO ADMITTED TO (OR WERE CONVICTED OF) HAVING SEX WITH TEENAGERS

William Breckinridge (D-KY)
Robert Bauman (R-MD)
Buz Lukens (R-OH)

Daniel Crane (R-IL)
Gerry Studds (D-MA)
Mel Reynolds (D-IL)

POLITICAL BOSSES:
The Men Behind the Machines

*"Politics is as much a regular business as the grocery
or the dry-goods or the drug business."*
—GEORGE WASHINGTON PLUNKITT,
Tammany Hall boss

Thurlow Weed (1797–1882)   Weed was the publisher of the
Anti-Masonic Enquirer and the *Albany Evening Journal* and
was a behind-the-scenes force for the Whigs and, later, the
Republicans. He dispensed all sorts of bribes and favors but
wasn't on the take himself. A supporter of New York senator
William Seward, William Henry Harrison, and Zachary Taylor, Weed also advised Abraham Lincoln on Cabinet appointments.

William M. Tweed (1823–1878)   Tammany Hall, founded in the
days of Aaron Burr, was perhaps the most powerful, long-
running, and greedy of all the machines. Boss Tweed squan-
dered his life savings to remove an enemy (Fernando Wood,
another Tammany member) from City Hall, but he made the
money back through graft as an antigraft member of the
Board of Supervisors of New York County. In 1863, Tweed
and his ring took over the Tammany organization and ran
New York City. During his career, Tweed served as alderman,
congressman, state senator, school commissioner, deputy
commissioner of public works, and deputy street commissioner, and he profited from each position. Newspapers and
cartoonists went after Tweed and Tammany. Tweed tried a
$500,000 bribe to silence *The New York Times,* but the paper
didn't take it. With a $6-million judgment against him,
Tweed escaped from custody in 1875 and ran away to Spain,
where he was recognized from his caricature in a political
cartoon. He was returned to jail, where he died.

Roscoe Conkling (1829–1888)   A hardware salesman by profession, Conkling ran the New York State Republican Party for many years. He served as district attorney of Albany, mayor of Utica, U.S. congressman, and U.S. senator and played a large role in the backroom politics of the national Republican organization. His support lay in the New York Customhouse, a corrupt patronage organization that Chester Arthur headed for a time. He fought the nomination of James Garfield in 1880, and to pacify him, Arthur was chosen to fill out the ticket.

James "King James" McManes (1822–1899) McManes worked his way up through the Philadelphia Republican organization until he became a trustee of the Gas Trust in 1865. He gained control of its board and from that position handed out tens of thousands of government and private patronage jobs. He used intimidation by police, violence, and threatened firings during elections to maintain his position. He fell from power in 1885 after a battle with another state Republican boss and an exposé of the Gas Trust graft and the exploding city debt. McManes's successors were no more honest; George, Edwin, and William Vare, brothers known as the Dukes, doubled the voting registry during a period when Philadelphia's population was declining.

Marcus Alonzo Hanna (1837–1904) Hanna was in the street-railway business in Cleveland when he began backing politicians sympathetic to his business needs. He supported James Garfield and then became a protector of William McKinley's. In six years he turned McKinley from a congressman who had lost his seat into a governor and a viable presidential candidate. Hanna backed the McKinley campaign and recruited other contributors, and he even rented a house in Georgia so the candidate could court southern Republicans. After McKinley was elected, Hanna became a senator. Though quiet in the Senate, Hanna was involved behind the scenes in the McKinley administration.

Abe Ruef (1864–1936) A lawyer, a dandy, and a gourmet, Ruef, a Jew, ran San Francisco as boss of the Union Labor

Party. He backed an orchestra leader, Handsome Gene Schmitz, as mayor in 1903. Pacific State Telephone and Telegraph, United Railroad, Pacific Gas and Electric, and other businesses retained Ruef as their municipal-law adviser and so kept their city contracts. Ruef geared up to run for the Senate but was tried for graft before he could and was sentenced to 14 years in San Quentin.

Thomas J. Pendergast (1872–1945)   Pendergast was a saloon-keeper and police officer until he took over the Kansas City Democratic organization in 1911, following in the footsteps of his brother Jim. He soon expanded his influence to the entire state of Missouri and, in the process, turned haberdasher Harry Truman into an administrative judge and sponsored his ascent to the Senate and beyond. In 1939, Pendergast was convicted of tax evasion and taking a bribe. His probation after a year and a day in Leavenworth stipulated that he was to avoid politics for five years. The Pendergast machine crumbled shortly before his death.

Edward Hull Crump (1874–1954)   Known as the Red Snapper, Ed Crump, a native of Holly Springs, Mississippi, became the virtual emperor of Memphis for most of the first half of the 20th century. Entering politics as a reformer in 1901, he ran for mayor as a law-and-order candidate at the end of the decade and won by 79 votes. His victory was assured by African American voters, whom he wooed by promising favors and having W. C. Handy write him a campaign song. After Crump became mayor, Memphis had decades of extremely lopsided elections. Crump himself was elected to various offices 26 times in 45 years, and the Crump organization never lost an election until 1950. Crump's decline began in 1948, when the boss compared Tennessee senatorial candidate Estes Kefauver to a pet coon. Kefauver turned the pejorative comment around, declaring that he wasn't Crump's pet coon and appearing in a coonskin cap throughout his campaign.

James Michael Curley (1874–1958)   Curley had no more than a sixth grade education. He lost his first election, for the Boston common council, in 1898 and his last, a tenth run for mayor, in 1955. In between he served four terms as mayor of Boston, four terms as a U.S. congressman, and one as governor of Massachusetts. He was convicted in 1903 of taking someone else's civil service exam and was elected alderman while in prison. In 1946, while mayor, he was convicted of mail fraud. He modeled his machine on Tammany Hall, paying for food, rent, and funerals for poor Irish immigrants and establishing public bathhouses. Curley was called everything from the Irish Mussolini to the Ambassador from South Boston.

Frank Hague (1876–1956)   Hague once modestly declared, "I am the law in Jersey City." Kicked out of school at 13, Hague ran for constable at 21. He then pushed to shrink the city council to a five-member city commission, saying that the new arrangement would reduce corruption when in fact it would facilitate Hague's consolidation of power. He became mayor in 1917 and for the next 30 years controlled Jersey City. Hague was no beneficent dictator; he raised taxes while diverting the city's funds into his cronies' pockets as well as his own. Elections had very high turnout rates, and members of the Hague machine were not above tearing up, smudging, or rewriting the opposition's ballots. In the 1920s, 200 Princeton students were sent in to monitor a local election; every monitor was kicked out of every polling place, and five of them landed in the hospital. Hague's hold over Jersey City was so strong that he had a large say in state races, and in 1928, out of spite, he was responsible for the election of a Republican governor.

Huey Pierce Long (1893–1935)   Long was a brilliant high school dropout who passed the Louisiana bar after only six months of school. As a member of the Louisiana Railroad Commission, and taking his inspiration from a political novel called *The Fakers,* Long railed against Standard Oil and other wealthy companies, promised aid to the poor for education, medicine, and other services, and thus became a popular public figure. He won the governorship on his second try and fired the election commissioners in the parishes that hadn't supported him. In 1930, in his run for the Senate, he forced state employees to give 10% of a month's salary to his campaign, which was built on vague promises of ending joblessness and reducing New Orleans's public debt. Toward the end of the campaign, he ordered the kidnapping of two men who were responsible for giving him bad press. He kept control of Louisiana while in the Senate, putting his own people in the other Senate seat and the governor's mansion. He tenaciously opposed the New Deal and might have run for president if he hadn't been shot and killed in 1935.

Richard Joseph Daley (1902–1976)   Daley, born to a working-class Irish family, won his first election as a Republican write-in candidate. He was chosen chairman of the Cook County Democratic Committee in 1953 and two years later was elected mayor, an office he held for the rest of his life. Daley helped fellow Illinoisan Adlai Stevenson win the Democratic presidential nomination in 1952 and 1956 and was responsible for John Kennedy's victory over Nixon in the tight 1960 presidential contest. He was embarrassed in 1968 by his handling of riots in the black ghettos and the violence at the Democratic National Convention. Nevertheless, he dominated Chicago politics until his death.

POLITICIANS WHO HAVE ADMITTED TRYING MARIJUANA

Those politicians who have come clean about past marijuana use make all sorts of excuses about their wayward past: I was young and stupid; I succumbed to peer pressure; I didn't inhale; it didn't have any affect on me.

Bruce Babbitt   Secretary of the Interior

Lawton Chiles   D-FL, governor

Bill Clinton   President

Howard Dean   D-VT, governor

Richard Gephardt   D-MO, House minority leader

Newt Gingrich   R-GA, Speaker of the House

Douglas Ginsberg   U.S. Appeals Court judge*

Al Gore   Vice president

Gary Hart   D-CO, former senator

Joseph Kennedy II   D-MA, congressman

Richard Lamm   D, Reform Party–CO, former governor

Michael McCurry   Clinton administration press secretary

Connie Mack   R-FL, senator

Susan Molinari   R-NY, former congresswoman

James Moran   D-VA, congressman

George E. Pataki   R-NY, governor

Claiborne Pell   D-RI, former senator

Dana Rohrabacher   R-CA, congressman

Donna Shalala   Secretary of Health and Human Services

Clarence Thomas   Supreme Court justice

William F. Weld   R-MA, former governor

---

* Nomination for Supreme Court justice withdrawn because of the marijuana issue.

POP POLITICS: LISTS FROM POPULAR CULTURE

AMERICANS TREAT POLITICIANS LIKE celebrities. We name candy bars and cocktails and ballparks and asteroids after them. We elect sports heroes and popular actors the way we used to elect war heroes. We read books and watch movies about politicians, both real and fictional, and the real ones sometimes get in on the act by performing and writing themselves. And why shouldn't they? As Shirley Chisholm observed, "Some members of Congress are the best actors in the world."

ASTEROIDS NAMED AFTER U.S. POLITICAL FIGURES

Eva Perón and Frank Zappa have celestial bodies that carry their names, but don't expect a Richard Nixon asteroid anytime soon. Current asteroid-naming regulations require people to be dead at least a century before they can be honored. Asteroids are identified by both name and number.

(886) Washingtonia Unclear whether named for the president or for the capital city

(932) Hooveria Named for Herbert Hoover in recognition of his aid to Austria after World War I

(1363) Herberta Also named for Herbert Hoover, in appreciation of his relief work for Belgium after World War I

(3153) Lincoln Named for Abraham Lincoln

(3154) Grant Named for Ulysses Grant

(4372) Quincy Named for John Quincy Adams

> *There is an asteroid called Johnadams (3726), but it was named for a scientist, not for the president.*

PROFESSIONAL BASEBALL PLAYERS WHO WERE/ARE ACTIVE IN POLITICS

In the 19th century, joining an amateur baseball club was good for making political and business connections, much like playing golf at a country club is today. The game soon went professional and athletic excellence became more important than social networking. Nevertheless, several alumni of the major and minor leagues have served their country in significant political capacities.

Fred Brown (D-NH, governor, 1923–1924; Senate, 1933–1939) Brown, a Dartmouth graduate, played seven games in the outfield in 1901 and 1902 for the National League's Boston

Beaneaters. While in the Senate he attended Senators
games.

Jim Bunning (R-KY, House, 1987–)   Hall of Famer Bunning
pitched for the Detroit Tigers, the Philadelphia Phillies, the
Pittsburgh Pirates, and the Los Angeles Dodgers between
1955 and 1971.

Mario Cuomo (D-NY, governor, 1982–1994)   Cuomo played
minor league ball in 1952 for Brunswick of the Georgia-
Florida League, a team in the Pittsburgh Pirates farm system.

Dwight Eisenhower (president, 1953–1961)   While a cadet at
West Point, Eisenhower played a little semipro ball. Ike used
a false name, Wilson, because playing professional sports vi-
olated National Collegiate Athletic Association rules and
would have interfered with his eligibility to play football.
President Eisenhower kept his diamond days a secret until
Mel Ott of the New York Giants, who had heard rumors
about Eisenhower and baseball, asked him about them.

Arthur Gorman (D-MD, Senate, 1881–1899, 1903–1906)   Gorman played right field for the Washington Nationals in the
1860s. It is because of Gorman that the Washington baseball
team was nicknamed the Senators.

Frank Lausche (D-OH, governor, 1945–1947, 1949–1957; Senate, 1957–1969)   Lausche played for two minor league
teams: Duluth, in the Northern League, in 1916 and
Lawrence, in the Eastern League, in 1917.

Scott Lucas (D-IL, House, 1935–1939; Senate, 1939–1951)   Between 1913 and 1915, Lucas played for Pekin of the Illinois-
Missouri League and Bloomington of the Three-I (Illinois,
Indiana, Iowa) League. In the Senate he served as majority
whip (1947–1949) and majority leader (1949–1951).

Wilmer "Vinegar Bend" Mizell (R-NC, House, 1969–1975)
Mizell, who was known by the name of his southern hometown ("a town so small the welcome signs are back to
back"), pitched in the major leagues for nine years. He had a
respectable 90-88 record and a 3.85 earned run average with

the St. Louis Cardinals, the Pittsburgh Pirates, and the New York Mets.

Pius Schwert (D-NY, House, 1939–1941)   Schwert spent two years in the major leagues. He was a Yankees catcher in 1914 and 1915, playing eleven games. He died in office, on March 11, 1941.

John Tener (R-PA, House, 1909–1911; governor, 1911–1915)   Tener was a pitcher for the Baltimore Orioles of the American Association in 1885, the Chicago White Stockings of the National League in 1888–1889, and the Pittsburgh Burghers of the Players League in 1890. He racked up a lifetime record of 25-31 and a 4.30 earned run average. During his last two years in the Pennsylvania state capital he was also president of the National League.

> *Though he never played professionally, George Bush was the captain of the Yale baseball team in 1948, his senior year.*

RUDOLPH GIULIANI'S FIVE MOST MEMORABLE OCTOBER MOMENTS WITNESSED IN YANKEE STADIUM

Rudolph Giuliani, mayor of New York since 1993, is a longtime New York Yankees fan.

1. **October 26, 1996**   In the sixth game of the World Series, the Yankees defeat the Atlanta Braves, 4 games to 2.

2. **October 18, 1977**   In the sixth game of the World Series, Reggie Jackson hits three home runs, each on the first pitch, and the Yankees defeat the Los Angeles Dodgers, 4 games to 2.

3. **October 1, 1961**   Roger Maris hits his record-breaking 61st home run.

4. **October 6, 1978**   Thurman Munson hits a 430-foot home run in the third game of the playoffs against the Kansas City Royals.

5. **October 13, 1978**   Graig Nettles makes four of the most spectacular plays at third base in the history of baseball.

POLITICIANS WHO THREW OUT THE FIRST BALL

In 1913, President William Howard Taft was the first president to throw out the first ball of the season at a Washington Nationals game, and from him to Richard Nixon, every president started at least one season for the Nationals. Then, after the 1971 season, Washington, D.C., finally lost its baseball franchise. Now presidents occasionally travel to the nearest stadium, in Baltimore, to throw out the first ball of the season. Here are other first-ball throwers of national prominence.

James Sherman   Vice president   1912

Champ Clark   Speaker of the House   1914

Thomas Marshall   Vice president   1917, 1920

Charles Dawes   Vice president   1926

John Garner   Vice president   1939

Henry Wallace   Vice president   1942, 1944

Paul McNutt   Manpower commissioner   1943

Sam Rayburn   Speaker of the House   1945

Richard Nixon   Vice president   1959

Hubert Humphrey   Vice president   1966, 1968

David Eisenhower   Grandson of Dwight Eisenhower and son-in-law of Nixon   1970

Madeleine Albright   Secretary of State   1997

THE RICHARD NIXON
ALL-STARS

Richard Nixon was an avid baseball fan. In June 1972, a month before the Watergate break-in, President Nixon was asked at a press conference to put together his all-time all-star baseball team. He came up with four teams, a prewar team and a postwar team for each league. In 1992, he revised his selections and submitted six lineups.

National League, 1925–1959

First base   Johnny Mize

Second base   Jackie Robinson

Third base   Ed Mathews

Shortstop   Ernie Banks

Outfield   Stan Musial, Willie Mays, Mel Ott

Catcher   Roy Campanella

Designated hitter   Rogers Hornsby

Pitchers   Carl Hubbell, Dizzy Dean, Warren Spahn, Robin Roberts, Elroy Face

Manager   Branch Rickey

American League, 1925–1959

First base   Lou Gehrig

Second base   Charlie Gehringer

Third base   George Kell

Shortstop   Phil Rizzuto

Outfield   Babe Ruth, Joe DiMaggio, Ted Williams

Catcher   Mickey Cochrane

Designated hitter   Jimmie Foxx

Pitchers   Lefty Grove, Bobo Newsom, Bob Feller, Early Wynn, Satchel Paige

Manager   Casey Stengel

National League, 1960—1991

First base Willie McCovey

Second base Joe Morgan

Third base Mike Schmidt

Shortstop Maury Wills

Outfield Hank Aaron, Lou Brock, Roberto Clemente

Catcher Johnny Bench

Designated hitter Pete Rose

Pitchers Sandy Koufax, Juan Marichal, Bob Gibson, Steve Carlton, Tom Seaver

Manager Walt Alston

American League, 1960—1991

First base Harmon Killebrew

Second base Bobby Grich

Third base Brooks Robinson

Shortstop Luis Aparicio

Outfield Carl Yastrzemski, Mickey Mantle, Reggie Jackson

Catcher Thurman Munson

Designated hitter Rod Carew

Pitchers Jim "Catfish" Hunter, Jim Palmer, Whitey Ford, Luis Tiant, Rollie Fingers

Manager Billy Martin

National League Players Active in 1992

First base Will Clark

Second base Ryne Sandberg

Third base Howard Johnson

Shortstop Ozzie Smith

Outfield Tony Gwynn, Darryl Strawberry, Andre Dawson

Catcher Gary Carter

Designated hitter Bobby Bonilla

Pitchers Dwight Gooden, Bret Saberhagen, David Cone, Rob Dibble, Lee Smith

Manager Tommy Lasorda

American League Players Active in 1992

First base Don Mattingly

Second base Roberto Alomar

Third base George Brett

Shortstop Cal Ripken Jr.

Outfield Rickey Henderson, Ken Griffey Jr., Kirby Puckett

Catcher Carlton Fisk

Designated hitter Jose Canseco

Pitchers Nolan Ryan, Jack Morris, Roger Clemens, Goose Gossage, Dennis Eckersley

Manager Tony LaRussa

POLITICIANS WHO PLAYED PROFESSIONAL FOOTBALL

Chester "Ted" Chesney (D-IL, House, 1949–1951) Center, Chicago Bears, 1939–1940

Winfield Kirkpatrick Denton (D-IN, House, 1949–1953, 1955–1967) Guard, Evansville, Indiana, Crimson Giants, 1922

LaVern Dilweg (D-WI, House, 1943–1945) End, Green Bay Packers, 1926–1934

Fob James Jr. (R-AL, governor, 1995–) Halfback, Montreal Alouettes, 1956–1957

Jack Kemp (R-NY, House, 1971–1989; George Bush's secretary of Housing and Urban Development, 1989–1993) Quarterback, Pittsburgh Steelers, 1957; San Diego Chargers, 1960–1962; Buffalo Bills, 1962–1969

Edward King (R-MA, governor, 1979–1983) Guard, Buffalo Bills, 1948–1949; Baltimore Colts, 1950

Steve Largent (R-OK, House, 1994–) Wide receiver, Seattle Seahawks, 1975–1989

J. C. Watts Jr. (R-OK, House, 1994–) Quarterback, Ottawa Rough Riders, 1981, 1983–1986, Toronto Argonauts, 1986

Byron "Whizzer" White (Supreme Court justice, 1962–1993) Runningback, Pittsburgh Pirates, 1938

> *Dwight Eisenhower, Richard Nixon, Gerald Ford, and Ronald Reagan played football in college. Reagan also worked as a football announcer for midwestern radio stations.*

BEN NIGHTHORSE CAMPBELL'S FIVE FAVORITE MOTORCYCLES

Senator Campbell (R-CO) is the only Native American in Congress. He is also a motorcycle fanatic.

1. **1997 Harley-Davidson Road King**
2. **1993 Harley-Davidson Custom Softail**
3. **1970 Harley-Davidson Chopper**
4. **1996 1200 Daytona Triumph**
5. **1943 WLA Harley-Davidson Military**

PRESIDENTS WHO GOLFED

William McKinley was the first president to try golf. Since William Howard Taft, all presidents except Herbert Hoover, Harry Truman, and Jimmy Carter played golf. The golfer Jimmy Demaret once said, "If the people wish to determine the best candidate, put all the contenders on a golf course. The one who can take five or six bad holes in a row without blowing his stack is capable of handling the affairs of the nation." The golfer presidents are ranked here according to the proficiency of their games.

1. **John Kennedy**   "A graceful rhythmic swing," "an indifferent putter," "often shot 40 or less for nine"

2. **Gerald Ford**   "A true golf zealot," "capable of outdriving professionals," "even as he approached the age of 80, had a handicap in the 15-to-17 range"

3. **Dwight Eisenhower** "A quality short-iron game," "a congenital slicer," "broke 80 three times in his life"

4. **Franklin Roosevelt** (prepolio) "A powerful swing that produced long drives," "once won his club championship," "scored in the high 80s fairly consistently"

5. **George Bush** "Great golfing genes," "short game needed work," "an 11-handicapper when he was younger; the figure soared to twice that during his White House years"

6. **Ronald Reagan** "A powerful, if wristy swing," "his attitude toward the game was more congenial than competitive," "a solid 12 at his peak; once he became president, his game faded"

7. **Richard Nixon** "A confident putter," "awkward swing," "generally in the low 90s or high 80s"

8. **Bill Clinton** "Capable of cranking out long drives," "a flying elbow and unorthodox posture at the top of his backswing," "scored in the 80s or low 90s, depending on how many mulligans he took"

9. **William Howard Taft** "A good putter," "a short, choppy swing," "generally in the middle to high 90s"

10. **Warren Harding** "A smooth, effective putting stroke," "a tendency to rush his swing," "struggled to break 100"

11. **Woodrow Wilson** ☞ "A fidgety player," "a wicked slice," "generally shot around 115"

12. **Lyndon Johnson** "Often took huge divots," "could uncork long (but wild) drives," "never broke 100 with his initial ball"

13. **Calvin Coolidge** "Pecked away at his fairway shots," "extremely short off the tee," "once took 11 strokes to reach a par 3"

Clinton, Ford, and Bush played golf together at the Bob Hope Classic at Indian Wells, CA. Though Clinton is here ranked the worst of the three, he was the only one not to hit a spectator with a golf ball. (Bush hit two.)

JAMES CLYBURN'S TOP TEN MOST FREQUENTED GOLF COURSES NEAR HIS CONGRESSIONAL OFFICES

Congressman Clyburn (D-SC) has been in the House since 1993.

Washington, DC

1. **TPC at Avanel**   Potomac, MD
2. **Robert Trent Jones Golf Club**   Lake Manassas, VA
3. **Army/Navy Country Club**   Arlington, VA
4. **Indian Springs Country Club**   Silver Spring, MD

South Carolina's Sixth Congressional District

5. **Santee-Cooper Country Club**   Santee, SC
6. **Old Hickory** (at Fort Jackson)   Columbia, SC
7. **Wrenwood** (at Charleston Air Force Base) Charleston, SC
8. **The Country Club of South Carolina**   Florence, SC
9. **Santee National Golf Course**   Santee, SC
10. **Lakewood Links**   Santee, SC

PRESIDENTS WHO FISHED

George Washington

Thomas Jefferson

Chester Arthur

Harry Truman

Dwight Eisenhower

Lyndon Johnson

Grover Cleveland

Calvin Coolidge

Jimmy Carter

George Bush

> *Coolidge enjoyed fishing at his South Dakota summer home, but he did little of the work. He wore white kid gloves while holding the rod and demanded that his Secret Service detail bait the hook and handle any fish he caught.*

★ ★ ★

BILL CLINTON'S CELEBRITY OVERNIGHT GUESTS, IN THE LINCOLN AND OTHER BEDROOMS

Kathleen Battle

Candice Bergen

Chevy Chase

Judy Collins

Ted Danson

Richard Dreyfuss

Jane Fonda

David Geffen

Doris Kearns Goodwin and
Richard Goodwin

Billy Graham

John Guare

Tom Hanks

Norman Jewison

Steven Jobs

Christine Lahti

Dr. Dean Ornish

Neil Simon

Steven Spielberg

Mary Steenburgen

Barbra Streisand

Marianne Williamson

OLYMPIANS IN PROMINENT POLITICAL POSITIONS

Dwight Filley Davis (Calvin Coolidge's secretary of War, 1925–1929)   Tennis, 1904; founder of the Davis Cup

Ralph Metcalfe (D-IL, House, 1971–1978)   100-meter and 200-meter runs, bronze medalist, 1932

Bob Mathias (R-CA, House, 1967–1975)   Decathlon, 1948, 1952

Wendell Anderson (D-MN, governor, 1971–1976; Senate, 1976–1978)   Ice hockey, 1956

Bill Bradley (D-NJ, Senate, 1979–1997)   Basketball, gold medalist, 1964

Ben Nighthorse Campbell (D-CO, House, 1987–1993; D/R-CO, Senate, 1993–)   Captain, U.S. judo team, 1964

Jim Ryun (R-KS, House, 1996–)   1,500-meter run, silver medalist, 1968

Tom McMillen (D-MD, House, 1987–1993)   Basketball, silver medalist, 1972

FOODS AND DRINKS NAMED AFTER POLITICIANS AND THEIR FAMILY MEMBERS

Washington Loaf Cake   Named for George Washington   3 cups sugar, 2 scant cups butter, 1 cup sour milk, 5 eggs, 1 teaspoon soda, 3 tablespoons cinnamon, half a nutmeg, 2 cups raisins, 1 cup currants, 4 cups sifted flour. Mix sugar and butter, add eggs, milk, and flour; coat fruit in flour and stir. Bake.

Dolly Madison   Named for Dolley Madison (wife of James Madison)   Ice cream brand

Old Hickory Nut Soup   Named for Andrew Jackson   Break open 1 gallon hickory nuts, remove meat, and crush. Add 1 quart boiling water, let stand for 10 minutes, add 4 tablespoons sugar, and serve.

Daniel Webster's Chowder   Named for Daniel Webster (congressman, senator, and Cabinet member)   Clean 5 or 6 pounds of cod; slice thick. Slice thinly ½ pound salt pork. Warm a kettle with the salt pork; then remove the salt pork. Layer the fish, potatoes, salt pork, and add salt and pepper. Fill with water and boil for 25 minutes. Add 1 pint boiling milk and crackers; cook another 10 minutes.

Jefferson Davis Pie   Named for Jefferson Davis (president of the Confederacy)   Blend 1 cup light cream with 4 beaten egg yolks. Mix 2 cups brown sugar and 2 tablespoons flour, and add to egg mixture. Add ½ cup melted butter. Pour into a pie shell; bake at 250° for 20 minutes. Add meringue top, and bake at 350° for 15 minutes.

Tilden Cake   Named for Samuel Tilden (presidential candidate)   Cream 1 cup butter and 2 cups sugar. Add 4 eggs, one at a time. Sift 3 cups flour, ½ cup cornstarch, 2 teaspoons baking powder, and ½ teaspoon salt. Add to butter and sugar along with 1 cup milk and 2 teaspoons lemon extract. Bake at 350° for 30 to 35 minutes.

Hancock Sour   Named for Winfield Hancock (presidential candidate)   4 dashes rock-candy syrup, juice of 1 lime, 3 dashes Jamaica rum, 1 jigger bourbon. Ice, stir, strain, and fill with carbonic.

Mark Hanna Hash   Named for Mark Hanna (Ohio senator and adviser to William McKinley)   Corned beef hash with a poached egg on top

Baby Ruth   Named for Ruth Cleveland (daughter of Grover Cleveland)   Candy bar

Roosevelt Punch   Named for Theodore Roosevelt   Juice of ½ lemon, ½ spoon sugar, 1 jigger apple whiskey. Shake, and add a dash brandy on top.

Gin Rickey   Named for Colonel Joe Rickey (Washington, DC, lobbyist)   Squeeze ½ lime over ice in a glass. Add 1 jigger gin, and fill with soda water. (The rye rickey and the nonalcoholic lime rickey followed.)

Nixonburgers   Named for Donald Nixon, brother of Richard   Hamburgers sold by the southern California restaurant chain owned by Donald Nixon

Billy   Named for Billy Carter (brother of Jimmy) A novelty beer from before the era of microbreweries

MORE POLITICAL FOODS

Hartford Election Cake
Confederate Pudding
Mugwump in a Hole
Electioneering Burgoo
Ward 8 (cocktail named for a Boston electoral district)

BILL MAHER'S AMERICAN POPULISTS BY WEIGHT (ESTIMATED POUNDS)

Carry Nation	185	Reverend Al Sharpton	240
William Jennings Bryan	190	Huey Long	275
Father Charles Coughlin	200	Michael Moore	330
John Brown	210	Rush Limbaugh	350
John L. Lewis	220		

A SAMPLER OF
PRESIDENTIAL RECIPES

Thomas Jefferson's Persimmon Beer   "Gather the persimmons perfectly ripe and free from any roughness, work them into large loaves, with bran enough to make them consistent, bake them so thoroughly that the cake may be brown and dry throughout, but not burnt, so they are fit to use; but if you keep them any time, it will be necessary to dry them frequently in an oven moderately warm. Of these loaves broken into coarse powder, take 8 bushels, pour over them 40 gallons of cold water; and after two or three days draw it off; boil it as other beer, hop it; this makes a strong beer. By putting 30 gallons of water to the same powder, and letting it stand two or three days longer, you may have a very fine small beer."

Dolley Madison Cake   Cream 1 pound butter and 1 pound sugar. Add 1 pound sifted flour, 6 eggs, ½ teaspoon baking soda, 2 ounces brandy, 2 ounces rosewater. Mix, add 1 ground nutmeg, 1 pound raisins, ½ pound citron. Bake at 300° for 40 minutes.

General Harrison Eggnog   Fold 4 whipped eggs into 1 pint heavy cream, 1½ quarts milk. Add bourbon and sweeten with sugar syrup.

Tyler Pudding Pie   Cream ½ cup butter and 6 cups sugar. Beat in 6 eggs, 1 cup heavy cream, and 1 grated coconut. Pour into 4 puff-pastry piecrusts. Bake at 450° for 10 minutes and then lower to 350° for 30 minutes.

James Polk's ☛ **Christmas Fruitcake**
Mix ½ pound chopped blanched almonds with the juice of 3 oranges. Cream 1 pound butter and 2 pounds sugar. Beat in 12 eggs. Sift together 4 cups flour, cloves, cinnamon, nutmeg, allspice, and mace, and mix dry and wet ingredients. Add citron, raisins,

dates, currants, candied pineapple, and almonds. Bake at 150° for 6 hours.

Coolidge Pickle Sauce   Boil 1 cup cider vinegar, add 2 teaspoons cinnamon, 1½ tablespoons cornstarch, 1 cup chopped pickles.

President Eisenhower's Beef Soup   Stew 20 pounds beef in 3 gallons beef stock for 2½ hours. Add salt, pepper, 8 pounds potatoes, 6 bunches carrots, 5 pounds onions, 15 tomatoes. Cook 30 minutes more. Serves 60.

A MENU FROM MARTHA WASHINGTON'S COOKBOOK

First Course	Second Course
Small Chicken Patties	Maids of Honor
Red Cabbage Stewed	Asparagus *à la Petit Poi*
Boiled Chickens	Sauce
Plain Butter	2 Teal
Shrimp Sauce	Crayfish
Dressed Greens	Sauce
Soup Purée (replaced by Salmon)	Fish in Jelly
Shoulder of Mutton in Epigram	2 Wild Ducks
Ham	Lambs Tails *au Bechamel*
Beef *Tremblongue*	Roasted Hare
Soup Santea (replaced by Stewed Carp)	Sweetbreads *à la Dauphin*
Scotch Collops	3 Partridges
Pork Cutlets	Rhenish Cream
Sauce Robert	Prawns
Mashed Potatoes	Sauce
Boiled Turkey	Plovers
French Beans Fricasséed	Sauce
Celery Sauce	Chardoons
Oyster Loaves	Fricasséed Birds
	Custards

Third Course

Fruits

Nuts

Wine

A BANQUET IN HONOR OF
WILLIAM HOWARD TAFT

Historians have observed that the roundest president got rounder in times of political crisis. In the White House, Taft's diet was monitored by the president's wife and his staff, but on the road he ate well. This menu is from a dinner in Jackson, Mississippi, on November 1, 1909.

Back Bay Plant Oysters
Clear Green Sea Turtle Soup
Celery Radishes   Green Olives
Salted Almonds
Fillet of Pompano *à la meunière*
Cucumbers *en gelée*
Filet Mignon of Mutton
Béarnaise Sauce
Tomatoes Stuffed with Corn
Roast Wild Turkey
Grilled Sweet Potatoes with Rice
Fritters
Lettuce and Artichoke Heart Salad
Cheese Biscuits
Cigars   Fancy Glacés   Bonbons
Cigarettes   Petits Fours   Coffee

RICHARD NIXON'S ETIQUETTE FOR SERVICE AT STATE DINNERS

President Nixon outlined these new rules in a memo to White House aide Rex Scouten, dated July 9, 1969.

1. If it is a stag dinner or lunch, with no guest of honor, the President will be served first.
2. If it is a stag affair, with a guest of honor, the guest of honor will be served first and the President next.
3. If it is a mixed dinner, with no guest of honor, Mrs. Nixon will be served first and the President next.
4. If it is a mixed dinner, with a guest of honor, the wife of the guest of honor will be served first simultaneously with Mrs. Nixon, and then the guest of honor and I will be served second.
5. If it is one of those rare occasions where it is a mixed dinner and the guest of honor is not accompanied by his wife, serve Mrs. Nixon first and simultaneously the woman who is assigned as my dinner partner, and then serve me and the guest of honor second.

POLITICIANS ON MONEY

The first of each denomination is the one currently in production. Unless otherwise stated, the currency is paper.

- **1¢** Abraham Lincoln (coin)
- **5¢** Thomas Jefferson (coin)
- **10¢** Franklin D. Roosevelt (coin). Also George Washington (1863), secretary of the Treasury William Merith
- **25¢** George Washington (coin). Also George Washington (1863), Cabinet members William Pitt Fessenden (1864) and Robert J. Walker

50¢ John Kennedy (coin). Also George Washington (1863), Abraham Lincoln (1863), secretary of War Edwin Stanton, secretary of the Treasury Samuel Dexter, and secretary of the Treasury William Crawford, Benjamin Franklin (1948–1963, coin)

$1 George Washington. Dwight Eisenhower (1971–1978, coin), Susan B. Anthony (1979–1981, coin)

$2 Thomas Jefferson. Also Alexander Hamilton (1862)

$5 Abraham Lincoln. Also James Garfield (1882), Benjamin Harrison (1902)

$10 Alexander Hamilton. Also Abraham Lincoln (1861), Daniel Webster (1869), William McKinley (1902), Andrew Jackson (1923)

$20 Andrew Jackson. Also Alexander Hamilton (1869), John Marshall (1890), secretary of the Treasury Hugh McCulloch (1902), Grover Cleveland (1914)

$50 Ulysses S. Grant. Also Alexander Hamilton (1862), Henry Clay (1869), Benjamin Franklin (1874), secretary of the Treasury John Sherman (1902)

$100 Benjamin Franklin. Also Abraham Lincoln (1869), James Monroe (1878)

$500 William McKinley. Also Albert Gallatin (1862), John Quincy Adams, (1869), Senator Charles Sumner (1878)

$1,000 Grover Cleveland. Also Senator Robert Morris (1862), DeWitt Clinton (1869), secretary of State William Marcy (1878), Alexander Hamilton (1918)

$5,000 James Madison

$10,000 Salmon P. Chase. Also Stephen Douglas (1872), Andrew Jackson (1878)

$100,000 Woodrow Wilson

FOREIGN COUNTRIES THAT HAVE ISSUED MILLARD FILLMORE STAMPS

*Other nations have remembered
one of the most forgettable presidents.*

Antigua and Barbuda
Bhutan
Dominica
Equatorial Guinea
Grenada
Laos
Liberia

Maldives
Montserrat
St. Lucia
St. Vincent and the Grenadines
Sierra Leone
Turks and Caicos Islands

FOREIGN COUNTRIES THAT HAVE ISSUED GERALD FORD STAMPS

Comoros
Dominica
Equatorial Guinea
Laos

Liberia
Nicaragua
St. Vincent
South Korea

FOREIGN COUNTRIES THAT HAVE ISSUED GEORGE BUSH STAMPS

Bermuda
Bolivia
Central African Republic
Colombia
Dominica
Guinea
Guyana
Liberia

Malta
Mongolia
Palau
Paraguay
St. Vincent
San Marino
Togo

COUNTRIES THAT HAVE ISSUED NANCY REAGAN STAMPS

Nancy Reagan usually appears side by side with her husband, Ronald.

Grenada

Paraguay

Philippines

St. Lucia

St. Vincent

POLITICAL ANIMAL WORDS

allegator   Person who makes allegations; used often by Senator Sam Ervin (D-NC, 1954–1974)

boll weevils   Members of the Conservative Democratic Forum, whose members are southern conservative Democrats

bull   Powerful chairperson of a House committee; also called *lion*

dark horse   Unlikely candidate for nomination who wins the nomination

donkey   Symbol of the Democratic Party

eagle   Republican on Wall Street who has given a lot of money to political campaigns

elephant   Symbol of the Republican Party

floo-floo bird   Backward-looking bird; pejorative term for a conservative

gerrymander   Creature with a pointed tongue, wings, and claws; named for Gilbert Stuart's drawing of an election district formed while Gerry Elbridge was governor of Massachusetts

gypsy moth   Republican moderate from the northeast and the Great Lakes region

horse   Chief sponsor of a bill or a cause

Kingfish   Nickname of Huey Long (D-LA, governor, 1928–1931; Senate, 1932–1935)

lame duck   Elected official who has not been reelected and is finishing the remainder of his or her term

lion   Powerful chairperson of a House committee; also called *bull*

mangy dog   Legislation with many flaws

mossback   Inactive conservative

old bull   Veteran members of Congress

old walrus   Veteran politician

rooster   Former symbol of the Democratic Party

sacrificial lamb   Candidate who runs for the sake of the party, usually against an incumbent, knowing he or she will lose

sparrow hawk   Liberal masquerading as hawk

stalking horse   Decoy candidate

yellow dog Democrat   Southerner who will vote for any Democratic candidate

FUNNY-SOUNDING POLITICAL WORDS

bafflegab   Intentionally confusing jargon. See *gobbledygook*

bloviate   To speechify pompously

boondoggle   Wasteful or crooked government-funded project

filibuster   Long-winded oration whose purpose is to obstruct the passage of a particular piece of legislation

flugie   Rule that helps only the rule maker

gerrymander   To redraw an election district for politically motivated reasons

gobbledygook   Roundabout, nonsensical explanation. See *bafflegab*

mollycoddle   Wimpy politician

mugwump   Political maverick

roorback   Invented rumor intended to smear an opponent

snollygoster   Politician who puts office holding ahead of principles

wonk   Nerd drawn to political details

14 DEFINITIONS FROM
THE DEVIL'S DICTIONARY

Ambrose Gwinnett Bierce (1842–1914?) was a journalist, critic, and editor with a fierce wit. He published The Devil's Dictionary *(originally titled* Cynic's Word Book*), a collection of humorous and cynical definitions, in 1906.*

administration, n.   An ingenious abstraction in politics, designed to receive the kicks and cuffs due to the premier or president. A man of straw, proof against bad egging and dead catting

alderman, n.   An ingenious criminal who covers his secret thieving with a pretense of open marauding

conservative, n.   A statesman who is enamored of existing evils, as distinguished from the liberal, who wishes to replace them with others

consul, n.   In American politics, a person who having failed to secure an office from the people is given one by the administration on condition that he leave the country

deliberation, n.   The act of examining one's bread to determine which side it is buttered on

impartial, adj.   Unable to perceive any promise of personal advantage from espousing either side of a controversy or adopting either of two conflicting opinions

nepotism, n.   Appointing your grandmother to office for the good of the party

politics, n.   A strife of interests masquerading as a contest of principles; the conduct of public affairs for private advantage

politician, n.   An eel in the fundamental mud upon which the superstructure of organized society is reared. When he wriggles, he mistakes the agitation of his tail for the trembling of the edifice. As compared with the statesman, he suffers the disadvantage of being alive

quorum, n.   A sufficient number of members of a deliberative body to have their own way and their own way of having it.

In the United States Senate a quorum consists of the chairman of the Committee on Finance and a messenger from the White House; in the House of Representatives, of the Speaker and the devil

recount, n. In American politics, another throw of the dice, accorded to the player against whom they are loaded

referendum, n. A law for submission of proposed legislation to a popular vote to learn the nonsensus of public opinion

representative, n. In national politics, a member of the lower house in this world and without discernible hope of promotion in the next

senate, n. A body of elderly gentlemen charged with high duties and misdemeanors

POLITICIANS WHO WROTE POETRY

John Quincy Adams
Jimmy Carter
William Cohen (R-ME, Senate, 1979–1997; secretary of Defense 1997–)
Orrin Hatch (R-UT, Senate, 1977–)
John Hay (secretary of State, 1898–1905)
Andrew Johnson
Abraham Lincoln
Eugene McCarthy (D-MN, House, 1949–1959; Senate 1959–1971)
James Madison
Donald Manzullo (R-IL, House, 1993–)
Humphrey Marshall (Whig-KY, House, 1849–1852; American-KY, Senate, 1855–1859)
Spark Matsunaga (D-HI, House, 1963–1977; Senate, 1977–1990)
John Tyler
George Washington

SOME TITLES OF POEMS
BY JIMMY CARTER

Jimmy Carter published his first collection of poetry,
Always a Reckoning, *in 1995.*

"A Committee of Scholars Describe the Future Without Me"

"The Day No One Came to the Peanut Picker"

"Considering the Void"

"Miss Lillian Sees Leprosy for the First Time"

"A Motorcycling Sister"

"My First Try for Votes"

"Of Possum and Fatback"

"Priorities of Some Mexican Children"

"Trout"

"Why We Get Cheaper Tires from Liberia"

POLITICIANS WHO WROTE NOVELS

Officeholders tend to turn to political themes in their fiction.

Neil Abercrombie (D-HI, House, 1986–1987, 1991–) *Blood of Patriots* (with Richard Hoyt)

William S. Cohen (R-ME, House, 1973–1979; Senate, 1979–1997; secretary of Defense (1997–) *The Double Man* (with Gary Hart); *Murder in the Senate* (with Thomas B. Allen); *One-Eyed Kings*

Newt Gingrich (R-GA, House, 1979–) *1945* (with William R. Forstchen)

Gary Hart (D-CO, Senate, 1975–1987) *The Double Man* (with William Cohen)

Ed Koch (D-NY, House, 1969–1977; mayor of New York, 1978–1989) *Murder at City Hall* (with Herbert Resnicow); *Murder on Broadway* (with Wendy Corsi Staub)

Richard Lamm (D-CO, governor, 1975–1987) *1988* (with Arnold Grossman)

Barbara Mikulski (D-MD, Senate, 1987–) *A Capitol Offense* (with MaryLouise Oates); *A Capitol Venture* (with MaryLouise Oates)

BARBARA MIKULSKI'S FIVE FAVORITE MYSTERY NOVELS

The heroine of Senator Barbara Mikulski's two mystery novels is Norie Gorzack, a Polish American senator from Pennsylvania who solves crimes.

1. **Murder on the Orient Express** (1934)   Agatha Christie
2. **The Little Drummer Girl** (1983)   John Le Carré
3. **The Hunt for Red October** (1984)   Tom Clancy
4. **Postmortem** (1990)   Patricia Cornwell
5. Any Nancy Drew book

SOME BOOKS BY PRESIDENTS ON NONPRESIDENTIAL MATTERS

Thomas Jefferson   *Notes on the State of Virginia* (1785)

John Quincy Adams   *Dermot MacMorrogh or, the Conquest of Ireland: An Historical Tale of the Twelfth Century* (1832)

Grover Cleveland   *Fishing and Shooting Sketches* (1906)

William McKinley   *The Tariff in the Days of Henry Clay and Since* (1896)

Theodore Roosevelt   *African Game Trails: An Account of the African Wanderings of an American Hunter Naturalist* (1910)

William Howard Taft   *Our Chief Magistrate and His Powers* (1916)

Woodrow Wilson   *A History of the American People* (1902)

Herbert Hoover   *Principles of Mining, Valuation, Organization, and Administration: Copper, Gold, Lead, Silver, Tin, and Zinc* (1909)

Franklin Roosevelt   *The Happy Warrior: Alfred E. Smith* (1928)

John Kennedy   *Why England Slept* (1940)

Gerald Ford   *Portrait of the Assassin* (1965)

Jimmy Carter   *An Outdoor Journal* (1988)

Ronald Reagan   *Where's the Rest of Me?* (1965)

MORE BOOKS BY THEODORE ROOSEVELT

In addition to being a politician, Theodore Roosevelt was a naturalist, a rancher, a big-game hunter, and a historian.

Big Game Hunting in the Rockies and in the Great Plains (1899)

A Book-Lover's Holidays in the Open (1916)

Gouverneur Morris (1888)

Hunting Trips of a Ranchman: Sketches of Sport on the Northern Cattle Plains (1885)

The Naval Operations of the War Between Great Britain and the United States, 1812–1815 (1882)

The New Nationalism (1910)

Notes on Some of the Birds of Oyster Bay, Long Island (1879)

Oliver Cromwell (1900)

Outdoor Pastimes of an American Hunter (1905)

The Rough Riders (1899)

Thomas Hart Benton (1886)

Through the Brazilian Wilderness (1914)

The Wilderness Hunter: An Account of the Big Game of the United States and Its Chase with Horse, Hound, and Rifle

The Winning of the West (4 volumes, 1889–1896)

RICHARD RIORDAN'S TEN FAVORITE BOOKS

Mayor Richard Riordan of Los Angeles belongs to a monthly reading group.

1. **The End of the Affair** (1951)   Graham Greene
2. **Brideshead Revisited** (1945)   Evelyn Waugh
3. **Six Great Ideas** (1981)   Mortimer Adler
4. **Parkinson's Law** (1957)   C. Northcote Parkinson
5. **Deep River** (1994)   Shusako Endo
6. **The Remains of the Day** (1989)   Kazuo Ishiguro
7. **Modern Times: The World from the Twenties to the Nineties** (1991)   Paul Johnson
8. **The Blue Nile** (1962)   Alan Moorehead
9. **Uncommon Law** (1935)   A. P. Herbert
10. **In the Classroom: Dispatches from an Inner-City School That Works** (1997)   Mark Gerson

BOOKS ON WATERGATE BY THOSE INVOLVED

Charles W. Colson (special White House counsel)   *Born Again* (1976)

Samuel Dash (chief counsel to the Senate Watergate Committee)   *Chief Counsel: Inside the Ervin Committee* (1976)

John W. Dean (counsel to Richard Nixon)   *Blind Ambition: The White House Years and Lost Honor* (1976)

Maureen Dean (wife of John Dean)   *"Mo": A Woman's View of Watergate* (1975)

James Doyle (press spokesman for the special prosecutors) *Not Above the Law: The Battles of Watergate Prosecutors Cox and Jaworski* (1977)

John Ehrlichman (Nixon's chief adviser on domestic affairs) *Witness to Power* (1982)

Gerald Ford (Nixon's vice president) *A Time to Heal* (1979)

H. R. Haldeman (White House chief of staff) *The Ends of Power* (1978)

G. Gordon Liddy (counsel to the Committee to Reelect the President and leader of Watergate break-in) *Will* (1980)

James W. McCord (former CIA officer charged with bugging the Democratic National Committee's Watergate headquarters) *A Piece of Tape: The Watergate Story Fact and Fiction* (1974)

Gail Magruder (wife of Jeb Magruder) *A Gift of Love* (1976)

Jeb Stuart Magruder (deputy director of the Committee to Reelect the President) *An American Life* (1979)

Maurice Stans (finance chairman of the Committee to Reelect the President) *The Terrors of Justice* (1978)

Fred Dalton Thompson (minority counsel to the Senate Watergate Committee) *At That Point in Time: The Story of the Senate Watergate Committee* (1975)

★ ★ ★

FIVE ALL-TIME POLITICAL BEST-SELLERS

The choice of books on this list was determined by the number of weeks a book spent on the New York Times *best-seller list.*

1. Allen Drury *Advise and Consent* (1959)	102
2. Theodore H. White *The Making of the President 1960* (1961)	56
3. Jack Lait and **Lee Mortimer** *Washington Confidential* (1950)	40
4. David Halberstam *The Best and the Brightest* (1972)	36
5. Bob Woodward and **Carl Bernstein** *All the President's Men* (1974)	34

POLITICS AND PROSE'S 12 TOP POLITICAL BOOKS

Politics and Prose is a 14-year-old independent bookstore in Washington, DC, that specializes in political books. The owners chose a dozen best-selling books that have been most discussed by, and most influential among, their inside-the-Beltway customers.

1. **Robert Bellah**   *Habits of the Heart* (1985)
2. **J. Anthony Lukas**   *Common Ground* (1985)
3. **Charles Murray**   *Losing Ground* (1985)
4. **Garry Wills**   *Reagan's America: Innocents at Home* (1987)
5. **Robert Bork**   *The Tempting of America* (1989)
6. **Kevin Phillips**   *The Politics of Rich and Poor* (1990)
7. **Haynes Johnson**   *Sleepwalking Through History: America in the Reagan Years* (1991)
8. **E. J. Dionne**   *Why Americans Hate Politics* (1991)
9. **Richard Ben Cramer**   *What It Takes* (1992)
10. **William Greider**   *Who Will Tell the People* (1992)
11. **David Maraniss**   *First in His Class* (1995)
12. **Anonymous**   *Primary Colors* (1996)

WOMEN WHO DATED HENRY KISSINGER

"I go out with actresses because I'm not apt to marry one,"
Kissinger once said. Richard Nixon's national security adviser
and secretary of State dated a lot after divorcing his first wife.
A 1972 poll of Playboy bunnies proved his quip that "power
is the ultimate aphrodisiac," ranking Kissinger as the man
they would most like to go on a date with.

Candice Bergen   Actress (*Carnal Knowledge*)

Judy Brown   Star of the X-rated film *Threesome*

Lana Edmund   Hollywood stuntwoman

Samantha Eggar   Actress (*The Collector*)

Barbara Howar   Television talk-show host

Karen Lerner   Ex-wife of lyricist Alan Jay Lerner

Shirley MacLaine   Actress (*Irma La Douce, Sweet Charity*)

Marsha Metrinko   Beauty pageant contestant named Miss Love
Bundle

Jill St. John   Actress (*The Oscar*)

Diane Sawyer   TV newscaster

Marlo Thomas   Actress (*That Girl*)

Liv Ullmann   Swedish actress

IMPROBABLE ASSASSINS: Celebrities with Secret Service Security Dossiers

Muhammad Ali	**Joe Louis**
Joan Baez	**Groucho Marx**
Harry Belafonte	**Tony Randall**
Marlon Brando	**Carl Reiner**
Jane Fonda	**Jackie Robinson**
Dick Gregory	**Hunter S. Thompson**

PERFORMER POLITICIANS

Politics is a form of performance. Politicians have to be good public speakers and, like singers and actors, have to win over their audience. Several men and women have made a successful transition from the theater stage or the soundstage to the political one.

Sonny Bono Singer in the pop duo Sonny and Cher, 1964–1974; on TV and in films (*Airplane II: The Sequel; Hairspray*); mayor of Palm Springs, CA, 1988–1992; R-CA, House, 1995–1998

Jimmy Davis Singer and songwriter; wrote "You Are My Sunshine"; member of the Country Music Hall of Fame; D-LA, governor, 1944–1948, 1960–1964

Helen Gahagan Douglas Star of Broadway shows in the 1920s and one film, *She*; D-CA, House, 1945–1951; lost nasty Senate race to Richard Nixon, 1950

Clint Eastwood Actor, director, and Academy Award winner; mayor of Carmel, CA, 1987–1989

Daniel Flood Shakespearean actor; D-PA, House, 1945–1947, 1949–1953, 1955–1980

Fred Grandy Played Burl "Gopher" Smith, the assistant purser on the TV series *The Love Boat*, 1977–1986; R-IA, House, 1987–1995

Ben Jones Played Cooter on *The Dukes of Hazzard*, 1979–1985; D-GA, House, 1989–1993

Sheila James Kuehl Played Zelda Gilroy on *The Many Loves of Dobie Gillis*, 1959–1963; CA State Assembly, speaker pro tem, 1994–

George Murphy Actor, dancer, and singer on Broadway and in Hollywood, 1927–1952; president of Screen Actors Guild; winner of special Academy Award; R-CA, Senate, 1965–1971

Ronald Reagan Movie actor; president of Screen Actors Guild; R-CA, governor, 1967–1975; president, 1981–1989

Fred Thompson Movie actor (*Cape Fear, The Hunt for Red October, In the Line of Fire*); R-TN, Senate, 1995–

ACTORS WHO PLAYED
RICHARD NIXON

Joe Alaskey *Forrest Gump* (1994)

Beau Bridges *Kissinger and Nixon* (TV, 1995)

John Byner *Will: G. Gordon Liddy* (TV, 1982)

Philip Baker Hall *Secret Honor* (1984)

Anthony Hopkins *Nixon* (1995)

Rich Little *Bebe's Kids* (1992)

Buck McDancer *Hot Shots!: Part Deux* (1993)

Peter Riegert *Concealed Enemies* (TV, 1984)

Lane Smith *The Final Days* (TV, 1989)

Harry Spillman *Born Again* (1978)

Rip Torn *Blind Ambition* (TV miniseries, 1979)

★ ★ ★

ACTORS WHO PLAYED
LYNDON JOHNSON

Nesbitt Blaisdell *Kennedy* (TV miniseries, 1983)

Andrew Duggan *The Private Files of J. Edgar Hoover* (1978)

John William Galt *JFK* (1991)

Kenneth Mars *Prince Jack* (1984)

Donald Moffat *The Right Stuff* (1983)

Randy Quaid *LBJ: The Early Years* (TV, 1987)

Brian Smiar *A Woman Named Jackie* (TV miniseries, 1991)

G. D. Spradlin *Robert Kennedy and His Times* (TV miniseries, 1985)

Rip Torn *J. Edgar Hoover* (TV, 1987)

12 FAMOUS ACTORS WHO PLAYED ABRAHAM LINCOLN

1. **F. Murray Abraham** *Dreams West* (TV miniseries, 1986)
2. **John Carradine** *Of Human Hearts* (1938)
3. **Henry Fonda** *Young Mr. Lincoln* (1939)
4. **Hal Holbrook** *North and South* (TV miniseries, 1985) and *North and South II* (TV miniseries, 1986)
5. **Walter Huston** *Two Americans* (1929), *Only the Brave* (1930), and *Abraham Lincoln* (1930)
6. **Victor Kilian** *Virginia City* (1940)
7. **Kris Kristofferson** *Tad* (TV, 1995)
8. **Raymond Massey** *Abe Lincoln in Illinois* (1940) and *How the West Was Won* (1962)
9. **Gregory Peck** *The Blue and the Gray* (TV miniseries, 1982)
10. **Jason Robards** *Abe Lincoln in Illinois* (TV, 1964), *The Perfect Tribute* (TV, 1991), and *Lincoln* (TV, 1992)
11. **Sam Waterston** *Gore Vidal's Lincoln* (TV, 1988), *The Civil War* (TV miniseries, 1990), and *Abe Lincoln in Illinois* (stage, 1994)
12. **Dennis Weaver** *The Great Man's Whiskers* (TV, 1971)

MOVIES IN WHICH FRANK McGLYNN PLAYED ABRAHAM LINCOLN

Character actor Frank McGlynn (1867–1951) played Abraham Lincoln in the John Drinkwater play Abraham Lincoln *on the New York stage in 1919. Like Lincoln, McGlynn trained as a lawyer. Besides appearing in many films as the 16th president, he played Andrew Jackson onstage in* That Awful Mrs. Eaton *in 1924.*

The Life of Abraham Lincoln (1915)

Are We Civilized? (1934)

The Littlest Rebel (1935)

The Roaring West (1935)

Custer's Last Stand (1936)

The Plainsman (1936)

The Prisoner of Shark Island (1936)

Hearts in Bondage (1936)

The Man Without a Country (1937)

Wells Fargo (1937)

Western Gold (1937)

The Lone Ranger (1938)

Land of Liberty (1939)

Lincoln in the White House (1939)

The Mad Empress (1939)

Hi-Yo Silver (1940)

ACTORS WHO PLAYED MORE THAN ONE PRESIDENT

Ed Beheler   Jimmy Carter in *Sextette* (1978); fictional president in *The Last Boy Scout* (1991)

Andrew Duggan   Dwight Eisenhower in *Backstairs at the White House* (TV miniseries, 1979); Lyndon Johnson in *The Private Files of J. Edgar Hoover* (1978); fictional president in *In Like Flint* (1967)

Ed Flanders   Calvin Coolidge in *Backstairs at the White House* (TV miniseries, 1979); Harry Truman in *MacArthur the Rebel General* (1977)

Henry Fonda   Abraham Lincoln in *Young Mr. Lincoln* (1939); fictional presidents in *Fail Safe* (1964) and *Meteor* (1979)

Larry Gates   Chester Arthur in *Cattle King* (1963); Herbert Hoover in *Backstairs at the White House* (TV miniseries, 1979)

Charlton Heston   Andrew Jackson in *The President's Lady* (1953) and *The Buccaneer* (1958); Franklin Roosevelt in *F.D.R.* (TV miniseries, 1965)

Hal Holbrook   John Adams in *George Washington* (TV miniseries, 1984); Lincoln in *North and South* (TV miniseries, 1985) and *North and South II* (TV miniseries, 1986); fictional president in *The Kidnapping of the President* (1980)

Ken Howard   Thomas Jefferson in *1776* (1972); fictional president in *OP Center* (TV, 1995)

Walter Huston   Lincoln in *Two Americans* (1929), *Only the Brave* (1930), and *Abraham Lincoln* (1930); fictional presidents in *Gabriel over the White House* (1933) and *Transatlantic Tunnel* (1935)

Alexander Knox   Woodrow Wilson in *Wilson* (1944); fictional president in *Crack in the Mirror* (1960)

Fredric March   Jackson in *The Buccaneer* (1938); fictional president in *Seven Days in May* (1964)

Harry Morgan   Ulysses Grant in *How the West Was Won* (1962);

Truman in *Backstairs at the White House* (TV miniseries, 1979)

Gregory Peck   Lincoln in *The Blue and the Gray* (TV miniseries, 1982); fictional president in *Amazing Grace and Chuck* (1987)

Jason Robards   Lincoln in *Abe Lincoln in Illinois* (TV, 1964), *The Perfect Tribute* (TV, 1991), and *Lincoln* (TV, 1992); Grant in *The Legend of the Lone Ranger* (1981) and *The Civil War* (TV miniseries, 1990); Franklin Roosevelt in *F.D.R.: The Last Year* (TV, 1980)

Rip Torn   Grant in *The Blue and the Gray* (TV miniseries, 1982); LBJ in *J. Edgar Hoover* (TV, 1987); Richard Nixon in *Blind Ambition* (TV miniseries, 1979)

13 POLITICAL-ASSASSINATION MOVIES

Assassination (1986)   Secret Service man (Charles Bronson) protects the first lady (Jill Ireland).

Black Sunday (1977)   Palestinian terrorists send an explosive blimp to the Super Bowl to blow up Jimmy Carter and tens of thousands more.

The Day of the Dolphin (1973)   Terrorists train dolphins to blow up the president's yacht.

The Dead Zone (1983)   Christopher Walken, who has visions of the future, shoots at a presidential candidate (Martin Sheen). The candidate shields himself with a baby, who is killed; his career ruined, he kills himself.

In the Line of Fire (1993)   Clint Eastwood and his fellow Secret Service agents protect the president from madman John Malkovich.

JFK (1991)   Oliver Stone's dramatization of Jim Garrison's search for a conspiracy behind the assassination of John Kennedy.

The Kidnapping of the President (1980)   A third world terrorist handcuffs himself to the president (Hal Holbrook) and threatens to blow him up; William Shatner is the Secret Service man who saves him.

The Manchurian Candidate (1962)   Laurence Harvey plays Raymond Shaw, who has been brainwashed by the Communists and so will assassinate a liberal presidential candidate at the command of his mother (Angela Lansbury). Frank Sinatra tries to stop him.

The Parallax View (1974) Witnesses to the assassination of a senator atop the Seattle Space Needle die under mysterious circumstances, and journalist Warren Beatty tries to expose the assassins.

Suddenly (1954)   Frank Sinatra plays an assassin who wants to kill the president when he passes through Suddenly, CA, on a fishing trip.

The Tall Target (1951)   A policeman foils an 1861 plot to assassinate Abraham Lincoln.

Taxi Driver (1976)   Alienated veteran Travis Bickle (Robert De Niro) tries to shoot a senatorial candidate.

Winter Kills (1979)   The younger half brother of an assassinated president (Jeff Bridges) discovers that their father (John Huston) was behind the murder.

MOVIES WITH UNUSUAL PRESIDENTS

The American President (1995)   Michael Douglas plays President Andrew Shepherd, who is single and starts dating while in the White House.

Dave (1993)   Kevin Kline plays Dave, who is hired as a presidential look-alike but ends up stepping in when the real president, Bill Mitchell, goes into a coma.

Dr. Strangelove; or, How I Learned to Stop Worrying and Love the Bomb (1963)   Peter Sellers plays several characters, including President Merkin Muffley, who presides over the United States as a doomsday machine is about to destroy the world.

First Family (1980)   Bob Newhart plays President Manfred Link, the patriarch of a very dysfunctional family.

Gabriel over the White House (1933)   Walter Huston plays President Judson Hammond, who starts out crooked but becomes noble when he learns that an angel has taken an interest in his conduct.

Kisses for My President (1964)   Polly Bergen plays Leslie Harrison McCloud, the first woman elected president. Her husband, Thad (Fred MacMurray), feels emasculated as first lady. President McCloud resigns when she becomes pregnant.

The Man (TV, 1973)   After a series of deaths, James Earl Jones, president pro tempore of the Senate, becomes the first African American president.

The President's Analyst (1967)   James Coburn plays the psychiatrist who treats an unseen president until spies try to capture him and learn the president's innermost thoughts.

Whoops Apocalypse (1986)   Loretta Swit, as another first female president, tries to avert nuclear catastrophe and gets little help from her staff.

Wild in the Streets (1968)   The Constitution is amended so that 14-year-old pop singer Max Frost (Christopher Jones) can become the youngest president ever.

GEORGE STEPHANOPOULOS'S FIVE BEST POLITICAL MOVIES

George Stephanopoulos was one of Bill Clinton's closest advisers in the 1992 campaign and during his first term in office. He was one of the subjects of the political documentary The War Room. *Stephanopoulos now teaches at Columbia University and is a commentator for ABC News.*

1. *The Seduction of Joe Tynan* (1979)
2. *The Candidate* (1972)
3. *Advise and Consent* (1962)
4. *The President's Analyst* (1967)
5. *The War Room* (1993) ("Sorry, had to.")

CAMPAIGN MOVIES

The Best Man (1964)   At the national party convention, honest Henry Fonda and slick Cliff Robertson vie for the nomination as successor to the dying outgoing president, played by Lee Tracy.

Bob Roberts (1992)   A Senate campaign pits faux populist Tim Robbins against patrician incumbent Gore Vidal.

The Candidate (1972)   Robert Redford, son of a former governor (Melvyn Douglas) runs for senator against the incumbent.

The Cowboy and the Lady (1938)   Henry Kolker plays a presidential candidate whose daughter, Merle Oberon, falls in love with rodeo star Gary Cooper. Kolker sacrifices his political ambitions for his daughter's happiness.

The Dark Horse (1932)   Guy Kibbee plays the slow-witted Zachary Hicks ("Hicks from the Sticks"), who is running for governor. A strip-poker match is set up to embarrass him, but he escapes in his long johns.

Hail the Conquering Hero (1944)   Eddie Bracken plays Woodrow Truesmith, a soldier discharged for being unfit who fibs about being a World War II hero and is drafted to run for mayor. He finally confesses and is elected for his honesty.

Home Town Story (1951)   Jeffrey Lynn plays Blake Washburn, a senatorial candidate running on an anti–big business platform until his sister is buried alive in a cave and big business saves her.

If I'm Lucky (1945)   Perry Como, as crooner Allen Clark, runs as a reform candidate for governor.

It's a Joke, Son! (1947)   Una Merkel, as Magnolia Claghorn, runs for state senate. Her husband, played by Kenny Delmar, is recruited to run, too. He is supposed to split the vote so that the third candidate wins, but he ends up coming in first.

Meet John Doe (1941)   Vagrant Gary Cooper is hired to represent the American Everyman in crooked politician Edward Arnold's presidential campaign.

Morgan Stewart's Coming Home (1987)   A gubernatorial candidate brings his son (Jon Cryer) home from boarding school to help his family-values campaign, but the boy is not so compliant.

The Phantom President (1932)   George M. Cohan plays T. K. Blair, a presidential candidate, and Doc Varney plays a huckster who doubles for him in political appearances.

The Senator Was Indiscreet (1947)   William Powell plays a pompous and vapid senator running for president. His campaign platform includes instituting eight days' pay for a three-day work week and breeding cows that secrete malted milk. The campaign comes to an abrupt end when his diary is found by an aide.

Under Western Stars (1938)   Roy Rogers campaigns for Congress on a platform of water rights for dust bowl farmers.

Young Philadelphians (1959)   Paul Newman plays a young lawyer born out of wedlock who dips his toe into the political arena only to face a blackmail plot.

ON-SCREEN POLITICAL BOSSES

Edward Arnold as Paul Madvig in *The Glass Key* (1935)

Ed Begley as Boss Finley in *Sweet Bird of Youth* (1962)

David Brian as a southern political boss in *Flamingo Road* (1949)

Broderick Crawford as Willie Stark in *All the King's Men* (1949) and as Harry Brock in *Born Yesterday* (1950)

Brian Donlevy as Paul Madvig in *The Glass Key* (1942)

Albert Finney as Leo in *Miller's Crossing* (1990)

John Huston as Hollis Mulwray in *Chinatown* (1974)

Adolphe Menjou as Jim Conover in *State of the Union* (1948)

John Payne as Matt Brady in *The Boss* (1956)

George Raft as Eddie Ace in *Mr. Ace* (1946)

Akin Tamiroff as the boss in *The Great McGinty* (1940)

MOVIES ABOUT POLITICAL LOVE STORIES

Adventure in Washington (1941)   A congressional page brings together a senator (Herbert Marshall) and a radio commentator (Virginia Bruce).

Beau James (1957)   Bob Hope plays New York City mayor Jimmy Walker, whose political career ends with his extramarital affair with the actress Betty Compton (Vera Miles).

Blaze (1989)   Louisiana governor Earl Long (Paul Newman) has a romance with stripper Blaze Starr (Lolita Davidovich).

The Farmer's Daughter (1947)   Katrin Holstrom (Loretta Young) moves to Washington and is hired by Congressman Glenn Morley (Joseph Cotten) as his maid. She unseats him and then marries him.

Goodbye My Fancy (1951)   Congresswoman Agatha Reed (Joan Crawford) receives an award from the college she was kicked out of and falls in love with an administrator (Robert Young).

Key to the City (1950)   At a mayoral convention in San Francisco, Steve Fisk (Clark Gable), mayor of a northern California city, and Clarissa Standish (Loretta Young), mayor of a Maine hamlet, fall in love.

Mr. Ace (1946)   Congresswoman Margaret Wyndham Chase (Sylvia Sidney) wants to run for governor. Boss Eddie Ace (George Raft) helps her win. They fall in love, but their happiness must be postponed when he is convicted of vote fraud.

Rockabye (1932)   Constance Bennett plays Judy Carroll, a Broadway star whose career is hurt when it is revealed that she is the mistress of a corrupt politician.

Speechless (1994)   Geena Davis and Michael Keaton are opposing speechwriters in a New Mexico Senate campaign who become lovers.

State of the Union (1948)   Spencer Tracy plays businessman Grant Matthews, who is drafted by his newspaper-mogul mistress (Angela Lansbury) to run for president. To do this, he must travel with his wife (Katharine Hepburn), who presses him to stick to his principles and wins him back.

Washington Masquerade (1932)   Upstanding senator Jeff Keane (Lionel Barrymore) marries a lobbyist (Karen Morley) who convinces him to take a bribe. The payoff to the senator is discovered, and Keane dies as a result.

Washington Story (1952)   Senator Joseph T. Gresham (Van Johnson) falls in love with a reporter (Patricia Neal).

★ ★ ★

MOVIES THE ROOSEVELTS ENJOYED IN THE WHITE HOUSE

Eleanor Roosevelt wrote an article for Photoplay *in July 1938 entitled "Why We Roosevelts Are Movie Fans," in which she named some of the family's favorite films.*

Arsène Lupin Returns (1938)

The Buccaneer (1938)

The Hurricane (1937)

The Life of Emile Zola (1937)

Snow White and the Seven Dwarfs (1937)

The Adventures of Tom Sawyer (1938)

FDR was also a great fan of Mickey Mouse cartoons.

★ ★ ★

MEMORABLE RONALD REAGAN MOVIES

Ronald Reagan was introduced to both his wives and to the American public through his work in films.

Love Is on the Air (1937) In his first film, Reagan played Andy McLeod, a small-town radio announcer who uncovers racketeering. He is demoted to children's programming but manages to unravel the collusion between businessmen and politicians.

Sergeant Murphy (1938) Reagan plays Private Dennis Murphy; the sergeant is his horse. Too skittish for army service, the horse stays with Murphy after his discharge and becomes a champion show jumper.

Brother Rat (1938) Reagan plays Dan Crawford, one of three mischievous cadets at the Virginia Military Institute; he falls in love with the commandant's daughter, played by Jane Wyman. *Brother Rat* spawned a sequel and a real-life marriage between Reagan and Wyman.

Dark Victory (1939)   Reagan plays Alex Hamm, a friend of Judith Traherne (Bette Davis), who is stricken with a brain tumor; Hamm's amorous longings for her amount to nothing.

Secret Service of the Air (1939)   Reagan plays Lieutenant Brass Bancroft, a commercial pilot who joins the Secret Service and busts an illegal-alien smuggling ring—the first in a series.

Knute Rockne, All American (1940)   Reagan plays George Gipp, the legendary Notre Dame running back who died of pneumonia and inspired his team to "win just one for the Gipper."

King's Row (1942)   Reagan plays Drake McHugh, a dashing playboy with money who loses both legs to amputation after an accident, thus bringing about the line "Where's the rest of me?"

The Hasty Heart (1949)   Reagan plays Yank, an American soldier in a military hospital in Burma during World War II who befriends a terminally ill Scottish soldier.

Bedtime for Bonzo (1951)   Reagan plays Peter Boyd, a psychology professor and the son of a thief. With chimp Bonzo as his subject, Boyd tries to prove that nurture plays a greater role than nature.

The Killers (1964)   Reagan plays Browning, a criminal boss secretly married to Sheila (Angie Dickinson), who attracts race car driver Johnny North (John Cassavetes) and cons him into driving the getaway car in a heist—Reagan's last film and his least likeable character.

★   ★   ★

FORGETTABLE RONALD REAGAN MOVIES

Ronald Reagan made 53 feature films during his Hollywood career. Some were better than others.

Swing Your Lady (1937)   Reagan plays Jack Miller, a small role in an early Humphrey Bogart film about a wrestling promoter.

Cowboy from Brooklyn (1938)   Reagan plays Pat Dunn, assistant to a producer who meets fish-out-of-water Brooklyn boy Elly Jordan (Dick Powell) on a dude ranch and finds he can sing. A musical.

Girls on Probation (1938)   Reagan plays Neil Dillon, a sharp young lawyer who defends Connie (Jane Bryan) on charges that she stole a fancy gown.

Hell's Kitchen (1939)   Reagan plays Jim, a social worker at a crooked boys' home; the Dead End Kids star.

The Bad Man (1940)   Reagan plays Gil Jones, who is about to lose his ranch. Mexian outlaw Pancho Lopez (Wallace Beery) helps him out.

Tugboat Annie Sails Again (1940)   Reagan plays Eddie King, sidekick to Tugboat Annie (Marjorie Rambeau), captain of a tugboat in the Pacific Northwest.

Desperate Journey (1942)   Reagan plays Johnny Hammond, an American officer in the Royal Air Force on an implausible mission.

That Hagen Girl (1947)   Reagan plays Tom Bates, a war veteran–attorney who falls in love with teenager Mary Hagen (Shirley Temple) despite rumors that he is her father.

Night unto Night (1949)   Reagan plays John, a sensitive biochemist with chronic epilepsy who seeks solitude on the Florida coast but falls in love with his landlady (Viveca Lindfors).

Hong Kong (1951)   Reagan plays Jeff Williams, an ex-GI in Asia after World War II who is down on his luck. He meets a young Chinese orphan, and they have adventures.

Tropic Zone (1953)   Reagan plays Dan McCloud, a farmer and political exile in the fictitious land of Puerto Barrancas.

THE HOLLYWOOD TEN

In 1947, the ten men listed here were subpoenaed by the House Un-American Activities Committee (HUAC), which was investigating Communist influence in the motion picture industry. When members of the committee asked each witness about his current or past connection with communism, the witness in turn questioned the committee's authority to ask him about his own political associations and refused to answer the question. The Hollywood Ten were convicted of contempt of Congress and sentenced to a year in prison and a $1,000 fine. After they were released, they were blacklisted by the Hollywood studios.

1. **Alvah Bessie** (screenwriter; credits include *Northern Pursuit*)   Bessie did not work in Hollywood again. He wrote a book, *Inquisition in Eden* (1965), about the blacklist.
2. **Herbert J. Biberman** (producer and director; credits include *Meet Nero Wolfe*)   In the 1950s, Biberman made *Salt of the Earth*, a mining drama starring miners and financed by a miners' union. The film was shown in only one theater, in New York City (other projectionists refused to show it), but it won prizes in France and Czechoslovakia. Biberman's wife, the actress Gale Sondergaard, was also blacklisted and didn't work in Hollywood for two decades.
3. **Lester Cole** (screenwriter; credits include *Objective Burma*)   In 1948, after MGM suspended him without pay, Cole filed a suit against the studio for his suspension and blacklisting,

which he eventually lost. He wrote the screenplay for *Born Free* (1966) under the pseudonym Gerald L.C. Copley.

4. **Edward Dmytryk** (director; credits include *Murder My Sweet; Crossfire*) After his release from prison, Dmytryk went to England, where he made three films. In 1951, Dmytryk was called before HUAC again and cooperated, naming two dozen Communists, including four of the Hollywood Ten—Scott, Lawson, Cole, and Biberman. He was removed from the blacklist and continued to work in Hollywood. His wife, Madelyn, committed suicide after he decided to name names.

5. **Ring Lardner Jr.** (screenwriter; credits include *Woman of the Year*) Lardner worked without credit or under pseudonyms until the mid-1960s. He wrote the screenplay for *M*A*S*H* (1970).

6. **John Howard Lawson** (screenwriter and founding president of the Screen Writers Guild) Lawson moved to Mexico, where he wrote books about film and theater and lectured on those subjects at American universities.

7. **Albert Maltz** (screenwriter; credits include *The Naked City*) Maltz did not receive an onscreen credit again until 1970, when he was credited with writing the screenplay for *Two Mules for Sister Sara*.

8. **Samuel Ornitz** (screenwriter) Ornitz finished proofreading his final novel, *Bride of the Sabbath* (1951) while in a prison hospital. He died in 1957.

9. **Adrian Scott** (writer and producer; credits include *Murder My Sweet; Crossfire*) Scott's wife left him when he first refused to testify, and he never produced a film again.

10. **Dalton Trumbo** (screenwriter; credits include *Kitty Foyle; Thirty Seconds over Tokyo*) Trumbo moved to Mexico and wrote scripts under false names. He won the 1956 Academy Award for *The Brave One,* written under the pseudonym Robert Rich. *Spartacus* and *Exodus,* both released in 1960, were the first films to credit him after the HUAC hearings.

An 11th witness at the 1947 HUAC hearings, German playwright Bertolt Brecht, moved back to Europe after being interrogated by the committee.

TEN HOLLYWOOD ANTI-COMMUNISTS

The movie-business personalities named here were executive committee members of the Motion Picture Alliance for the Preservation of American Ideals. In September 1950, Alliance president John Wayne wrote, "We didn't make 'Hollywood' and 'Red' synonymous—the Communists, their fellow travellers and their dupes did that damaging job. We foresaw this result and tried to persuade our fellow workers of the need for cleaning our own house. We intend to continue doing so."

1. Ward Bond
2. Charles Coburn
3. Gary Cooper
4. John Ford
5. Clark Gable
6. Hedda Hopper
7. Leo McCarey
8. Adolphe Menjou
9. Robert Taylor
10. John Wayne

SOME POLITICIAN CHARACTERS ON TELEVISION

Laurie Bey   Mayor played by Marlee Matlin on *Picket Fences* (CBS, 1992–1996)

Ted Burnside   Mayor of Clinton Corners, GA, played by Richard Paul on *Carter Country* (ABC, 1977–1979)

Cooper   Mayor played by David Huddleston on *Hizzoner* (NBC, 1979)

Mickey Dolenz   Mayor played by Mickey Dolenz on *Pacific Blue* (USA, 1996–)

Michael Flaherty   Deputy mayor played by Michael J. Fox on *Spin City* (ABC, 1996–)

Gene Gatling   Governor played by James Noble on *Benson* (ABC, 1979–1986)

Otis Harper   Mayor played by George Gobel on *Harper Valley P.T.A.* (1981–1982)

Wayne Joplin   Senator played by Jack Dodson on *All's Fair* (CBS, 1976–1977)

Josephus "Joe" Kelley   Senator played by Jack Albertson on *Grandpa Goes to Washington* (NBC, 1978–1979)

Julia Mansfield President played by Patty Duke on *Hail to the Chief* (ABC, 1985)

Max White House mouse, whose voice was supplied by Neil Patrick Harris, on *Capitol Critters* (ABC, 1992)

Socrates "Sock" Miller City councilman played by Jackie Cooper on *The People's Choice* (NBC, 1955–1958)

Louise Plank Mayor played by Barbara Bosson on *Cop Rock* (ABC, 1990)

William F. Powers Senator played by John Forsythe on *The Powers That Be* (NBC, 1992–1993)

Diamond Joe Quimby Mayor voiced by Dan Castellaneta, on *The Simpsons* (Fox, 1990–)

Jack Tanner Presidential candidate played by Michael Murphy on *Tanner '88* (HBO, 1988)

Samuel Arthur Tresch President played by George C. Scott on *Mr. President* (Fox, 1987–1988)

Strobe Smithers Senator played by George Gaynes on *Hearts Afire* (CBS, 1992–1995)

Suzanne Sugarbaker Congresswoman played by Delta Burke on *Women of the House* (CBS, 1995)

POLITICIANS ON
SATURDAY NIGHT LIVE

Several major politicians have hosted or cohosted the weekly late-night comedy revue.

Ralph Nader (reformer) January 15, 1977

Ed Koch (mayor) May 14, 1983; May 12, 1984

George McGovern (senator) April 14, 1984

Jesse Jackson (former presidential candidate) October 20, 1984

George Bush (former president) October 15, 1994

Bill Bradley (senator) and **Lamar Alexander** (presidential candidate) October 28, 1995

George Pataki (governor) and **Rudolph Giuliani** (mayor) January 11, 1996

Bob Dole (senator and former presidential candidate) November 16, 1996

Rudolph Giuliani (mayor) November 22, 1997

TELEVISION KENNEDYS

*These actors played major and minor members of the
Kennedy family.*

Jason Bateman   Joseph P. Kennedy III in *Robert Kennedy and
His Times* (miniseries, 1985)

Blair Brown   Jacqueline Kennedy in *Kennedy* (miniseries,
1983)

Patrick Dempsey   John Kennedy in *JFK: Reckless Youth*
(miniseries, 1993)

William Devane   John Kennedy in *The Missiles of October*
(1974)

Shannen Doherty   Kathleen Kennedy in *Robert Kennedy and
His Times* (miniseries, 1985)

Geraldine Fitzgerald   Rose Kennedy in *Kennedy* (miniseries,
1983)

E. G. Marshall   Joseph Kennedy in *Kennedy* (miniseries, 1983)

River Phoenix   Robert F. Kennedy Jr. in *Robert Kennedy and
His Times* (miniseries, 1985)

Campbell Scott   Joseph Kennedy Jr. in *The Kennedys of Massachusetts* (miniseries, 1990)

Martin Sheen   Robert Kennedy in *The Missiles of October*
(1974) and John Kennedy in *Kennedy* (miniseries, 1983)

Jaclyn Smith   Jacqueline Kennedy in *Jacqueline Bouvier
Kennedy* (1981)

Jack Warden   Joseph Kennedy in *Robert Kennedy and His
Times* (miniseries, 1985)

POLITICIANS WHO MADE GUEST APPEARANCES ON NONPOLITICAL TELEVISION SHOWS

Willie Brown   *Suddenly Susan*

James Carville   *Boston Common*

Bob Dole   *Suddenly Susan* and *Murphy Brown*

Gerald Ford   *Dynasty*

Rudolph Giuliani   *Seinfeld* and *The Cosby Show*

Orrin Hatch   *Murphy Brown*

Jesse Jackson   *A Different World*

Ted Kennedy   *Chicago Hope*

Henry Kissinger   *Dynasty*

Ed Koch   *All My Children* and *Picket Fences*

Richard Nixon   *Laugh-In*

Tip O'Neill   *Cheers*

Ronald Reagan   *The Sonny and Cher Comedy Hour*

Alan Simpson   *Murphy Brown*

George Stephanopoulos   *Spin City*

Willie Brown, mayor of San Francisco, played poker on Sud-denly Susan with Donald Trump and actors Mr. T and Judd Nelson.

★ ★ ★

THE FIVE LONGEST-RUNNING POLITICAL TELEVISION PROGRAMS

1. *Meet the Press*   NBC, 1947–

2. *Face the Nation*   CBS, 1954–1961, 1963–

3. *Firing Line*   Syndicated, 1966–1971; PBS, 1971–

4. *Washington Week in Review*   PBS, 1967–

5. *This Week with David Brinkley*   ABC, 1981–

THE POLITICIANS WHO HAVE MADE THE MOST GUEST APPEARANCES ON *MEET THE PRESS*

Meet the Press *has been a Sunday fixture on NBC since 1947.*

Bob Dole	57	Henry "Scoop" Jackson	23
Sam Nunn	29	James A. Baker III	21
Richard Gephardt	27	Jesse Jackson	20
George Mitchell	27	George Shultz	20
Hubert Humphrey	25	Howard Baker	19
Richard Lugar	25	Tom Foley	19
Pat Moynihan	24	Al Gore	19

POLITICIANS WHO APPEARED IN ADVERTISEMENTS AFTER LEAVING OFFICE

The best-known political advertisement was losing vice presidential candidate William Miller's "Do You Know Me?" television spot for American Express. Since then many well-respected politicians have earned a little money after leaving public office by trading on their recognizable faces and trust-inspiring voices.

Howard Baker Jr. *USA Today*

Bill Bradley ESPN

Mario Cuomo Doritos

Bob Dole Air France; Visa

Sam Ervin American Express

Geraldine Ferraro Diet Pepsi

Barbara Jordan American Express

Ed Koch Health Insurance Plan; Dunkin' Donuts

William Miller American Express

Tip O'Neill Commodore Amiga computers; American Express; Quality Inns; Miller light beer; Hush Puppies; the Trump Shuttle

Dan Quayle Wavy Lay's potato chips

Ann Richards Doritos

Donna Rice (of Gary Hart fame) and Paula Jones (of Bill Clinton fame) have appeared in ads for No Excuses jeans.

TOM TOLES'S FIVE FAVORITE CLINTON CARICATURES

Toles is a cartoonist for The Buffalo News *and the* New Republic.

1. **Mine** "This is the way Clinton should be drawn. If it wasn't, I wouldn't draw him that way."
2. **Pat Oliphant's** "For his portrayal of Clinton as proprietor of White House of Ill Repute"
3. **Richard Thompson's** "So evocative, you can almost hear Clinton's accent"
4. **Tom Tomorrow's** (Dan Perkins's) "For the only Xerox-assisted Clinton caricature I'm aware of"
5. **Ted Rall's** "For the only Clinton caricature not based upon Clinton's actual features"

STRANGE BEDFELLOWS: HISTORICAL AND MISCELLANEOUS LISTS

Here we have some last-minute odds and ends, including some less-familiar American presidents, some well-known political figures who survived assassination attempts, and some proposals for amendments that didn't quite make it into the Constitution. We include some people who say they are incarcerated because of their political views, and others who avoided part or all of a prison term because of the good will of the chief executive who pardoned them. There is even a selection from the best-known political list of the last fifty years, Richard Nixon's 1971 list of his political enemies.

EARLY U.S. CAPITALS

Before Washington, DC, was established as the permanent capital city in 1800, the Continental Congress and the U.S. Congress met in these cities for time periods noted in the second column.

Philadelphia	September 5, 1774–December 12, 1776
Baltimore	December 20, 1776–March 4, 1777
Philadelphia	March 5, 1777–September 18, 1777
Lancaster, PA	September 27, 1777
York, PA	September 30, 1777–June 27, 1778
Philadelphia	July 2, 1778–June 21, 1783
Princeton, NJ	June 30, 1783–November 4, 1783
Annapolis, MD	November 26, 1783–June 3, 1784
Trenton, NJ	November 1, 1784–December 24, 1784
New York	January 11, 1785–August 12, 1790
Philadelphia	December 6, 1790–May 14, 1800

PRESIDENTS BEFORE WASHINGTON

The Continental Congress (1774–1789) was the federal legislative body of the thirteen American colonies under British rule and of the independent states under the Articles of Confederation. The presidents and their election dates are listed here.

Peyton Randolph	September 5, 1774
Henry Middleton	October 22, 1774
Peyton Randolph	May 10, 1775
John Hancock	May 24, 1775

Henry Laurens	November 1, 1777
John Jay	December 10, 1778
Samuel Huntington	September 28, 1779
Thomas McKean	July 10, 1781
John Hanson	November 5, 1781
Elias Boudinot	November 4, 1782
Thomas Mifflin	November 3, 1783
Richard Henry Lee	November 30, 1784
John Hancock	November 23, 1785
Nathaniel Gorham	June 6, 1786
Arthur St. Clair	February 2, 1787
Cyrus Griffin	January 22, 1788

★ ★ ★

OTHER AMERICAN PRESIDENTS

The republics of Texas and Hawaii were independent republics before their admission as states and the Confederacy had their own governments—including their own presidents.

David Burnet President of the Republic of Texas, 1836

Samuel Houston President of the Republic of Texas, 1836–1838, 1841–1844

Mirabeau Buonaparte Lamar President of the Republic of Texas, 1838–1841

Anson Jones President of the Republic of Texas, 1844–1846

Jefferson Davis President of the Confederate States of America, 1861–1865

Sanford Ballard Dole President of the Republic of Hawaii, 1894–1900

19TH-CENTURY POLITICAL FACTIONS

Antisnappers   Anti-Tammany Democrats in 1892

Barn Burners   New York Democrats who opposed slavery

Black and Tans   Southern Republicans who favored giving African Americans the vote

Carpetbaggers   Democrats' nickname for northerners who went south to carry out the policies of Reconstruction

Chloroformers   New York supporters of Stephen Douglas

Copperhead Democrats   Northerners who wanted an immediate armistice in the Civil War

Half-Breeds   Liberal Republicans who supported James Blaine ☞ in 1880

Hunkers   Conservative, proslavery New York Democrats

Lily-Whites   Southern Republicans who were opposed to letting African Americans vote

Mugwumps   Republicans who opposed Blaine in 1884

Scalawags   Democrats' nickname for southerners who carried out the policies of Reconstruction

Silver Grays   Proslavery Whigs

Stalwarts   Conservative Republicans who wanted to draft Grant to run again in 1880

Wide-Awakes   Lincoln supporters

Woolly Heads   Antislavery Whigs who supported William Seward

WETS AND DRYS:
Supporters and Opponents of Prohibition and Temperance

Alcohol was a major political issue from the second half of the 19th century until the repeal of Prohibition, in 1933. Today few politicians publicly support the legalization of such drugs as marijuana and cocaine, but the debate over alcohol had voluble supporters among both politicians and their constituents, on both sides.

Wets

James Cox In the 1920 presidential election, Cox lost to Harding, an avowed dry, but a big drinker.

Clarence Darrow Darrow was a big-name lawyer perhaps best remembered for his defense of John T. Scopes, who was accused of teaching evolution in the Tennessee public schools.

Pierre Samuel du Pont Du Pont was chairman of General Motors and E. I. du Pont de Nemours companies.

William Faulkner The novelist was listed as an executive committee member of an antiprohibition group. A quarter century later he did not recall any activism and guessed he was drunk when he signed the petition.

Marshall Field Department store owner

Samuel Gompers As President of the American Federation of Labor, Gompers was concerned about the jobs of brewery workers.

Fiorello La Guardia Congressman, then mayor of New York

H. L. Mencken Journalist and editor

John J. Raskob Chairman of the Democratic National Committee

Elihu Root A lawyer, senator, and Cabinet member, Root argued before the Supreme Court that the 18th Amendment was unconstitutional.

Paula Morton Sabin Head of the Women's Organization for National Prohibition Reform

Charles Scribner Book publisher

Woodrow Wilson Wilson was protemperance but antiprohibition.

Drys

James Cannon A bishop, Cannon was a member of the executive committee of the Anti-Saloon League of America and the Methodist Board of Temperance. He also led southern Democrats in their opposition to Al Smith's candidacy in the 1928 presidential election.

Josephus Daniels Daniels was secretary of the Navy during World War I.

Lucy Hayes Rutherford Hayes's wife earned the nickname Lemonade Lucy for refusing to serve alcohol in the White House.

Carry Nation Nation's activism led her to take a hatchet to the saloon at the Kansas state senate. She was often attacked, shot at, and arrested, and for a time enjoyed success on the lecture circuit.

Edgar Allan Poe A well-known alcoholic, Poe made a public appearance in support of temperance shortly before his death.

John D. Rockefeller Billionaire

John L. Sullivan The bare-knuckle boxer was a showy drinker until he became a temperance speaker.

William Ashley "Billy" Sunday "You were God's worst enemy, you were Hell's best friend," the evangelist said in a eulogy to alcoholic beverages as the 18th Amendment went into effect.

William Howard Taft As president and as chief justice of the United States Taft opposed prohibition in theory but sought to uphold the law of the land.

Andrew J. Volstead Congressman Volstead (R-MN) sponsored the law prohibiting the manufacture, sale, and transportation of any beverage with an alcohol content of 0.5%.

Wayne Bidwell Wheeler Wheeler, general counsel of the Anti-Saloon League of America, claimed to be the author of the Volstead Act.

Frances E. Willard Willard was a college professor and dean who devoted herself to the temperance movement. She was president of the National and the World's Women's Christian Temperance Union.

Jess Willard Willard, a heavyweight boxing champion, was no relation to Frances.

"SNOW WHITE AND THE SIX DWARFS"

In a speech in the Senate on June 1, 1950, Margaret Chase Smith (R-ME) condemned Senator Joseph McCarthy (R-WI) and his campaign to weed out alleged Communists in government service, and she presented a Declaration of Conscience, which was signed by six other Republican senators. McCarthy dismissed Smith and her supporters, referring to them as "Snow White and the Six Dwarfs." McCarthy's reign of terror continued until the Senate censured him in 1954.

Margaret Chase Smith (ME)

George D. Aiken (VT)	**Wayne Morse** (OR)
Robert C. Hendrickson (NJ)	**Edward J. Thye** (MN)
Irving M. Ives (NY)	**Charles W. Tobey** (NH)

★ ★ ★

THE CHICAGO SEVEN

The Chicago Seven were charged with conspiracy for their part in organizing the protests at the 1968 Democratic National Convention in Chicago. An eighth defendant, Black Panther leader Bobby Seale, was tried separately.

1. **Rennie Davis**
2. **David Dellinger**
3. **John Froines**
4. **Tom Hayden**
5. **Abbie Hoffman**
6. **Jerry Rubin**
7. **Lee Weiner**

PEOPLE ON NIXON'S ENEMIES LIST

In 1971, George Bell, an assistant to Special White House Counsel Charles Colson, made a list of opponents of Richard Nixon's administration. It was the people on this list whom Nixon lawyer John Dean was referring to when he spoke of "us[ing] the available federal machinery to screw our political enemies." The so-called Enemies List became another nail in the Watergate coffin.

Jack Anderson Newspaper columnist

Ramsey Clark Lyndon Johnson's attorney general

John Conyers Congressman (D-MI)

Maxwell Dane Retired chairman of Doyle Dane Bernbach, an advertising firm

Sidney Davidoff Former aide to John V. Lindsay, mayor of New York

Ron Dellums Congressman (D-CA)

S. Harrison Dogole President of Globe Security Systems, a Philadelphia company

Jane Fonda Actress

Harold J. Gibbons Vice president of the Teamsters union

Dick Gregory Comedian

Edwin O. Guthman National editor of the *Los Angeles Times*

Morton Halperin Brookings Institution staff member; former member of the National Security Council; former Common Cause executive

Samuel M. Lambert Former National Education Association executive

Steve McQueen Actor

Stewart R. Mott New York philanthropist

S. Sterling Munro Jr. Administrative assistant to Senator Henry Jackson (D-WA)

Joe Namath Football player

Paul Newman Actor

Arnold M. Picker ("public enemy number 1") Fund-raiser for Senator Edmund Muskie (D-ME) and an executive at United Artists

Daniel Schorr Newscaster for CBS

Howard Stein Dreyfus Corporation executive

Barbra Streisand Singer and actress

George H. Talbot President of Charlotte Liberty Mutual Insurance Company

Arthur R. Taylor President of CBS

Thomas J. Watson Jr. Chairman of the board of IBM

Leonard Woodcock President of the United Auto Workers

ORGANIZATIONS ON NIXON'S ENEMIES LIST

National Welfare Rights Organization
The New York Times
St. Louis Post-Dispatch
Socialist Workers' Party
The Washington Post

MARCHES ON WASHINGTON:
The Largest Political Demonstrations

The following are official estimates by the U.S. Parks Police. As of the fiscal year 1997, Congress no longer provided funds for counting crowds on federal land, so an organization now has to hire a private counting service if it wants to know how many people came to its rally. This policy should suit most organizations, since most complain that the National Park Service has underreported the size of their gatherings. This list does not include events like presidential inaugurations or the annual Fourth of July festivities, which regularly draw several hundred thousand celebrants.

Demonstration, Date	National Park Service Estimate	Organizer's Estimate
Vietnam Moratorium Rally (March Against Death), November 15, 1969	600,000	800,000
Vietnam "Out Now," April 24, 1971	500,000	–
NOW March for Women's Lives, April 5, 1992	500,000	700,000
Million Man March, October 16, 1995	400,000	close to 1 million
March on Washington II, August 20, 1983	300,000	–
Pro-choice rally, April 9, 1989	300,000	600,000
Lesbian and gay rights rally, April 25, 1993	300,000	–
Solidarity Day labor rally, September 19, 1981	260,000	–
Solidarity Day for Labor, August 31, 1991	250,000	–
March on Washington, August 28, 1963	250,000	–
Pro-life rally, April 28, 1990	200,000	700,000
Pro-choice II, November 12, 1989	200,000	300,000
Gay and lesbian rights rally, October 11, 1987	200,000	500,000
Washington for Jesus, April 29, 1980	200,000	–

POLITICAL ASSASSINATIONS

Abraham Lincoln (president)   April 14, 1865, in Washington, DC   Shot by John Wilkes Booth, an actor.

Thomas Haughey (AL congressman)   July 31, 1869, in Courtland, AL   Shot while giving a speech.

James Garfield (president)   July 2, 1881, in Washington, DC   Shot by Charles J. Guiteau, a mentally disturbed office seeker.

William Goebel (KY governor)   January 30, 1900, in Frankfort, KY   In a close gubernatorial race, Goebel, a reform, anti-railroad Democrat, made enemies. After Congressman William S. Taylor (R-KY) was declared the winner, the election was given to the state legislature to decide. Goebel was shot by an unknown assassin; then, on his deathbed, he was sworn in.

William McKinley (president)   September 6, 1901, in Buffalo   Shot by Leon Czolgosz, an anarchist.

Anton J. Cermak (Chicago mayor)   February 15, 1933, in Miami   Shot by Giuseppe Zangara, an anarchist, who was aiming for Franklin Roosevelt.

Huey Long (LA senator)   September 8, 1935, in Baton Rouge, LA   Shot 61 times by Dr. Carl Austin Weiss, who was slain by Long's bodyguards.

Medgar W. Evers (civil rights leader)   June 12, 1963, in Jackson, MS   Shot by Byron De La Beckwith.

John Kennedy (president)   November 22, 1963, in Dallas   Shot by Lee Harvey Oswald, who was subsequently shot by Jack Ruby. Governor John Connally (TX) was wounded in the attack on JFK.

Malcolm X (black nationalist)   February 21, 1965, in New York   Shot by members of the Nation of Islam after Malcolm had left that group in favor of mainstream Islam.

George Lincoln Rockwell (neo-Nazi leader)   August 25, 1967, in Arlington, VA   Shot by John Patsilos (aka John Patler).

Martin Luther King Jr. (civil rights leader)   April 4, 1968, in Memphis   Shot with a 30.06 rifle by James Earl Ray.

Robert Kennedy (NY senator)   June 5, 1968, in Los Angeles   Shot by Sirhan Sirhan.

George Moscone (San Francisco mayor) and **Harvey Milk** (city supervisor)   November 27, 1978, in San Francisco   Shot by former city supervisor Dan White.

Leo J. Ryan (CA congressman)   November 18, 1978, in Port Kaituma, Guyana   Shot by followers of the Reverend Jim Jones during a fact-finding tour. Three journalists were also killed.

Adolph Dubs (ambassador)   February 14, 1979, in Kabul, Afghanistan   Shot by Muslim extremists.

ATTEMPTED POLITICAL ASSASSINATIONS

Andrew Jackson (president)   January 30, 1835, in Washington DC   Unharmed. The ammunition fell out of Richard Lawrence's guns before Lawrence had a chance to pull the trigger.

William Seward (Abraham Lincoln's secretary of State)   April 13, 1865   Attacked by Lewis Powell (or Paine), a coconspirator of John Wilkes Booth.

William J. Gaynor (New York mayor)   August 9, 1910, aboard the *Kaiser Wilhelm* en route to Europe   Shot by James Gallagher. Gaynor blamed William Randolph Hearst for the assassination attempt.

Theodore Roosevelt (former president and presidential candidate)   October 14, 1912, in Milwaukee   Shot by John Schrank.

Franklin Roosevelt (president-elect)   February 15, 1933, in Miami   Shot at by Joseph Zangara, an anarchist, who killed Anton Cermak instead.

John Bricker (OH senator)   July 12, 1947, in Washington, DC   Shot at just outside the Senate chamber.

Hubert Humphrey (Minneapolis mayor)   February 6, 1947, in Minneapolis   Shot at outside his home.

Harry Truman (president)   November 1, 1950, in Washington, DC   Unharmed when Puerto Rican nationalists Griselio Torresola and Oscar Collazo attempted to storm Blair House, where the president was staying while the White House was under repair; Blair House guard Leslie Coffelt was killed in the mêlée, as was Torresela.

Lindsay Almond (VA governor)   April 10, 1959, in Richmond, VA   Shot at near state capitol after receiving threats because of his position on desegregating public schools.

George Wallace (AL governor and presidential candidate)   May 15, 1972, in Laurel, MD   Shot, and permanently crippled, by Arthur Bremer.

Richard Nixon (president)   February 22, 1974   Samuel Byck planned to hijack a plane, shoot the pilot, and fly it into the White House, thereby killing Nixon, himself, and everyone onboard the aircraft. As a first step, he killed a Delta Airlines security guard and a copilot; after being shot at by law-enforcement agents, he shot himself.

Gerald Ford (president)   (1) September 5, 1975, in Sacramento   Unharmed when Secret Service agents grabbed a gun from Lynette "Squeaky" Fromme, a follower of Charles Manson; (2) September 22, 1975, in San Francisco   Unharmed when Sara Jane Moore fired a revolver in his direction.

Alexander M. Haig Jr. (Supreme Allied Commander in Europe)   June 25, 1979, in Brussels   Members of West Germany's Red Army Faction detonated 100 pounds of explosives, which damaged the armored car Haig was riding in but left Haig unhurt.

Vernon E. Jordan Jr. (civil rights leader)   May 29, 1980, in Fort Wayne, IN   Shot and wounded by Joseph Paul Franklin, a white supremacist. Jordan recovered from his injuries.

Ronald Reagan (president)   March 30, 1981, in Washington, DC   Wounded by John W. Hinckley Jr., who was hoping the assassination would impress the actress Jodie Foster. Presidential press secretary James Brady was permanently crippled in the attack; Secret Service agent Timothy J. McCarthy was wounded.

Bill Clinton (president)   October 29, 1994, in Washington, DC   Unharmed when Francisco Duran, on the sidewalk outside the White House, shot at a tourist who resembled the president.

FAILED CONSTITUTIONAL AMENDMENTS

Thousands of attempts to change the Constitution have been made, but only 27 of these have become amendments. Some of the unsuccessful ones led to changes at the statutory level, while others have never been implemented in any form.

Abortion restrictions   Since the 1970s, amendments to declare that life begins at conception and to permit states to restrict and prohibit abortion have been proposed. None has been approved by Congress.

Amendment-ratification reform   The Wadsworth-Garrett amendment, proposed in 1921 in reaction to women's suffrage and Prohibition, would have made it more difficult to pass new amendments. It proposed that states be allowed to hold referenda on ratification and thus change their vote and that a waiting period be instituted so that new state legislators could be elected before any votes were taken on the ratification of an amendment. The amendment never made it out of its Senate committee.

Anti-Antislavery measures   In 1861, Lincoln endorsed the Corwin amendment, which held that the Constitution could not be amended to abolish slavery. Three states approved the amendment after it was ratified by Congress, but it was forgotten once the Civil War was under way.

Antipolygamy measures   In 1898, shortly after Utah became a state, 26 other states requested that a federal convention be held to discuss an amendment to ban polygamy and bar polygamists from serving in Congress.

Apportionment reform in state legislatures   In 1965, Senator Everett Dirksen (R-IL) proposed that each state be permitted to base apportionment in one house of its legislature on factors other than population. Some states voiced support, but the proposed amendment never passed the Senate.

Budget reform   Proposals to balance the federal budget were first made in the 1950s. Recently the House has approved a balance-budget amendment, but the measure has fallen short in the Senate.

Child labor reform   An amendment limiting child labor, passed by Congress in 1924, was eventually ratified by 28 states.

Electoral college reform   Since 1789, more than 500 proposals have been made to reform or replace the electoral college. These have included direct presidential elections, a winner-take-all system in each congressional district, and the assignment of electoral votes according to the proportion of the vote won by each candidate.

Equal rights   The first proposed amendment guaranteeing equal rights for men and women surfaced in 1923. In the 1970s, Congress sent an equal rights amendment to the states; it fell three states short of ratification when a built-in time limit ran out in 1982.

Establishment of state religion   Between 1870 and 1910, there were no fewer than ten proposals for an amendment recognizing the primacy of Christianity.

Federal regulation of marriage and divorce   In the late 19th century and early 20th century, several proposed amendments called for marriage to be made a federal, rather than a state, matter. These proposals never had much support.

Flag-burning prohibition   In the 1980s, an amendment was put forth calling for the protection of the U.S. flag. It passed the House in 1995 but did not pass the Senate.

Foreign office prohibition   In 1810, an amendment extending to all U.S. citizens the Article 1, Section 9, injunction against "holding any Office of Profit or Trust" or accepting a foreign title or office without the consent of Congress fell one state short of ratification.

Foreign policy reform   In 1952, Senator John Bricker (R-IL) proposed an amendment limiting the foreign policy powers of the president by making treaties subject to judicial scrutiny and requiring legislative approval of executive agreements. The Bricker amendment failed in the Senate by one vote.

Income tax reform   In 1938, the American Taxpayer Association and 28 states requested that a federal convention be held to discuss an amendment that would cap federal taxes at 25%. Congress never considered the proposal.

School-prayer measures   A proposed amendment to allow prayer in public schools first came to the House floor in 1971, but no such measure has been approved by either house.

Shifting-terms measures   In 1886, the Senate passed an amendment that called for the commencement of presidential and congressional terms to be shifted to the end of April, around the time of the anniversary of George Washington's first inauguration. The proposal didn't pass the House, and in 1933 the 20th amendment moved the commencement of terms from March to January.

Term-limit measures   A 1995 congressional term-limit proposal did not win a two-thirds majority in either house.

War referenda   Amendments proposed before World War II and between the two world wars would have required a referendum to declare war unless U.S. territory was under attack. None was ever approved by Congress.

12 POLITICAL PRISONERS IN THE UNITED STATES

The Interfaith Prisoners of Conscience Project of the National Council of Churches keeps track of people it considers to be political prisoners in the United States. The project's roster includes largely left-wing political activists, many of them people of color. (The National Council of Churches does not consider right-wing political prisoners to be prisoners of conscience.) Many have been treated especially harshly in prison.

1. **Mumia Abu-Jamal** In December 1981, the journalist and former Black Panther was shot on a Philadelphia street, as was a policeman. The policeman died; Abu-Jamal was convicted of the killing. He was sentenced to death and is seeking a new trial.

2. **Sundiata Acoli** In 1973, Acoli, a computer analyst and Black Panther subject to FBI suveillance, was driving on the New Jersey Turnpike with two other men in the car when they were stopped by state troopers. One of Acoli's companions was killed, and so was one of the troopers. Acoli, convicted of the trooper's murder, received a sentence of life plus 30 years.

3. **Silvia Baraldini** An Italian citizen who became active in Students for a Democratic Society (SDS) and the black nationalist movement while at the University of Wisconsin, Baraldini refused to testify before a grand jury investigating Puerto Rican independence activists. She was arrested in 1982, convicted of conspiracy and criminal contempt, and sentenced to 43 years in prison.

4. **Marilyn Buck** Buck was an SDS organizer who became involved in various anti-imperialist movements. In 1973, she was arrested for gunrunning and sentenced to ten years in prison. She was granted a furlough in 1977, did not return to prison, was involved in the 1981 Brink's-truck robbery attempt, and was captured in 1985. She was convicted on charges related to the robbery and the prison break and was sentenced to 50 years.

5. **Mark Cook** In the mid-1970s, after serving time for a string of robberies, Cook founded a labor-rights group in the Seattle area. Local police believed Cook was linked to the George Jackson Brigade, a violent local revolutionary group. After the brigade pulled a bank heist in 1976, three people were arrested, one of whom escaped custody with the help of brigade members. Cook was arrested two days after the heist and charged with federal and state crimes related to the bank robbery and escape. He received a 30-year sentence.

6. **Ricardo Jimenez** Jimenez was a student at the Illinois Institute of Technology and a member of the FALN (the Armed Forces of National Liberation, a Puerto Rican separatist group) when he was convicted of seditious conspiracy in connection with a series of bombings and attempted bombings of Chicago public buildings. He was sentenced to 98 years in prison.

7. **Carl Kabat** A Catholic priest and antinuclear activist, Kabat was involved in a disarmament protest and convicted of a parole violation related to a previous protest-related conviction. He was sentenced to three and a half years and is due to be released in August 1998.

8. **Sekou Odinga** A Black Muslim and Black Panther, Odinga was living underground in 1969 when his home was surrounded by police. He managed to escape and lived in Algeria. In October 1981, he was arrested and convicted of six counts of attempted murder and two counts under the Racketeer Influenced and Corrupt Organizations (RICO) Act. He received 25 years to life in federal prison.

9. **Leonard Peltier** A Native American involved in the activist American Indian Movement (AIM), Peltier was convicted of the 1975 deaths of two FBI special agents in a shootout on the Pine Ridge Reservation in South Dakota and given two life sentences. He continued his activism in the notorious Marion, IL, prison by going on a hunger strike for religious rights.

10. **Alberto Rodriguez** A Puerto Rican nationalist in Chicago,

Rodriguez was arrested in 1983 and, as a member of the FALN, was charged with seditious conspiracy against the U.S. government. He was sentenced to 35 years in prison and 5 years' probation.

11. **Juan Segarra Palmer** Segarra, a Harvard graduate and Puerto Rican nationalist, was arrested for his participation in a $7.1-million Wells Fargo heist in Hartford, CT, and sentenced to 55 years in prison.

12. **Mutulu Shakur** Shakur, an acupuncturist, was a member of the provisional government of the Republic of New Afrika, an organization devoted to establishing a black nation in the southern United States. In 1981, he was convicted of theft, helping prisoners to escape, conspiracy against the government, and other crimes and was sentenced to 60 years in prison.

PRESIDENTIAL PARDONS

Article 2, Section 2, of the Constitution says that the president "shall have Power to Grant Reprieves and Pardons for Offences against the United States, except in Cases of Impeachment." Presidents have traditionally pardoned war deserters shortly after the wars, and Ulysses Grant pardoned tens of thousands of Confederate soldiers.

George Burdick Woodrow Wilson pardoned Burdick, a journalist, in order to remove his 5th Amendment protections and force him to testify and reveal his sources. Burdick refused the pardon, and the Supreme Court upheld his right to do so.

Eugene Debs Debs was pardoned in 1921 by Warren Harding (☞), thereby cutting short a ten-year sentence for sedition that was the result of an antiwar speech Debs had given in 1918. (Prison had not stopped the Socialist from running for president in 1920.)

Armand Hammer   George Bush pardoned Hammer for making illegal contributions to Richard Nixon's 1972 presidential campaign. Hammer, who never served time in prison, lobbied hard for the pardon because he thought the conviction was keeping him from winning the Nobel Peace Prize.

Samuel Mudd   Mudd, pardoned by Ulysses Grant (☞) in 1869, had treated the broken ankle of Lincoln assassin John Wilkes Booth when Booth was on the lam.

Richard Nixon   Gerald Ford pardoned Nixon for Watergate-related crimes a month after becoming president.

Oliver North   Bush pardoned North for crimes related to the Iran-contra affair. The president also pardoned Caspar W. Weinberger, Robert Mc-Farlane, Elliott Abrams, and other participants in the Iran-contra affair, hailing them as "patriots all."

Vuco Perovich   William Howard Taft (☞) commuted Perovich's death sentence to life in prison. Twenty years later, Perovich decided he wanted to be put to death. The Supreme Court did not allow him to refuse the pardon.

George Steinbrenner   On his last day in office, Ronald Reagan pardoned shipping magnate and New York Yankees owner Steinbrenner for making illegal contributions to Nixon's 1972 presidential campaign.

Iva Toquri D'Aquino   Toquri D'Aquino was pardoned by Ford for treason charges connected with her World War II radio broadcasts as Tokyo Rose.

15 FLAG NO-NOS

This list was compiled by Colonel James A. Moss in a 1933 book devoted to the flag. Moss did not rule out flag burning. He wrote, "When a Flag is in such condition that it is no longer a fitting emblem to display, it should be destroyed as a whole, privately, preferably by burning or by some other method lacking in any suggestion of disrespect." Then again, he probably would not have approved of the Yippies.

1. Do not permit disrespect to be shown to the Flag of the United States.

2. Do not dip the Flag of the United States to any person or anything. The regimental color, State flag, organization or institutional flag will render this honor.

3. Do not display the Flag with the blue field down except as a signal of distress.

4. Do not place any other flag or pennant above, or, if on the same level, to the right of the Flag of the United States.

5. Do not let the Flag touch the ground or the floor, or trail in the water.

6. Do not place any object or emblem of any kind on or above the Flag of the United States.

7. Do not use the Flag as drapery in any form whatsoever. Use bunting of blue, white, and red.

8. Do not fasten the Flag in such manner as will permit it to be easily torn.

9. Do not drape the Flag over the hood, top, sides or back of a vehicle, or of a railway train or boat.

10. Do not use the Flag as a covering for a ceiling.

11. Do not carry the Flag flat or horizontally, but always aloft and free.

12. Do not use the Flag as a portion of a costume or of an athletic uniform. Do not embroider it upon cushions or handkerchiefs nor print it on paper napkins or boxes.

13. Do not put lettering of any kind upon the Flag. (Note. In nearly all the States the placing of letters on the Flag is prohibited by law.)

14. Do not use the Flag in any form of advertising, nor fasten an advertising sign to a pole from which the flag is flown. (In nearly all the States the use of the Flag for advertising purposes is prohibited by law.)

15. Do not display, use or store the Flag in such a manner as will permit it to be easily soiled or destroyed.

11 ELECTED OFFICIALS WHO WERE MEMBERS OF THE KU KLUX KLAN

There have been many local politicians who were members of the Ku Klux Klan, an anti-Catholic, anti-Semitic, white supremacist secret society founded after the Civil War and revived in the early 20th century. The Klan was partly responsible for the defeat of Alfred Smith, the first Catholic presidential candidate, in 1928. Some Klansmen and former Klansmen have risen to the highest levels of politics despite (or because of) their odious beliefs.

1. **Theodore Gilmore Bilbo** (D-MS, governor, 1916–1920, 1928–1932; senator, 1935–1947) Bilbo was reelected to the Senate in 1946 despite his admission of KKK membership.

2. **Robert C. Byrd** (D-WV, senator, 1959–) Byrd admits that he was a Klan member from 1942 to 1943.

3. **David Bibb Graves** (D-AL, governor, 1927–1931, 1935–1939) Graves was an unabashed Klansman.

4. **Warren Harding** (President, 1921–1923) Harding was reportedly inducted into the Klan early in his presidency, in a ceremony in the Green Room of the White House.

5. **Thomas Heflin** (D-AL, senator, 1920–1931) A proud segregationist, Heflin was an uncle of former senator Howell Heflin.

6. **Earle B. Mayfield** (D-TX, senator, 1923–1929) Mayfield was the first active Klansman elected to the upper house of Congress.

7. **Ben Paulen** (R-KS, governor, 1925–1929) During the gubernatorial campaign, Paulen claimed he was not a Klan member "at this time."

8. **John Rarick** (D-LA, congressman, 1967–1975) Once served as the Exalted Cyclops of his local Klan chapter in St. Francisville, Louisiana.

9. **Louis Rawls** (mayor of Bogalusa, Louisiana, 1970–1978) Rawls accepted hood and honorary membership in a 1976 ribbon-cutting ceremony at the opening of the Bogalusa Klan headquarters.

10. **Friend W. Richardson** (R-CA, governor, 1923–1927) Richardson evaded inquiries about Klan membership and won with Klan support. He appointed the Kludd (Klan chaplain) of Sacramento as chaplain of the state senate.

11. **Fuller Warren** (D-FL, governor, 1949–1953) Active in the Klan before World War II, Warren later spoke out against it.

Hugo Black, a Supreme Court justice appointed by Franklin Roosevelt in 1937, was a member of the KKK from 1923 to 1925. He broke with the organization while working on the presidential campaign of Al Smith, a Catholic.

AL FRANKEN'S
FIVE FUNNIEST POLITICIANS

Al Franken is a political humorist and author of
Rush Limbaugh Is a Big Fat Idiot.

1. **Chuck Grassley** (R-IA, Senate)
2. **Paul Sarbanes** (D-MD, Senate)
3. **William Roth** (R-DE, Senate)
4. **Rick Santorum** (R-PA, Senate)
5. **David McIntosh** (R-IN, House)

THOMAS JEFFERSON'S DOZEN CANONS OF CONDUCT IN LIFE

Jefferson sent this list in 1811 to his granddaughter Cornelia J. Randolph.

1. Never put off to tomorrow what you can do to-day.
2. Never trouble another with what you can do yourself.
3. Never spend your money before you have it.
4. Never buy a thing you do not want because it is cheap; it will be dear to you.
5. Take care of your cents; dollars will take care of themselves.
6. Pride costs us more than hunger, thirst, and cold.
7. We never repent of having eat too little.
8. Nothing is troublesome that one does willingly.
9. How much pain have cost us the evils which have never happened!
10. Take things always by their smooth handle.
11. Think as you please & so let others, & you will have no disputes.
12. When angry, count 10 before you speak; if very angry, 100.

POLITICIANS WHO WERE BORN ON JULY 4

Ethan Allen Brown (b. 1776) No party–OH, governor, 1818–1822; senator, 1822–1825

Green Smith (b. 1826) Union-KY, congressman, 1863–1866; Montana Territory, governor, 1866–1869; Prohibition Party presidential candidate, 1876

Calvin Coolidge ❦ (b. 1872) Vice president, 1921–1923; president, 1923–1929

George Murphy (b. 1902) R-CA, senator, 1965–1971

Sam Farr (b. 1941) D-CA, congressman, 1993–

POLITICIANS WHO DIED ON JULY 4

John Adams (d. 1826)   President, 1797–1801

Thomas Jefferson (d. 1826)   President, 1801–1809

James Monroe (d. 1831)   President, 1817–1825

William Marcy (d. 1857)   Secretary of War, 1845–1849; secretary of State, 1853–1857; senator (D-NY), 1831–1833; governor (D-NY), 1833–1839

Hannibal Hamlin (d. 1891)   Congressman (D-ME), 1843–1847; senator (D-ME), 1848–1857; governor (R-ME), 1857; senator (R-ME), 1857–1861; vice president, 1861–1865

Melville Weston Fuller (d. 1910)   Supreme Court chief justice, 1888–1910

ELDERLY STATESMEN: Politicians Who Refused to Die

Adelbert Ames (1835–1933)   Union general in the Civil War; R-MS, governor, 1868–1870, 1874–1876; senator, 1870–1874. Lived to be 98

Ezra Taft Benson (1899–1994)   Secretary of Agriculture, 1953–1961. Lived to be 95

Charles Carroll (1737–1832)   Signer of the Declaration of Independence; delegate to the Continental Congress; no party–MD, senator, 1789–1792. Lived to be 95

Rebecca Ann Felton (1835–1930)   D-GA, first female senator, 1922. Lived to be 95

Hamilton Fish (1888–1991)   D-NY, congressman, 1920–1945. Lived to be 103

John Garner (1868–1967)   D-TX, congressman, 1903–1933 and Speaker of the House, 1931–1933; vice president, 1933–1941. Lived to be 99

William Averell Harriman (1891–1986) Secretary of Commerce, 1947–1948; D-NY, governor, 1955–1959. Lived to be 95

Carl Hayden (1877–1972) D-AZ, congressman, 1912–1927; senator, 1927–1969. Lived to be 95

Alfred Landon (1887–1987) R-KS, governor, 1933–1937; Republican presidential candidate, 1936. Lived to be 100

Levi Parsons Morton (1824–1920) R-NY, congressman, 1879–1881; vice president, 1889–1893; governor, 1895–1897. Lived to be 96

Milward Lee Simpson (1897–1993) R-WY, governor, 1955–1959; senator, 1962–1967; father of former senator Alan Simpson. Lived to be 96

Nellie Tayloe Ross (1876–1977) D-WY, governor, 1925–1927; first female governor. Lived to be 101

Margaret Chase Smith (1897–1995) R-ME, congresswoman, 1940–1949; senator, 1949–1973. Lived to be 98

Carl Vinson (1883–1981) D-GA, congressman, 1914–1965. Lived to be 98

POLITICIANS WHO DIED IN ACTION

John Quincy Adams (president, 1825–1829; F-MA, congressman, 1831–1848) Suffered a stroke while making a speech in the House, February 21, 1848; died two days later in the Speaker's office at the Capitol

Elisha Hunt Allen (Whig-ME, congressman, 1841–1843) Died at a White House reception, January 1, 1883

Chet Blaylock (D-MT, state senator, 1975–1994) While running for governor, suffered a heart attack on his way to a debate and died, October 23, 1996

Thomas Tyler Bouldin (D-VA, congressman, 1829–1833, 1833–1834) Died while making a speech on the House floor, February 11, 1834

William John Browning (R-NJ, congressman, 1911–1920)   Died in the Capitol, March 24, 1920

John Caldwell (Kentucky state senator)   Died while presiding over the Kentucky state senate, 1804.

Morris Edelstein (D-NY, congressman, 1940–1941)   After giving a speech on the House floor, died in the House cloakroom, June 4, 1941

Edward Eslick (D-TN, congressman, 1925–1932)   Died while making a speech on the House floor, June 14, 1932

Augustus Hill Garland (D-AZ, governor, 1874–1877; senator, 1877–1885; attorney general, 1885–1889)   Died while arguing a case before the Supreme Court, January 26, 1899

Earl Long (D-LA, governor, 1939–1940, 1948–1952, 1956–1960)   Suffered a heart attack while campaigning for a seat in Congress but would not go to a hospital until after the election; died on September 5, 1960

Russell Vernon Mack (R-WA, congressman, 1947–1960)   Died on the House floor, March 28, 1960

Martin Madden (R-IL, congressman, 1905–1928)   Died in the Capitol, in the meeting room of the House Appropriations Committee, April 27, 1928

Henry Wilson (R-MA, senator, 1855–1873; vice president, 1873–1875)   Suffered a stroke while presiding over the Senate and died in the Capitol twelve days later, November 22, 1875

Many people believe former vice president Nelson Rockefeller also died in action, though of another sort. He was "working late" with a 25-year-old female aide in his midtown Manhattan town house on January 26, 1979, when he died suddenly. The young woman called a friend rather than an ambulance, and the exact cause of death was never determined.

POLITICIANS WHO DIED IN PLANE CRASHES

George Joseph Bates (R-MA, congressman, 1937–1949) Died November 1, 1949, at National Airport near Washington, DC

William Becker (mayor of St. Louis, Missouri, 1941–1943) Died August 1, 1943, in an army glider

Nicholas Begich (D-AK, congressman, 1971–1972) Disappeared October 16, 1972, between Anchorage and Juneau, AK, and presumed dead

Hale Boggs Sr. (D-LA, congressman, 1941–1943, 1947–1972) Disappeared October 16, 1972, between Anchorage and Juneau, AK, and presumed dead

Ron Brown (secretary of Commerce, 1993–1996) Died April 3, 1996, in Croatia

William Byron (D-MD, congressman, 1939–1941) Died February 27, 1941, in Jonesboro, GA

Robert L. Coffey Jr. (D-PA, congressman, 1949) Died April 20, 1949, in Albuquerque, NM

George Collins (D-IL, congressman, 1970–1972) Died December 8, 1972, at Chicago Midway Airport

John William Ditter (R-PA, congressman, 1933–1943) Died September 21, 1943, near Columbia, PA

H. John Heinz III (R-PA, congressman, 1971–77; senator, 1977–1991) Died April 4, 1991, in a small plane near Philadelphia

William Kirk Kaynor (R-MA, congressman, 1929) Died December 20, 1929, near Washington, DC

Jerry Litton (D-MO, congressman, 1973–1976) Died August 3, 1976, in Chillicothe, MO

Larry McDonald (D-GA, congressman, 1975–1983) Died September 5, 1983, on Korean Airlines Flight 007, shot down by the Soviets near Sakhalin Island

Donald Nutter (R-MT, governor, 1961–1962) Died January 25, 1962, over Montana in a snowstorm

Thaddeus C. Sweet (R-NY, congressman, 1923–1928) Died May 1, 1928, at Whitney Point, NY

THE CLINTON BODY COUNT:
People Who Conspiracy Theorists Believe Were Killed to Preserve the President's Image and Power

To those who distrust the president, the "mysterious" death of Vincent Foster is just the tip of the iceberg. The following people, many of whom had tenuous connections to the president, died in circumstances that the preternaturally suspicious find suspicious, including car crashes, plane crashes, skiing accidents, and "apparent" suicides. The conspiracy theorists' list of Clinton victims also includes more than a dozen federal agents and military officers who had been charged with protecting the president.

James Bunch Claimed to have kept records on prominent Texans and Arkansans who frequented prostitutes. Apparent suicide by gunshot, date unconfirmed.

Suzanne Coleman Alleged to have had an affair with Clinton while he was attorney general of Arkansas and was pregnant at the time of her death. Apparent suicide by gunshot, February 15, 1977.

Steve Dickson Counsel to Stanley Heard (see below). Both died in plane crash, September 10, 1993.

Kathy Ferguson Ex-wife of the Arkansas state trooper who is a codefendant in Paula Jones's lawsuit against Clinton. Apparent suicide by gunshot, May 1994.

Vincent Foster White House counsel. Apparent suicide by gunshot, July 21, 1993.

Herschel Friday Attorney and Clinton fund-raiser. Plane explosion, March 1, 1994.

Paula Grober Clinton's longtime sign-language interpreter. Automobile accident, December 9, 1992.

Stanley Heard Chairman of the National Chiropractic Health Care Advisory Committee and doctor to members of the Clinton family. Plane crash, September 10, 1993.

Mary Mahoney Young White House intern. Shot in possible robbery attempt at Starbucks, July 6, 1997.

Luther "Jerry" Parks Head of Clinton's gubernatorial security team in Little Rock. Shot to death while driving home, September 26, 1993.

C. Victor Raiser II National finance cochairman of Clinton for President. Private plane crash, July 30, 1992.

Montgomery Raiser Son of C. Victor Raiser. Private plane crash, July 30, 1992.

Ronald Rogers Arkansas dentist who died in a plane crash on his way to meet a British tabloid reporter, March 3, 1994.

Bill Shelton Arkansas state trooper and fiancé of Kathy Ferguson (see above). Apparent suicide by gunshot, June 1994.

Paul Tully Political director of the Democratic National Committee. Found dead in hotel room in Little Rock, cause unknown, September 24, 1992.

Jon Walker Investigator for the Resolution Trust Corporation. Fell or jumped from an apartment balcony, August 15, 1993.

Paul Wilcher Washington, DC, attorney investigating corruption. Found dead on toilet, no cause listed, June 22, 1993.

Jim Wilhite vice chairman of Arkla, Incorporated, Mack McClarty's former firm. Skiing accident, December 21, 1992.

Ed Willey Attorney and Clinton fund-raiser. Apparent suicide by gunshot, November 30, 1993.

John Wilson Former Washington, DC, city council member. Apparent suicide by hanging, May 18, 1993.

UNLIKELY CANDIDATES

Pediatricians, revolutionaries, con men, and journalists have all run for office. A few of them have even won.

Jello Biafra (lead singer of the Dead Kennedys) Ran for mayor of San Francisco, 1979

Jimmy Breslin (journalist) Ran for New York city council president, 1969

Heywood Broun (journalist) Ran for Congress on the Socialist ticket, 1930

William F. Buckley Jr. (editor and author)   Ran for mayor of New York, 1965

Henry Ford (industrialist)   Ran for the Senate from Michigan on the Democratic ticket, 1918

Dick Gregory (comedian)   Ran for mayor of Chicago, 1966; ran for president on the New Party ticket, 1968

Jack London (author)   Ran for mayor of Oakland, CA, 1901, 1905

Norman Mailer (author)   Ran for mayor of New York, 1969

Huey Newton (cofounder of the Black Panthers)   Ran for governor of California

Pat Paulsen (comedian)   Ran for president in every election 1968–1996 on the Straight Talking American Government (STAG) Party ticket

Upton Sinclair (author)   Ran for Congress from New Jersey, 1906; ran for governor of California, 1934

Benjamin Spock (physician and author)   Ran for president on the People's Party ticket, 1972

Howard Stern (radio talk-show host)   Planned to run for governor of New York in 1994 on the Libertarian Party ticket but dropped out after a judge ruled that he must file a financial-disclosure statement

Gore Vidal (author)   Ran for Congress from California, 1960; ran for the Senate from California, 1982

Wavy Gravy (aka Hugh Romney; hippie communitarian)   His Hog Farm ran a pig for president, 1968; has sponsored the Nobody for President campaign in every election since 1972; ran for Berkeley, CA, city council, 1990

Showman P. T. Barnum served in the Connecticut state legislature 1865–1869 and was elected mayor of Bridgeport in 1875.

PRESIDENTIAL NAMESAKES

Many politicians have been named after presidents, but not everyone bearing a presidential name goes into politics.

Grover Cleveland Alexander   Major league pitcher

James Buchanan "Diamond Jim" Brady
Financier and bon vivant

Chester Arthur Burnett (aka Howlin' Wolf) Blues musician

George Washington Carver Botanist

William Harrison "Jack" Dempsey Heavyweight boxer

Woodrow Wilson "Woody" Guthrie Folksinger and songwriter

Ulysses S. Grant "Lil" Stoner Major league pitcher

19TH-CENTURY JEWISH POLITICIANS

Some states once had laws against Jews holding political office; the last of these was repealed by New Hampshire in 1876. Still, dozens of Jewish Americans held elective and appointive offices, particularly in the South. Some notable examples are listed below.

Judah Philip Benjamin (state legislature, LA, 1842–1852; Whig-LA, Senate, 1853–1861; attorney general of the Confederacy, 1861; secretary of War for the Confederacy, 1861–1862; secretary of State for the Confederacy, 1862–1865) Said to be the "brains behind the Confederacy," Benjamin married a Catholic and was not a practicing Jew. He became extremely unpopular because of his plan to induct slaves into the Confederate army and arm them, and so he left the country, ending up in Great Britain, where he achieved success as a queen's counsel.

David Emanuel (no party–GA, governor, 1801) Emanuel, who is believed to have come from a Jewish family, was a practicing Presbyterian. He lived in Burke County and in a neighboring Georgia county that was later named for him.

Michael Hahn (Free-Soil–LA, House, 1862–1863; governor, 1864; House, 1885–1886)

Emanuel B. Hart (New York alderman, 1845; chairman of Tammany Hall, 1849; D-NY, House, 1851–1853; surveyor of the Port of New York during James Buchanan's administration)

After the Civil War, Hart served as a presidential elector and an emigration commissioner and held various other NYC offices.

Solomon Hirsch (state senate, OR, 1874–1886; Benjamin Harrison's minister to Turkey, 1889–1892)   Hirsch's brothers Mayer and Edward were also active in Oregon politics.

David Spangler Kaufman (Republic of Texas's chargé d'affaires to the United States; D-TX, House, 1846–1851)   Kaufman became chairman of the House Rules Committee at the age of 38.

Louis Charles Levin (American-PA, House, 1845–1851)   Levin was a founder of the American (Know-Nothing) Party and the first Jew to be elected as a voting member of Congress.

Adolph Meyer (Confederate soldier; brigadier general in the national guard, postwar; D-LA, House, 1891–1908)   Meyer died in office.

Mordecai Manuel Noah (consul to Tunis, 1813; special agent to Algiers, 1813–1815; surveyor of the Port of New York during Andrew Jackson's administration; Tammany Hall grand sachem)   A journalist by profession, Noah was also a playwright and a mystic.

Philip Phillips (D-AL, House, 1853–1855)   Phillips was an active abolitionist who was placed under house arrest in Washington, DC, during the Civil War because of the "seditionist" activities of his wife, Eugenia Levy Phillips, and his daughter.

Isidor Rayner (state legislature, MD, 1878–1884, 1885–1886; D-MD, House, 1887–1889, 1891–1895; Senate, 1905–1912)   Rayner died in office.

Myer Strouse (D-PA, House, 1863–1867)   Strouse was the only Jewish member of Congress during the Civil War. Later he was an attorney for the Molly Maguires, a secret miners' union that was active in Pennsylvania in the 1870s and whose members were charged with murder.

David Levy Yulee (D-FL, House, 1841–1845; Senate, 1845–1851, 1855–1861)   The first Jew elected to Congress, Yulee resigned from the Senate to join the Confederacy. Though called "the Jew delegate" by John Quincy Adams, he was not an observant Jew.

| *Portland, OR, elected two Jewish mayors before 1880.*

MEXICAN AMERICAN POLITICIANS

Mexican Americans have been active in southwestern and California politics since the 19th century. Several Mexican Americans represented New Mexico as congressional delegates before it received statehood in 1912. Some notable examples are listed below.

Toney Anaya   D-NM, governor, 1983–1987

Jerry Apodaca   D-NM, governor, 1975–1979

Xavier Becerra   D-CA, House, 1993–

Ezequiel Cabeza de Baca   D-NM, governor, 1917

Raul Castro   D-AZ, governor, 1975–1977

Lauro F. Cavazos   George Bush's secretary of Education, 1989–1991

Dennis Chavez   D-NM, House, 1931–1935; Senate, 1935–1962

Henry Cisneros   Mayor of San Antonio, 1981–1988; Bill Clinton's secretary of Housing and Urban Development, 1993–1997

Eligio "Kika" de la Garza   D-TX, House, 1965–1997

Henry B. Gonzalez   D-TX, House, 1962–

Octaviano Larrazolo   R-NM, governor, 1919–1921

Manuel Lujan   R-NM, House, 1969–1989; Bush's secretary of the Interior, 1989–1993

Joseph Montoya   D-NM, House, 1957–1964; Senate, 1964–1977

Nestor Montoya   R-NM, 1921–1923

Solomon Ortiz   D-TX, 1983–

Romualdo Pacheco   R-CA, governor of California, 1875; House, 1877–1878, 1879–1883

Ed Pastor   D-AZ, House, 1991–

Federico F. Peña   Mayor of Denver, 1983–1991; Clinton's secretary of Transportation, 1993–1997; secretary of Energy, 1997–

Edward Roybal   D-CA, House, 1963–1993

Lucille Roybal-Allard   D-CA, House, 1993–

★ ★ ★

MARIO CUOMO'S GREATEST ITALIAN AMERICAN POLITICIANS

Fiorello La Guardia   Mayor of New York

John Pastore   The first Italian American senator and governor

Geraldine Ferraro   The first female major-party vice presidential candidate

Francis B. Spinola   The first Italian American congressman

Charles J. Bonaparte   Secretary of the Navy and attorney general

Salvatore Cotillo   The first Italian American judge on the New York State Supreme Court

Pete Domenici   Senator (R-NM)

GAY POLITICIANS

Undoubtedly there were gay politicians before the 1969 Stonewall Rebellion, but figuring out who was and who wasn't is a gossipy guessing game. James Buchanan, the only bachelor president, and his friend and sometime roommate William Rufus DeVane King are often mentioned as possible homosexuals. King, who was vice president under Franklin Pierce, wore foppish clothing and had an effeminate manner; Andrew Jackson referred to him derisively as Miss Nancy. But there is no concrete evidence of either man's sexual orientation.

Jim Kolbe R-AZ, House, 1985–

Barney Frank D-MA, House, 1981–

Steve Gunderson R-WI, House, 1981–1996

Gerry Studds D-MA, House, 1973–1997

Jon Hinson R-MS, House, 1979–1981

Robert Bauman R-MD, House, 1973–1981

Jim Giuliano Mayor of Tempe, AZ, 1995–

Harvey Milk San Francisco city council, 1975–1978

Stewart McKinney (R-CT, House) died of AIDS-related complications in 1987. The McKinney family claimed his death was caused by a 1979 blood transfusion, but The Washington Post *and other papers reported that McKinney was known to frequent gay nightspots in Washington, DC.*

GAYS AND LESBIANS
IN STATE GOVERNMENT

Ken Cheuvront   AZ State Assembly

Sheila James Kuehl   CA State Assembly

Carole Migden   CA State Assembly

Art Feltman   CT House of Representatives

Larry McKeon   IL House of Representatives

Tim Van Zandt   MO House of Representatives

Diane Sands   MT House of Representatives

David Parks   NV House of Representatives

Deborah Glick   NY State Assembly

Chuck Carpenter   OR House of Representatives

Georgia Eighmey   OR House of Representatives

Cynthia Wooten   OR House of Representatives

Mike Pisaturo   RI House of Representatives

Glen Maxey   TX House of Representatives

Ed Flanagan   VT state auditor

Ed Murray   WA House of Representatives

Tammy Baldwin   WI State Assembly

ED KOCH'S TEN
MOST ADMIRABLE POLITICIANS

Ed Koch, mayor of New York from 1978 to 1989, is an author, movie reviewer, radio talk-show host, and the presiding judge on TV's The People's Court.

1. **"President Harry S Truman,** a relatively ordinary human being who grew into the presidency and became one of the United States' best."

2. **"Governor Adlai Stevenson,** who ran for president twice, in 1952 and 1956, and would have made a terrible president. With his brilliant and intellectual speeches, he thrilled America's youth."

3. **"Senator Bob Kerrey** of Nebraska, a war hero who oozes integrity from every pore."

4. **"Senator Bill Bradley,** brilliant, a great athlete with enormous common sense."

5. **"President Franklin Delano Roosevelt,** who saved the U.S. from fascism and the world from Nazi Germany."

6. **"Governor Hugh Carey.** When he concentrated—which was not always the case—he understood problems and conceptualized their solutions, saving both the city and state of New York from fiscal chaos."

7. **"Mayor Fiorello La Guardia,** a great mayor and mythic figure. Though unpopular at the end of his third term, he ultimately became the mayor against whom all other mayors are judged."

8. **"Mayor Robert Wagner.** A great mayor for his time, he never lost his composure or his ability to outwait and outsmart every opponent."

9. **"Speaker Stanley Fink,** speaker of the New York Assembly, defender of the city. He brought both the state senate and the governor to accept his important proposals. He was an oak among saplings."

10. **"Senator Al D'Amato,** underrated and scorned by the literati and other snobs, he overwhelms his political opponents. He protects the people of the city and state of New York as a pit bull protects his master."

SOURCES

PRESIDENTIAL LISTS

PAGE 7   Related and non-related presidents: Gary Boyd Roberts, *Ancestors of American Presidents* (Carl Boyer, 1995), p. 328.

PAGE 8   Presidents with royal blood: Ibid., pp. 214–15.

PAGE 9   *Mayflower* presidents: Ibid., p. 333.

PAGE 10   Presidents with Irish ancestors: John Joseph Concannon and Francis Eugene Cull (eds.), *The Irish American Who's Who* (Port City Press, 1984), pp. 939–43.

PAGE 12   Phi Beta Kappa presidents: Joseph Nathan Kane, *Facts About the Presidents*, 5th ed. (H. W. Wilson, 1989), p. 324, and other sources.

PAGE 24   Inclement inaugurations: Kane, p. 376.

PAGE 25   Inaugural Verbiage: Kane, p. 377.

PAGE 26   Secret Service code names: Truman and Eisenhower presidential libraries, and other sources.

PAGES 26–27   Vetoes and overridden vetoes: Howard W. Stanley and Richard G. Niemi, *Vital Statistics on American Politics*, 3d ed. (Congressional Quarterly, 1992), p. 276.

PAGE 29   War declarations: Congressional Research Service, "A Compendium of Records and Firsts of the United States House of Representatives," Doc 75-96 GGR, 1975, p. 31.

PAGE 31   Presidents with less than 50% of popular vote: Gil Troy, *See How They Ran* (Free Press, 1991), p. 269; and Michael Nelson (ed.), *Congressional Quarterly's Guide to the Presidency* (Congressional Quarterly, 1989), p. 417.

PAGES 34–35   Presidents not in power in Congress: Kane, p. 393; *Congressional Quarterly's Guide to U.S. Elections*, 3d ed. (Congressional Quarterly, 1994).

PAGE 37   Ill or injured presidents: Robert E. Gilbert, *The Mortal Presidency* (Basic, 1992); William A. DeGregorio, *The Complete Book of U.S. Presidents*, 3d ed. (Barricade, 1991); Jack Mitchell, *Executive Privilege: Two Centuries of White House Scandals* (Hippocrene, 1992).

PAGE 40   Public schools: Market Data Retrieval (a division of Dun & Bradstreet).

PAGE 44   Interpresidential insults: Elizabeth Frost (ed.), *The Bully Pulpit* (Facts on File, 1988); DeGregorio.

PAGE 48   Presidents' last words: Kane, p. 338; Paul F. Boller, Jr., *Presidential Anecdotes* (Penguin, 1981), p. 27.

PAGE 49   Presidential burial grounds: Carl Wheeless, *Landmarks of American Presidents* (Gale, 1996).

Basic presidential facts culled from sources including Boller; *Congressional Quarterly's Guide to the Presidency;* DeGregorio; Kane; Troy.

FIRST FAMILY LISTS

PAGE 52   Presidents who married older women: Lu Ann Paletta, *The World Almanac of First Ladies* (World Almanac, 1990), p. 198.

PAGE 52   First ladies, oldest and youngest: Kane, *Facts About the Presidents,* p. 307.

PAGE 53   First ladies who lived the longest: Kane, pp. 307–8.

PAGE 53   First lady college graduates: Paletta, p. 200.

PAGE 54   First ladies in DAR: Paletta, p. 201.

PAGE 56   Women who rejected presidents: DeGregorio, *The Complete Book of U.S. Presidents.*

PAGE 58   Presidential mistresses: Wesley O. Hagood, *Presidential Sex: From the Founding Fathers to Bill Clinton* (Carol, 1995); DeGregorio; Boller, *Presidential Anecdotes.*

PAGE 63   Presidents' children in government: Sandra L. Quinn and Sanford Kanter, *America's Royalty: All the Presidents' Children* (Greenwood, 1983); DeGregorio; Kane, p. 313.

PAGE 64   Fatherless presidents: DeGregorio; David Maraniss, *First in His Class: A Biography of Bill Clinton* (Simon and Schuster, 1995).

PAGE 66   Presidents' fathers: Kane, pp. 295–96.

PAGE 67   White House weddings: *American Presidential Families* (Macmillan, 1993); Kane.

PAGE 68   Embarrassing presidential relatives: Bill Adler with Norman King, *All in the First Family* (G. P. Putnam's Sons, 1982); DeGregorio.

PAGES 73–76   White House dogs, birds, other pets, and TR's menagerie: Margaret Truman, *White House Pets* (David McKay, 1969), pp. 169–74.

VICE PRESIDENTS AND CABINET MEMBERS LISTS

PAGE 84   Older vice presidents: Kane, *Facts About the Presidents,* p. 409.

PAGES 85–86 Vice presidents in Congress and Senate: Kane, p. 405; *Congressional Quarterly's Guide to the Congress*, 4th ed. (Congressional Quarterly, 1991).

PAGE 86 Tiebreaking votes cast by vice presidents: Louis Clinton Hatch, *A History of the Vice-Presidency of the United States* (Greenwich, 1934), p. 101, and other sources.

PAGE 89 Proposed order of succession: Provided by Bill Maher.

PAGE 92 Foreign-born cabinet members: Robert Sobel (ed.), *Biographical Dictionary of the United States Executive Branch* (Greenwood Press, 1990), p. 551.

PAGE 94 Cabinet nominations rejected by Senate: Stanley and Niemi, *Vital Statistics on American Politics*, p. 278; Robert C. Byrd, *The Senate 1789–1989*, vol. 2 (U.S. Government Printing Office, 1991), pp. 25–44.

PAGE 96 Shady advisers: Mitchell, *Executive Privilege;* Shelley Ross, *Fall from Grace: Sex, Scandal and Corruption in American Politics from 1702 to the Present* (Ballantine, 1988); *Congressional Quarterly's Guide to Congress.*

PRESIDENTIAL POLLS

PAGES 100–101 Ridings-McIver polls: William J. Ridings and Stuart B. McIver, *Rating the Presidents* (Citadel Press, 1997).

PAGES 105–7 Also-rans and their running mates: Provided by Leslie Southwick.

PAGE 108 First ladies rankings: Siena Research Institute, Siena College, Loudonville, NY.

CONGRESSIONAL LISTS

PAGE 112 Speakers of the House: *History of the United States House of Representatives* (U.S. Government Printing Office, 1994), pp. 401–3.

PAGE 114 Speakers in Cabinet: Congressional Research Service, "A Compendium of Records and Firsts of the United States House of Representatives," pp. 63-64.

PAGE 115 Speakers with ethics problems: *Congressional Quarterly's Guide to Congress*, pp. 388–96, 769–71, and other sources.

PAGES 116–18 Senate leaders, whips: *Congressional Quarterly's Guide to Congress*, pp. 99A–100A.

PAGE 119 Senators who served longest: Senate Historical Office.

PAGE 119 Oldest senators reelected: Senate Historical Office.

PAGE 120 Five most outstanding senators: Robert J. Dole, *Historical Almanac of the United States Senate* (U.S. Government Printing Office, 1989), p. 269.

PAGE 121   Limbless Legislators' League: Senate Historical Office.

PAGE 122   Longest filibusters: Senate Minute Books, National Archives.

PAGE 123   Fleecings: Provided by William Proxmire, based on his book *The Fleecing of America* (Houghton Mifflin, 1980).

PAGES 124–27   House leaders, whips: *History of the United States House of Representatives*, pp. 404–8.

PAGE 127   Congressmen who served longest: Congressional Research Service.

PAGES 128–31   Congressional widows: Susan J. Tolchin, *Women in Congress 1917–1976* (U.S. Government Printing Office, 1976).

PAGE 131   Congressional couples: *Congressional Quarterly's Guide to Congress*, p. 701, and other sources.

PAGE 134   American Indian congressmen: Roger Walke and Jennifer E. Manning, "Members of Congress of American Indian Descent," Congressional Research Service report, February 9, 1993.

PAGE 135   African Americans in Congress during Reconstruction: Carol M. Swain, *Black Faces, Black Interests* (Harvard University Press, 1993), pp. 21–22, 29.

PAGE 137   Polish Americans in Congress: "Poles in the United States Congress," *New Horizon*, vol. XXI (September/October 1996), pp. 11–14.

PAGE 138   Informal organizations: *Federal Yellow Book* (Washington Monitor, 1997).

PAGE 139   Members of Congress who were pages: Congressional Research Service.

PAGE 140   Old-boy network: *Baird's Manual of American College Fraternities*, 20th ed. (Baird's Manual Foundation, 1990).

PAGE 141   Congressional firsts: Congressional Research Service, "A Compendium of Records and Firsts of the United States House of Representatives."

PAGE 144   Congressional exclusions: *Congressional Quarterly's Guide to Congress*, pp. 762–65.

PAGE 145   Congressional expulsions: Ibid., pp. 768–70.

PAGE 147   Congressional censures: Ibid., pp. 775–79.

PAGE 150   House reprimands: Ibid., pp. 780–83.

PAGE 152   Worst yearly congressional attendance records since 1987: *Congressional Quarterly Almanac* (Congressional Quarterly, 1987–1995); *Congressional Quarterly Weekly Report*, December 21, 1996.

PAGE 154   Worst midterm elections: Norman J. Ornstein et al., *Vital Statistics on Congress 1995–1996* (Congressional Quarterly, 1996), p. 55.

PAGE 155   Congressional salaries since 1789: Congressional Research Service.

PAGE 156   Luther Patrick's rules: Paul F. Boller, Jr., *Congressional Anecdotes* (Oxford University Press, 1991), pp. 21–22.

PAGE 158   Nine Commandments of Health: Dole, p. 253.

PAGE 158   Ten postterm perks: Mildred Amer, "Selected Privileges and Courtesies Extended to Former Members of the House of Representatives," Congressional Research Service report, November 4, 1994; Amer, "Selected Privileges and Courtesies Extended to Former Senators," Congressional Research Service report, November 8, 1994.

PAGE 159   Cemeteries: The Political Graveyard website (www.potifos.com/tpg).

PAGE 160   McCarthy's ten commandments: Eugene McCarthy, *Required Reading: A Decade of Political Wit and Wisdom* (Harcourt Brace Jovanovich, 1988), pp. 114–16.

Basic congressional facts from sources including United States Congress, *Biographical Directory of the United States Congress 1774–1989* (U.S. Government Printing Office, 1989); *Congressional Quarterly's Guide to Congress.*

CURRENT CONGRESSIONAL LISTS

PAGE 168   Harvard graduates in the 105th Congress: Office of News and Public Affairs, Harvard University.

PAGE 169   Yale graduates in the 105th Congress: Office of Public Information, Yale University.

PAGE 173   Best political journalists: Provided by Alan Simpson.

PAGE 180   Mencken on democracy: Mayo DuBasky, *The Gist of Mencken* (Scarecrow: 1990), pp. 351–71.

Some of the information in this chapter was compiled from Michael Barone and Grant Ujifusa, *The Almanac of American Politics 1998* (National Journal, 1997), and *Congressional Quarterly's Politics in America 1996* (Congressional Quarterly, 1996).

SUPREME COURT LISTS

PAGES 186–87   Nominations rejected, withdrawn, postponed, not acted on: Stanley and Niemi, *Vital Statistics on American Politics*, p. 291.

PAGE 188   Nominations declined by appointee: J. Myron Jacobstein and Roy M. Mersky, *The Rejected* (Toucan Valley, 1993), p. 172.

PAGE 190   Justices appointed across party lines: *Congressional Quarterly's Guide to the Presidency*, p. 625.

PAGE 190   Justices in Cabinet: Sobel, *Biographical Dictionary of the United States Executive Branch*, pp. 457–58.

PAGE 192   Justices in Congress: Congressional Research Service, "A Compendium of Records and Firsts of the United States House of Representatives."

CAMPAIGN LISTS

PAGE 194   McCarthy's subtle signs of demagoguery: Eugene McCarthy, *Required Reading*, pp. 19–20.

PAGE 196   Elections Clinton lost: Maraniss, *First in His Class*.

PAGE 197   Best American politicians who never ran for president: Provided by Mario Cuomo.

PAGE 197   Three-time losers: Keith Melder, *Hail to the Candidate: Presidential Campaigns from Banners to Broadcasts* (Smithsonian Institute Press, 1992), pp. 199–202.

PAGE 203   Voter turnout: Committee for the Study of the American Electorate, Washington, D.C.

PAGE 205   Faithless electors: *Congressional Quarterly's Guide to U.S. Elections*, p. 351, and other sources.

PAGE 206   New Hampshire endorsements: Provided by the *Manchester Union-Leader*.

PAGE 207   Super Tuesday: Barbara Norrander, *Super Tuesday: Regional Politics and Presidential Primaries* (University Press of Kentucky, 1992), pp. 36–39, 208.

PAGE 208   Most ballots at conventions: Congressional Quarterly, *National Party Conventions 1831–1992* (Congressional Quarterly, 1995).

PAGE 211   Convention keynote speakers: Ibid., pp. 8, 10.

PAGE 212   Cities that have hosted multiple conventions: Ibid., p. 12.

PAGE 214   Favorite campaign activities: Provided by Bill Bradley.

PAGE 215   Rare campaign badges: Provided by Ted Hake.

PAGE 216   Campaign songs: Irwin Silber, *Songs America Voted By* (Stackpole, 1988).

PAGE 220–22   Campaign slogans: Fay M. Blake and H. Morton Newman, *Verbis Non Factis: Words Meant to Influence Political Choices in the United States, 1800–1980* (Scarecrow, 1984).

PAGES 222–23   Anti-FDR slogans, anti-Reagan slogans: Roger A. Fischer, *Tippecanoe and Trinkets Too: The Material Culture of American Presidential Campaigns* (University of Illinois Press, 1988), pp. 217–18, 295–96.

PAGE 223   Candidate sobriquets: Blake and Newman.

PAGE 224   Haynes platform: Glenn Day, *Minor Presidential Candidates and Parties of 1988* (McFarland, 1988), pp. 68–69.

PAGE 225   Nicest things about not being elected: Provided by Bob Dole.

THIRD-PARTY LISTS

PAGE 228   Significant third parties: Earl Kruschke, *Encyclopedia of Third Parties in the United States* (ABC-CLIO, 1991); J. David Gillespie, *Politics at the Periphery: Third Parties in Two-Party America* (University of South Carolina Press, 1993).

PAGE 231   Most popular third-party candidates: Gillespie; DeGregorio, *The Complete Book of U.S. Presidents.*

PAGE 235   Third-party issues that changed America: Gillespie, pp. 26–27.

PAGE 236   Qualified status in 1998: *Ballot Access News*, November 12, 1996, p. 5.

PAGE 237   State-ballot access for minor-party candidates: *Ballot Access News.*

PAGE 238   Greens on city councils: The Greens/Green Party USA.

PAGE 239   States in which Nader did best: European Green Federation.

PAGE 239   Reforms: Provided by John Anderson.

STATE AND LOCAL LISTS

PAGE 242   Best- and worst-paid governors: *Book of the States 1996–97* (Council of State Governments, 1996), p. 48; figures as of January 1996.

PAGE 243   Female governors: National Governors' Association.

PAGE 244   Most rewritten and amended state constitutions: *Book of the States 1990–1991* (Council of State Governments, 1990), p. 3.

PAGE 245   Professionalism of state legislatures: Karl T. Kurtz, "Understanding State Legislatures: Research and Commentary," *Legislative Studies Quarterly*, June 1992.

PAGE 246   Size of state legislatures: *Book of the States 1990–1991*, p. 68.

PAGE 246   Most uncontested seats: *Ballot Access News*, March 10, 1997, p. 3.

PAGE 247   Term limits: U.S. Term Limits.

PAGE 248   Initiative, recall: Stanley and Niemi, *Vital Statistics on American Politics*, pp. 23–24.

PAGE 250   Highest-paid mayors, unpaid mayors: U.S. Conference of Mayors.

PAGE 251   African American mayors before 1965: *Profiles of Black Mayors in America* (Joint Center for Political Studies, 1977), pp. 215–21.

PAGE 253   Preference voting: Center for Voting and Democracy.

PAGE 254   "Nobody's a Winner": Nevada secretary of State.

THE GOOD, THE BAD, AND THE IMPEACHABLE

PAGE 258   Code of ethics: *History of the United States House of Representatives*, p. 297.

PAGE 259   Washington's *Rules of Civility: George Washington's Rules of Civility & Decent Behaviour in Company and Conversation* (Mount Vernon Ladies' Association, 1989).

PAGE 260   Impeachments: Byrd, *The Senate 1789–1989*, vol. 2, pp. 76–92.

PAGE 266   Duels, etc.: Ross, *Fall from Grace;* Boller, *Congressional Anecdotes;* DeGregorio, *The Complete Book of U.S. Presidents;* Richard B. Morris and Jeffrey B. Morris, *Encyclopedia of American History*, 7th ed. (HarperCollins, 1996); Paul Dickson, *The Congress Dictionary* (John Wiley, 1993); Congressional Research Service, "A Compendium of Records and Firsts of the United States House of Representatives," p. 69.

PAGES 270–77   Sex scandals: Ross; Boller, *Congressional Anecdotes;* Mitchell; and other sources.

PAGE 278   Political bosses: Noal Solomon, *When Leaders Were Bosses: An Inside Look at Political Machines and Politics* (Exposition, 1975); Ralph G. Martin, *The Bosses* (G. P. Putnam's Sons, 1964); Alfred Steinberg, *The Bosses* (Macmillan, 1972).

PAGE 283   Marijuana: National Organization for the Reform of Marijuana Laws.

POP POLITICS

PAGE 286   Asteroids: Brian Marsden, Minor Planet Center, Harvard University.

PAGE 286   Baseball-playing politicians: National Baseball Hall of Fame Library, Cooperstown, NY; the Society for American Baseball Research, *Minor League Baseball Stars*, vol. 3 (SABR, 1992).

PAGE 288   Memorable Yankee Stadium moments: Provided by Rudoph Giuliani.

PAGE 289   First ball: National Baseball Hall of Fame Library.

PAGE 290   Nixon All-Stars: "Nixon the Fan Chooses Own All-Stars," *Sporting News*, July 15, 1972; William B. Mead and Paul Dickson, *Baseball: The Presidents' Game* (Farragut Publishing Co., 1993), pp. 210–11.

PAGE 292   Football-playing politicians: National Football Hall of Fame, Canton, OH.

PAGE 293   Motorcycles: Provided by Ben Nighthorse Campbell.

PAGE 293   Golfing presidents: Shepherd Campbell and Peter Landau, *Presidential Lies: The Illustrated History of White House Golf* (Macmillan, 1996), pp. 245–47.

PAGE 295   Golf courses: Provided by James Clyburn.

PAGE 296   Fishing presidents: Kane, *Facts About the Presidents.*

PAGE 297   Olympians: U.S. Olympic Committee.

PAGE 298   Food and drink: Poppy Cannon and Patricia Brooks, *The Presidents' Cookbook* (Funk & Wagnalls, 1968), and other sources.

PAGE 299   American populists by weight: Provided by Bill Maher.

PAGE 300   Recipes: Cannon and Brooks.

PAGE 301   Martha Washington menu: Ibid., p. 7.

PAGE 302   Taft banquet: Ibid., p. 371.

PAGE 303   Nixon etiquette: Bruce Oudes (ed.), *From: The President: Richard Nixon's Secret Files* (HarperCollins, 1989), p. 36.

PAGE 303   Money: Gene Hessler, *Comprehensive Guide to U.S. Paper Money* (Henry Regnery, 1974).

PAGES 305–6   Stamps: Melvin Morris, editor of the *Americana Philatelic News.*

PAGES 306–7   Political animal words, funny-sounding words: Dickson, *The Congress Dictionary;* William Safire, *Safire's New Political Dictionary* (Random House, 1993).

PAGE 308   *Devil's Dictionary:* Ambrose Bierce, *The Devil's Dictionary.*

PAGE 309   Poet-politicians: David Kresh, Library of Congress.

PAGE 310   Carter poem titles: Jimmy Carter, *Always a Reckoning and Other Poems* (Times Books, 1995).

PAGE 311   Favorite mystery novels: Provided by Barbara Mikulski.

PAGE 312   Books by TR: *Theodore Roosevelt: A Bibliography* (Charles Scribner's Sons, 1920).

PAGE 313   Favorite books: Provided by Richard Riordan.

PAGE 314   All-time political best-sellers: *The New York Times,* February 17, 1997, p. D1.

PAGE 315   Top political books: Politics and Prose bookstore, Washington, D.C.

PAGE 316   Women who dated Kissinger: Walter Isaacson, *Kissinger: A Biography* (Simon and Schuster, 1992), pp. 355–70.

PAGE 316   Improbable assassins: George Rush, *Confessions of an Ex–Secret Service Agent: The Marty Venker Story* (Donald I. Fine, 1989), p. 59.

PAGES 317–22   Actors who played presidents: Internet Movie Database (www.us.imdb.com).

PAGE 325   Best political movies: Provided by George Stephanopoulos.

PAGE 329   Movies enjoyed by the Roosevelts: Eleanor Roosevelt, "Why We Roosevelts Are Movie Fans," *Photoplay*, July 1938, pp. 16–17.

PAGES 329–31   Reagan movies: Tony Thomas, *The Films of Ronald Reagan* (Citadel Press, 1980).

PAGE 332   Favorite musicals: Provided by George McGovern.

PAGE 332   Hollywood Ten: Eric Bentley (ed.), *Thirty Years of Treason: Excerpts from Hearings Before the House Committee on Un-American Activities 1938–1968* (Viking, 1971); Ephraim Katz, *The Film Encyclopedia*, 2d ed. (HarperCollins, 1994).

PAGE 334   Hollywood anti-Communists: Bentley, pp. 291–93.

PAGE 334   Politician characters on TV: Research Services Department, Museum of Television and Radio, New York, NY.

PAGE 335   *Saturday Night Live*: NBC.

PAGE 336   TV Kennedys: Internet Movie Database.

PAGE 337   Politicians on TV, longest-running political shows: Research Services Department, Museum of Television and Radio, New York, NY.

PAGE 338   *Meet the Press:* NBC News; figures as of December 1, 1997.

PAGE 339   Favorite Clinton caricatures: Provided by Tom Toles.

STRANGE BEDFELLOWS

PAGE 342   Early capitals: *American Places Dictionary*, vol. 1 (Omnigraphics, 1994), pp. xxxiii–xxxiv.

PAGE 342   Presidents before Washington: Sobel, *Biographical Dictionary of the United States Executive Branch*, p. 431.

PAGE 344   19th-century factions: Blake and Newman, *Verbis Non Factis*.

PAGE 345   Wets and Drys: David E. Kyvig, *Repealing National Prohibition* (University of Chicago Press, 1979); Larry Englemann, *Intemperance* (Free Press, 1979); John Kobler, *Ardent Spirits* (Da Capo, 1993).

PAGE 350   Marches on Washington: U.S. Parks Police.

PAGES 351–52   Assassinations and attempts: Carl Sifakis, *Encyclopedia of Assassinations* (Facts on File, 1993); James Clarke, *American Assassins* (Princeton University Press, 1982).

PAGE 354   Failed amendments: David E. Kyvig, *Explicit and Authentic Acts* (University of Kansas Press, 1996).

PAGE 357   Political prisoners: Rev. S. Michael Yasutake, Interfaith Prisoners of Conscience Project, *Can't Jail the Spirit: Political Prisoners in the U.S.*, 3d ed. (n.p., 1992).

PAGE 359   Pardons: Kathleen Dean Moore, *Pardons: Justice, Mercy, and the Public Interest* (Oxford University Press, 1989), and other sources.

PAGE 361   Flag no-nos: Col. James A. Moss (ret.), *The Spirit of the American Flag* (United States Flag Association, 1933), p. 162.

PAGE 362   Ku Klux Klan: Anti-Defamation League of B'nai Brith. Compiled from Michael Newton and Judy Ann Newton, *The Ku Klux Klan: An Encyclopedia* (Garland, 1991).

PAGE 363   Funniest politicians: Provided by Al Franken.

PAGE 364   Jefferson's canons of conduct: Monticello Research Library.

PAGES 365–66   Fourth of July: The Political Graveyard website.

PAGES 366–69   Elderly statesmen, politicians who died in action, and plane crashes: The Political Graveyard website, among others.

PAGE 370   Clinton body count: The War Room website (www.warroom.com), among others.

PAGE 373   19th-century Jewish politicians: *The Jewish Encyclopedia* (Ktav, 1901); Lawrence Fuchs, *The Political Behavior of American Jews* (Free Press, 1956); Nathaniel Weyl, *The Jew in American Politics* (Arlington House, 1968); Rabbi Kurt Stone.

PAGE 375   Mexican American politicians: Matt S. Meier, *Mexican American Biographies: A Historical Dictionary 1836–1987* (Greenwood Press, 1988).

PAGE 376   Greatest Italian American politicians: Provided by Mario Cuomo.

PAGE 379   Most admirable politicians: Provided by Ed Koch.

ACKNOWLEDGMENTS

Thanks to the politicians who took a few minutes off from matters of state to contribute to the book.

Thanks to the always helpful research librarians at the New York Public Library.

Thanks to Eden Eskin, Doni Gewirtzman, Nina Morrison, Aaron Retica, Robert Schonberg, Steve Ury, and everyone else who suggested ideas for lists or looked over the manuscript.

Thanks to Ron Bigler and Kris McNeil for their research assistance.

Thanks to Peter Canby for enabling me to devote so much time to this project, and thanks to Martin Baron for the de-accessioned reference books and for the spiritual guidance.

Thanks to Beth Pearson, David Rosenthal, Bruce Tracy, Eliza Truitt, Jennifer Webb, Abigail Winograd, and Zoe Wolff at Villard Books.

Thanks to my agent, John Hodgman at Writers House, for his persistence and his wise counsel.

Thanks to Mom, Dad, and Devra.

Thanks to Rachel.

BLAKE ESKIN is arts editor for the *Forward*. He has written for magazines including *The New Yorker* and *Lingua Franca,* and for the public radio program *This American Life.* He lives in New York City.